✝

To Mary + Joe –

May Jesus + Mary
bless you!

Fr Andrew

FATIMA FOR TODAY

Father Andrew Apostoli, C.F.R.

Fatima for Today

The Urgent Marian Message of Hope

Foreword by Raymond Cardinal Burke

IGNATIUS PRESS   SAN FRANCISCO

Cover art:
Pilgrims Participate in a Religious Procession at the Shrine of Our Lady of Fatima
© Paulo Novias/epa/Corbis

Cover design by Roxanne Mei Lum

© 2010 Ignatius Press, San Francisco
All rights reserved
ISBN 978-1-58617-523-8
Library of Congress Control Number 2010927110
Printed in the United States of America ∞

This book is lovingly dedicated
to
the Immaculate Heart of Mary,
Mother of God and our Mother,
and to
Pope John Paul II
who made the Consecration of Russia
and to
Pope Benedict XVI
who has told us to
learn, live and spread the message of Fatima!

CONTENTS

FOREWORD

During his historic visit to the Shrine of Our Lady of Fatima on May 13, 2010, His Holiness Pope Benedict XVI spoke of the maternal instruction of the Blessed Virgin Mary to all mankind, which she communicated through her chosen messengers, Blessed Francisco Marto, Blessed Jacinta Marto, and the Servant of God Lucia dos Santos. Summarizing the content of the teaching conveyed through her six apparitions between May and October of 1917, which were prepared by the three apparitions of the Angel of Peace, His Holiness described Our Lady of Fatima as "the Teacher who introduced the little seers to a deep knowledge of the Blessed Trinity and led them to savor God Himself as the most beautiful reality of human existence".[1] His Holiness continued by quoting expressions of the most tender and profound love of God, which were inspired in the seers by the apparitions and message of Our Lady of Fatima and of the Angel of Peace.

Through her apparitions and message, the Mother of God, as she always does, led Francisco, Jacinta, and Lucia more surely and fully to our Lord Jesus Christ, God the Son Incarnate, and through him to God the Father and God the Holy Spirit, with whom he is one in being. In the words of Pope Benedict XVI, "Our Lady helped them to open their hearts to universal love", that is, to the love of God the Father,

[1] Pope Benedict XVI, "Homily during Mass celebrated in the square at the Marian Shrine: Prophetic mission of Fatima for the salvation of the world", *L'Osservatore Romano*, English ed., May 19, 2010, p. 11.

the Son and the Holy Spirit, who loves all men and desires only their eternal salvation.[2]

The Blessed Virgin Mary came to visit mankind at Fatima at a time when many had grown forgetful of God and his all-loving plan for our salvation, and many had grown rebellious before the Law of God by which he orders all things for our good. Having alienated themselves from the universal love that comes to us from God alone, they fell prey to a destructive selfishness of heart, which was most dramatically and tragically manifested in the horror of the First World War. The great temptation in a world beset with the gravest of evils was to lose hope in divine love and thus to cease responding to divine love with pure and selfless love. Knowing the severity of the temptation that his children were suffering, God the Father sent to earth the Blessed Virgin Mary, the mother of his only-begotten Son, in fidelity to her mission as Mother of God, which she first accepted at the Annunciation and which she expressed so clearly at the Wedding Feast of Cana. When the wine stewards of the newly married couple at Cana found themselves in a most distressful situation, it was the Blessed Virgin who was immediately aware of their distress; who interceded with her Divine Son to save the newlyweds from embarrassment; and who, with total confidence, instructed the wine stewards: "Do whatever he tells you."[3]

In all our times of crisis, both personally and as a society, the Virgin Mother of God is always immediately aware of our distress and is always interceding on our behalf before the throne of God. She also faithfully counsels us, with deepest motherly love, to do what our Lord Jesus Christ tells us, to turn over our lives to him through prayer and penance.

[2] Ibid.
[3] Jn 2:5.

In the most critical moments of our earthly pilgrimage, God the Father has favored us with an extraordinary sign of the Virgin Mary's maternal love, that is, with her visits to us by way of apparitions and messages. Regarding her appearances at Fatima, the Holy Father observed: "At a time when the human family was ready to sacrifice all that was most sacred on the altar of the petty and selfish interests of nations, races, ideologies, groups and individuals, our Blessed Mother came from heaven, offering to implant in the hearts of all those who trust in her the Love of God burning in her own heart." [4]

Through the third apparition of the Angel of Peace and the July apparition of our Lady, the little seers saw before their eyes both the indescribable beauty of the Mystery of Faith—the Body and Blood of Christ sacramentally offered and poured out for us, for our eternal salvation—and the unspeakably ugly emptiness of hell, of a life lived without God and in rebellion against his pure and selfless love for us. The Angel of Peace, like the angels in the Holy Scriptures, was God's messenger to prepare the children to receive the miraculous visits of the Mother of God, and to become her messengers to the world, most of all by the example of their lives, even to our day.

Prepared by the Angel of Peace, the little seers were enabled to place, to an heroic degree, their hearts, one with the Immaculate Heart of Mary, into the Most Sacred Heart of Jesus and thus to be purified of sin and inflamed with the pure and selfless love that flows without cease and without measure from the glorious pierced Heart of Jesus. In his Consecration of Humanity to the Immaculate Heart of Mary, in October of 1942, the Venerable Pope Pius XII

[4] "Homily during Mass celebrated in the square at the Marian Shrine ...", p. 11.

expressed in a striking manner the mystery of the Immaculate Heart of Mary, drawing us to the glorious pierced Heart of Jesus in which mankind finds the victory over sin and death, and the triumph of divine love and eternal life:

> Finally, as the Church and the whole human race were consecrated to the Sacred Heart of Jesus, so that placing in Him all its hopes it might have a pledge of victory and salvation, thus from to-day may they be perpetually consecrated to your Immaculate Heart, Oh Mother and Queen of the world, that your love and protection may hasten the triumph of the Kingdom of God and that all generations of mankind, at peace with themselves and with God, may proclaim you Blessed and with you may intone, from pole to pole, the eternal Magnificat of glory, love and thanksgiving to the Heart of Jesus where alone may be found Truth, Life and Peace.[5]

Through the Consecration of Humanity to the Immaculate Heart of Mary, the Shepherd of the Universal Church, the Venerable Pope Pius XII, prayed that the maternal care of the Blessed Virgin Mary, most perfectly represented in her sinless Heart, might lead all men to the Heart of Jesus, the font of their eternal salvation.

Reflecting upon the human context, individual and societal, of the apparitions of the Mother of God at Fatima, it is not difficult to perceive the critical importance of our Lady's message for our own time, an importance strongly underlined for us by the Venerable Pope John Paul II and by his successor Pope Benedict XVI. We too live in a time when many are ready to sacrifice all, including the lives of innocent and defenseless unborn brothers and sisters; the lives of those who have the first title to our care—the aged,

---

[5] Quoted in John de Marchi, *Fatima: From the Beginning*, 2nd ed., trans. I. M. Kingsbury (Fatima: Edições Missões Consolata, 1980), p. 233.

the critically ill and those suffering with special needs; and the great good of marriage and the family, the first cell of the life of society, on the altar of selfish individualism and tyrannical relativism. Many in our day have turned away from God and have rebelled against the most fundamental teachings of his life-giving Law—the teaching regarding the inviolable dignity of innocent human life and the teaching on the integrity of the faithful, indissoluble and procreative union of one man and one woman in marriage—and have thus found themselves profoundly unhappy and without hope, gazing into the terrifying emptiness of hell.

We can be certain that the Mother of God is keenly aware of our situation and that she seeks to draw us to herself and thereby place our hearts, one with her Immaculate Heart, into the Sacred Heart of Jesus. In her maternal love, she draws us to the Heart of Jesus, in which alone we will find both the purification of our sins and the inspiration and strength of the immeasurable and ceaseless love of God for us. Ultimately, she desires to lead us to the Mystery of Faith, to the Holy Eucharist, the medicine and nourishment that heal us of sin and strengthen us against the temptation to sin, thus rescuing us from the fruit of sin: everlasting death, the horror of which the Mother of God permitted the three little seers to contemplate during her July apparition.

Father Andrew Apostoli of the Franciscan Friars of the Renewal has understood the desire of Our Lady of Fatima to speak to us today. With great care and thoroughness, he provides for us the full context of the events at Fatima and then describes the three apparitions of the Angel of Peace and the six apparitions of the Mother of God to Lucia, Francisco, and Jacinta. He also describes the apparitions to Sister Lucia at Pontevedra and Tuy in Spain, through which Our Lady of Fatima made ever clearer what she asks of us for the conversion of our lives and the transformation of our world in anticipation of the Final Coming of our Lord Jesus in glory to inaugurate "new heavens and a new earth".[6] In a manner which is most accessible and, at the same time, complete and accurate, Father Apostoli helps us to know the maternal instruction of Our Lady of Fatima and, following it, to know and "savor", in the words of Pope Benedict XVI, the mystery of divine love in our lives.[7]

Two principal controversies surround the apparitions and message of Our Lady of Fatima, namely, the controversy over the consecration of Russia to the Immaculate Heart of Mary and the controversy over the Third Secret. These controversies sadly have distracted some from our Lady's maternal instruction and have hindered others from attending to it. Father Apostoli addresses both with the greatest respect and care. Placing them within the context of the complete account of the apparitions and message of Fatima, he resolves them through the careful consideration of all that was taught to the three little seers by the Mother of God.

Regarding the Third Secret, also known as the third part of the Secret of Fatima, Father Apostoli's treatment of the controversy called to mind the sage discussion of the matter by Fr. C. C. Martindale, S.J., in his classic presentation of the apparitions and message of Our Lady of Fatima. Father Martindale, referring to the great curiosity regarding the third part of the Secret, which, at the time of his writing had not yet been published, commented upon it in the light of the first and second parts of the Secret, observing:

> Now the first two parts of the secret contain, as we saw, nothing new. 'Hell' is no new doctrine; nor that our Lady is Immaculate. It is not novel or startling *information*

---

[6] 2 Pet 3:13.
[7] "Homily during Mass celebrated in the square at the Marian Shrine", p. 11.

that our Lady proposed to impart to us, but rather, a challenge to look more deeply into what we already know. It
need not surprise us that the children were told to say
nothing about what had been granted to them; Lucia quite
frankly said that she would not have had words in which
to express herself properly, and, to the end, that she could
give only the 'sense' of our Lady's message. This encour-
ages one to think that the 'secrecy' of that message may
have concerned the *intensity* with which the children were
made to understand certain truths, rather than anything
which could be crystallised into clear ideas or put into
forms of words.[8]

In a similar way, referring to his "Theological Commentary" on the Secret, Pope Benedict XVI observed that Our
Lady of Fatima invites us to cultivate what he calls "the
interior watchfulness of heart which, for most of the time,
we do not possess on account of the powerful pressure exerted
by outside realities and the images and concerns which fill
our soul".[9]

Father Martindale has rightly noted that Our Lady of
Fatima invites us to a deeper reflection upon the Mystery
of Faith, a reflection inspired by divine love. Pope Benedict
concludes that the Secret is, in the end, "the exhortation
to prayer as the path of 'salvation for souls' and, likewise,
the summons to penance and conversion".[10] In other words,
the Mother of God at Fatima leads us to her Divine Son
and instructs us to respond with all our being to his

[8] C. C. Martindale, S.J., *The Meaning of Fatima* (New York: P.J. Kenedy
and Sons, 1950), pp. 178–79.

[9] "Homily during Mass celebrated in the square at the Marian Shrine",
p. 11.

[10] Cardinal Joseph Ratzinger, "Theological Commentary" in Congregation for the Doctrine of the Faith's, *The Message of Fatima* (Città del Vati-
cano: Libreria Editrice Vaticana, 2000), p. 43.

preaching: "The time is fulfilled, and the kingdom of God
is at hand; repent, and believe in the gospel." [11]

As Pope Benedict XVI declared in his homily at Fatima
on May 13, 2010, and as Father Apostoli illustrates so fully
and well in this book, Our Lady of Fatima leads us to enter
more deeply into the mystery of the Holy Trinity, the mystery of the love of God—Father, Son, and Holy Spirit—
poured out for all mankind without cease and without
boundary. Father Apostoli helps us, in a most sound and
thorough manner, to hear more clearly the instruction of
Our Lady of Fatima and to follow it faithfully. His book,
which you will now be blessed to read, is truly a most worthy
instrument by which Our Lady of Fatima continues to speak
to our hearts from her Immaculate Heart.

In the second part of the Secret of Fatima, the Mother
of God promised: "My Immaculate Heart will triumph." [12]
The then Cardinal Joseph Ratzinger has helped us to understand the profound meaning of the promise made by Our
Lady of Fatima to the three little seers. Asking what may
be the meaning of our Lady's promise, he declared:

> The Heart open to God, purified by contemplation of God,
> is stronger than guns and weapons of every kind. The *fiat*
> of Mary, the word of her heart, has changed the history of
> the world, because it brought the Saviour into the world—
> because, thanks to her *Yes*, God could become man in our
> world and remains so for all time. The Evil One has power
> in this world, as we see and experience continually; he has
> power because our freedom continually lets itself be led away
> from God. But since God himself took a human heart and
> has thus steered human freedom towards what is good, the
> freedom to choose evil no longer has the last word. From

[11] Mk 1:15.
[12] *The Message of Fatima*, p. 16.

that time forth, the word that prevails is this: "In this world you will have tribulation, but take heart; I have overcome the world" (Jn 16:33). The message of Fatima invites us to trust in this promise.[13]

It is my hope and prayer that, through your study of Father Apostoli's handbook on Our Lady of Fatima, our Lady will draw you ever closer to her Immaculate Heart and that, one with her Heart, your heart, resting in the Most Sacred Heart of Jesus, will know the triumph of divine love and eternal life.

> ✝ Raymond Leo Burke
> Archbishop Emeritus of Saint Louis
> Prefect of the Supreme Tribunal of the Apostolic Signatura
> Solemnity of All Saints, 2010

---

[13] Ibid., p. 43.

PREFACE

I AM VERY GRATEFUL to Ignatius Press for the invitation to write this book on Our Lady of Fatima and her important message for our time. All throughout my life I have been devoted to Our Lady of Fatima. I heard about her message when I was a young boy, and it made a deep impression on me. Like Lucia, Francisco and Jacinta, I have prayed for the salvation of souls as our Lady asked. I also have practiced the devotion of the Five First Saturdays for many years and have tried to encourage others to do the same. So it was a delightful challenge to write this book. The publishers asked me to "put everything about Fatima in it". I tried to do that within the limits of my time, ability and resources.

My intention was to write a book that would combine three essential elements about Our Lady of Fatima. First, there are the historical facts of the apparitions by our Lady and by the Angel of Peace. I tried to present these facts as fully as possible, especially stressing the words our Lady and the Angel of Peace spoke during each of their apparitions. Second, there is the message of prayer, sacrifice, suffering and holiness of life. I am sure more people will be drawn to this message when they understand its meaning and importance. The message of Fatima has often been described as a brief summary of the essentials of Christian living. Our Lady of Fatima has given us a great reminder of these essentials for our difficult times. Third, there are certain questions and objections that have been raised concerning the message of Fatima, such as: Was the consecration of Russia to the Immaculate Heart of Mary made properly by Pope John

Paul II? Was the third secret of Fatima fully revealed by the Vatican? For years people have been asking me these questions. In this book I have tried to present clear evidence that both of these tasks have been fulfilled. The Pope has done his part; now we must do our part by good Christian living, by prayers for the conversion of sinners, by the fulfillment of our duties in life and by using the graces the Holy Spirit has been pouring forth into our hearts. Our Lady had told the children at Fatima that God wanted devotion to the Immaculate Heart of Mary to be spread throughout the world. If this book can contribute in any small way to the spreading of this devotion, the author will be richly rewarded for the efforts involved in writing this book. I have tried to write in the same spirit as Sister Lucia when she wrote about the message of Fatima, namely, "for the glory of God and the salvation of souls".

I want to give thanks to Almighty God for the graces needed to accomplish this undertaking. May this book give honor and glory to the Most Holy Trinity. I also want to thank the Blessed Virgin Mary, whom I felt was asking me to write this book to assist in bringing about the triumph of her Immaculate Heart.

I also want to thank the many people who have contributed in various ways to the writing of this book. First, I would like to express my gratitude to His Excellency Raymond Cardinal Burke for taking time out of his busy schedule to write the foreword. Next, I want to thank all the Franciscan Friars of the Renewal, especially those in my local community, who assisted me in so many ways in preparing this manuscript. I also wish to thank all the Franciscan Sisters of the Renewal and the many other people who supported me with their prayers and encouragement. Finally, I wish to thank Elaine Curzio, who helped with typing some of the manuscript; Tiffiny Gulla, who edited the text; Penny Wolfe, who helped with important research for the book; and, Gerri Kearns, who reviewed the text. May Jesus and his Blessed Mother reward all who have helped to make this work, as Mother Teresa of Calcutta would say, "something beautiful for God".

Father Andrew Joseph Apostoli, C.F.R.
Saint Leopold Friary
Yonkers, New York
March 2, 2010

MARY

The Only Woman Whose Coming Was Foretold

ARCHBISHOP FULTON J. SHEEN OFTEN SAID that Jesus was the only man whose coming into the world was pre-announced. No other great world leader or religious figure ever had his coming foretold. Even Jesus' mission was known before he entered the world. His mission was to overcome evil by his saving death on the Cross. In a very similar way, we can say that the Blessed Virgin Mary was the only woman whose coming into the world was foretold: "Behold, a virgin shall conceive and bear a son ..." (Is 7:14). Her mission was also known before she came into this world; she was to share in the saving sacrifice of her Divine Son. Hers was to be a mission of spiritual warfare in order to help obtain the final victory over evil prophesied in God's curse of the serpent:

> I will put enmity between you and the woman, and between your seed and her seed; he shall bruise your head, and you shall bruise his heel. (Gen 3:15)

The Blessed Virgin Mary plays a pivotal role in the great struggle between good and evil—between her Divine Son and his disciples, and Satan and his followers. In the Book of Revelation, we see powerful images depicting the hatred of the devil for the woman who bears the Savior, for the Lord himself, and for the Lord's followers:

> And a great sign appeared in heaven, a woman clothed with the sun, with the moon under her feet, and on her head a crown of twelve stars; she was with child and she cried out in her pangs of birth, in anguish for delivery. And another sign appeared in heaven; behold, a great red dragon, with seven heads and ten horns, and seven diadems upon his heads. His tail swept down a third of the stars of heaven, and cast them to the earth. And the dragon stood before the woman who was about to bear a child, that he might devour her child when she brought it forth.... Then the dragon was angry with the woman, and went off to make war on the rest of her offspring, on those who keep the commandments of God and bear testimony to Jesus. (Rev 12:1–4, 17)

The Blessed Virgin Mary is a central figure in God's plan of salvation. She plays a major role, second only to her son, in the work of redeeming the world. This role involves her in continuous conflict with Satan. At Fatima, however, our Lady assured us that the final victory would be hers: "In the end my Immaculate Heart will triumph!"

Mary's Important Role as the New Eve

Our Lady's role is so significant because God wants to defeat the devil by the same means with which the devil had conquered our first parents. This divine plan was a favorite theme among the Fathers of the Church. Here is how Saint John Chrysostom, a great bishop in the early church, expressed the role of Mary:

> Christ conquered the Devil using the same means and the same weapons that the Devil used to win. The symbols of

our fall were a virgin, a tree and death. The virgin was Eve (for she had not yet known man); then there was the tree; and death was Adam's penalty. And again these three tokens of our destruction, the virgin, the tree and death, became the tokens of our victory. Instead of Eve, there was Mary; instead of the tree of knowledge of good and evil, the cross of the Lord; instead of Adam's death, the death of Christ.[1]

Eve played a very important part in the Fall. The serpent never spoke to Adam; he only spoke to Eve. He first planted a doubt in her mind by questioning her about God's command: "Did God say, 'You shall not eat of any tree of the garden'?" (Gen 3:1). When Eve said they could eat of all the trees except the tree of the knowledge of good and evil, the devil then deceived her with the promise that, if she ate the forbidden fruit, she and Adam would "be like God, knowing good and evil" (Gen 3:5). This lie tempted Eve with a promise of greatness, which led to pride, followed by disobedience to God's command.

> So when the woman saw that the tree was good for food, and that it was a delight to the eyes, and that the tree was to be desired to make one wise, she took of its fruit and ate; and she also gave some to her husband, and he ate. Then the eyes of both were opened... (Gen 3:6–7)

Adam, as head of the human family, was our representative before God. So only his disobedience became the original sin for mankind. Eve, however, was an accomplice in the wrongdoing. She did not deserve the name Eve, which means mother of all the living (Gen 3:20), because she helped bring about the spiritual death of her children.

---

[1] "On the Cemetery and the Cross" (*De coemeterio et cruce*), in *The Liturgy of the Hours*, vol. 4 (New York: Catholic Book Publishing, 1975), p. 1660.

Our Lady, on the other hand, deserves to be called the New Eve. She does not represent us in the work of redemption; that role belongs to Jesus Christ, the New Adam who alone is our eternal high priest and victim for our sins. However, Mary was as much an accomplice in the work of redemption as Eve had been in the Fall.

At the Annunciation

At the Annunciation, Mary fully accepted God's will for her life in humility and obedience, as can be seen in her response to the archangel Gabriel. She had been told by the archangel that she would conceive and bear a son, who would be called Son of the Most High. When her question about how she would conceive because she did not have relations with Saint Joseph was clarified by the archangel, our Lady did not hesitate to respond humbly and trustingly: "Behold, I am the handmaid of the Lord; let it be to me according to your word" (Lk 1:38). As the sin of Eve contributed to bringing spiritual death into the world, the total obedience of our Lady brought Jesus, the source of our spiritual life, into the world. Mary's humility and obedience erased Eve's pride and disobedience, meriting her the title of the New Eve. Saint Irenaeus of Lyon explained this title in the second century:

> As Eve was seduced by the word of an angel and so fled from God after disobeying his word, Mary in her turn was given the good news by the word of an angel, and bore God in obedience to his word. As Eve was seduced into disobedience to God, so Mary was persuaded into obedience to God; thus the Virgin Mary became the advocate of the virgin Eve.[2]

---

[2] "Against Heresies" (*Adversus haereses*), in *Liturgy of the Hours*, vol. 1, p. 244.

At Cana and at Calvary

Mary is also the New Eve in the way she joins in the redemptive mission of her son to save the world. Just as Eve moved Adam toward his sin of disobedience by giving him the forbidden fruit, so Mary at the wedding feast at Cana led Jesus toward his "hour" by moving him to work his first miracle of changing water into wine. Once he manifested his glory, Jesus was on the road to the Cross and our redemption. Mary's role deepens at the foot of the Cross, when Jesus confides the care of his beloved disciple to her: "Woman, behold your son!" (Jn 19:26). We should note that twice in the Gospel of Saint John, Jesus addresses his mother as "Woman", namely, at Cana and Calvary. This title links Mary with Genesis 3:15: "I will put enmity between you and the woman, and between your seed and her seed."

The Meaning of Mary's Apparitions

By her exemplary virtues, by her powerful prayers and by her motherly protection, our Lady is even now fulfilling her role as the New Eve, which is marked by her ongoing opposition to evil and her concern for us. These features of Mary's role that we see in the Gospels can also be seen in her apparitions.

In the Gospels are examples of our Lady's concern for those in need. At the wedding feast of Cana she made known to Jesus the young couple's need for wine in order that their wedding celebration might continue. But probably the most striking example of our Lady's charity was her visit to her aged cousin Elizabeth. Once she had learned from the archangel that Elizabeth was six months into her pregnancy, Mary went quickly to help her (Lk 1:39). In Mary's visitation we find a beautiful pattern for the many apparitions she would make throughout the course of Christian history. In each case, our Lady appeared in order to help, guide and console her children.

Our Lady has appeared many times through the centuries. One of the first known of her apparitions (recorded by Saint Gregory of Nyssa) was to Saint Gregory the Wonderworker (d. 270). Our Lady appeared along with Saint John the apostle, whom she told to make known to Gregory "the mystery of true piety". Many other apparitions have occurred since, mostly to one person or a small group, and the messages on most of these occasions were meant for the individuals involved. However, beginning in the sixteenth century there have been a few great apparitions with signs and wonders witnessed by many people and messages intended for the whole world. These apparitions have been approved by Church authority for the benefit of the faithful. Though we are not obliged to believe in them, we can grow in faith, hope and charity if we do.[3]

Guadalupe

In 1531, Our Lady of Guadalupe appeared in Mexico City to Juan Diego, an Indian convert to the faith. Her message brought to the native peoples of Mexico a sense of their own dignity as children of a loving God. As a result, over nine million natives were baptized in ten years. The Aztec worship of false gods, such as the sun god and the serpent god, was abandoned, and the practice of human sacrifice ended. We see clearly our Lady as God's instrument, breaking the power Satan had for centuries over the native people of Mexico before Christianity came to the Americas.

[3] See Appendix E for a further explanation of private revelation in the life of the Church.

Rue du Bac, Paris

Our Lady appeared again in 1830 to Saint Catherine Labouré, a novice of the Daughters of Charity living at her motherhouse in Paris on the street called Rue du Bac. Mary gave Catherine a message of warning and of hope, especially regarding events that would happen in France. She also revealed the form of a medal she wanted made. It was to show Mary crushing the serpent beneath her feet and bear the inscription: "Oh Mary, conceived without sin, pray for us who have recourse to Thee!" So many blessings, including some amazing conversions, came from this medal that it soon became popularly known as the Miraculous Medal. Once again Mary was recognized as being our powerful intercessor and an adversary against Satan.

Lourdes

In a series of eighteen apparitions during the year 1858, the Blessed Mother appeared to fourteen-year-old Bernadette Soubirous near Lourdes, a French village at the base of the Pyrenees. In her messages our Lady asked for prayer, penance and reparation for sinners. Our Lady also provided the special spring for which Lourdes is so famous. Many who have bathed in its waters have been miraculously healed. Thousands who have visited this Marian shrine have found their faith renewed. A major part of our Lady's message at Lourdes is the revelation of her identity to Saint Bernadette: "I am the Immaculate Conception." The title brings us back to Genesis, when God spoke to the serpent: "I will put enmity between you and the woman." It was Mary's Immaculate Conception that made her the bitter enemy of Satan. Because she was kept free from the stain of original sin, Mary possessed a fullness of grace that even Satan could not overcome.

Fatima: A Special Apparition

Of all the messages of our Lady, none are as important as
those given at Fatima, Portugal. Our Lady of Fatima appeared
six times between May 13 and October 13, 1917, to three
shepherd children: Lucia dos Santos and her younger cousins Francisco and Jacinta Marto. She gave them a message
of peace and hope for a world engulfed by war.

World War I, called the "war to end all wars", was threatening to annihilate Europe. To end the conflict, Pope Benedict XV began a novena to the Queen of Peace on May 5,
1917. On that same day, the Pope wrote the following in a
letter to Cardinal Gasparri, his Vatican secretary of state:

> Our earnestly pleading voice, invoking the end of this vast
> conflict, the suicide of civilized Europe, was then and has
> remained ever since unheard. . . . Since all graces which the
> Author of all good deigns to grant to the poor children of
> Adam, by a loving design of His Divine Providence, are
> dispensed through the hands of the most holy Virgin, we
> wish that the petition of her most afflicted children, more
> than ever in this terrible hour, may turn with lively confi-
> dence to the august Mother of God.[4]

On Sunday, May 13, the eighth day of the novena, our
Lady responded to the prayers of the Pope and her children
in this valley of tears by appearing for the first time at Fatima.
Her message, with its hopeful promise, as well as its strong
warnings, was meant for the whole world. Pope John Paul II,
who has been named the Pope of Fatima, recognized the
necessity of our Lady's message for our times when he said
that it was more urgent and important in our day than it
was in 1917. He added that the popes have given the events

[4] Henry Rope, *Benedict XV: The Pope of Peace* (London: Trinity Press, 1940),
pp. 122–23.

of Fatima a special recognition, as its messages were more prophetic than those of any other apparition. The aim of this book is to present the full story and meaning of Fatima and explain the way we must now respond to our Lady's call for peace in the world through the salvation of souls.

2

Fatima, Portugal

A Message Revealed to Little Ones

Part I: Background on Portugal

PORTUGAL IS LOCATED ON THE IBERIAN PENINSULA in the extreme southwest of Europe. It is bordered to the west and south by the Atlantic Ocean; to the north and east lies Spain. Its large oceanfront has made navigation a major part of the country's history. During the exploration of the New World, Portugal boasted some great explorers, such as Henry the Navigator (d. 1460), who organized voyages along the west coast of Africa, and Vasco da Gama, who in 1498 became the first European to travel by sea to India. Two years later, Pedro Cabral discovered Brazil and claimed it for Portugal.

Our Lady Plays a Major Role in the History of Portugal

Christianity seems to have arrived in Portugal during the first Christian centuries when Saint James the apostle traveled over the lands of Portugal and Spain preaching the gospel. In the eighth century, the Muslim Moors invaded the Iberian Peninsula and took general control of Portugal and Spain. The Portuguese won a decisive victory over the

Moors in 1139 and became an independent country. In gratitude to the Blessed Virgin Mary for her help in gaining the victory, King Alfonso, the first king of Portugal, built a magnificent church and monastery, Santa Maria de Alcobaca, to house almost one thousand Cistercian monks. Saint Bernard of Clairvaux was there the day the monastery was dedicated and given to his order.

In the fourteenth century, Spain made claims to the throne of Portugal. The Portuguese did not want to surrender their liberty and autonomy, and so they made preparations to resist a Spanish invasion. Though outnumbered, the Portuguese turned to our Lady for her prayers and fought valiantly under the inspiring leadership of Saint Nuno Alvares. They successfully repelled the Spanish at the Battle of Aljubarrota on August 14, 1385. In gratitude to our Lady for her intercession, King John I built the beautiful monastery of Batalha, the Royal Convent of Saint Mary of Victory in the Battle, and gave it to the Dominican Order.

Crediting Mary with protecting them from many disasters, the Portuguese have a strong Marian devotion. From its foundation, Portugal has been referred to as the Land of Holy Mary. In 1646 King John IV and all his people promised their fidelity to the most holy Virgin under her title of the Immaculate Conception. Since that time, the Mother of God has been proclaimed the Queen and Patroness of Portugal. For this reason, the Portuguese kings did not wear a crown, since it was reserved exclusively for the Immaculate Virgin.

Where Did the Name Fatima Come From?

When the last Moors were leaving Portugal, a young Muslim princess named Fatima was captured by the Christian knight Don Goncalo. They fell in love, and after she converted to the Catholic faith they married. Princess Fatima, the daughter of a powerful Muslim prince, was named after Muhammad's first and most beloved daughter, Fatima. Upon becoming a Christian, Fatima was baptized with the name Oureana (after which is named the district capital Ourem, where the visionaries of Fatima were imprisoned in August 1917). Don Goncalo loved his wife very much, but within a year of their marriage she died. He then decided to become a Cistercian monk at Alcobaca. When later he was sent to a small priory, he took along the remains of the wife he loved so deeply and named the place Fatima in her memory. Many believe that Mary's appearance at Fatima can be of great importance in the Christian outreach to the Muslim people. Archbishop Sheen, for example, saw in our Lady's choice of Fatima a great significance for her message. She did not come down from heaven to the only place in all of Portugal with a Muslim name simply to convert Russia, he said. Unless we have the conversion of hundreds of millions of Muslims, there will never be world peace.

The Impact of Freemasonry

From the time of King John IV (1603–1656), the Catholic Church enjoyed relative peace in Portugal for about two hundred years. Then Freemasonry entered Portuguese politics. Its followers were against the Christian monarchy as well as the Catholic Church. They wanted to establish a godless, humanistic republic totally built upon Masonic ideals, and so they passed a series of anti-Catholic laws. Religious orders were outlawed and many religious were expelled from the country. Churches were sacked, church property was confiscated, convents and monasteries were closed and seminaries were controlled. The public celebration of religious feasts and the public wearing of clerical garb were forbidden. Divorce was legalized and religious instruction in all the schools was prohibited. These anti-Catholic measures culminated in the Law of Separation of Church and State that passed on April 20, 1911. The leader of the Freemasons, Alfonso Costa, boasted: "Thanks to this law of separation, in two generations Catholicism will be completely eliminated in Portugal." [1] Catholic loyalists attempted to overthrow the Masonic government but were unsuccessful. Once World War I began, nothing could be done until the war ended. The anti-Catholic government leaders in the district capital of Ourem were to cause great problems for the three little visionaries, imprisoning them, threatening them with a most painful death and preventing them from being at the apparition site on August 13, 1917. However, what the Masons never figured on was that our Blessed Mother would intervene once again to save Portugal.

The Village of Fatima

Fatima was a small village in 1917. One of the main buildings in the village was Saint Anthony's Church, where the three visionaries were baptized and where Lucia received her First Holy Communion. Most of the people living in Fatima were poor peasants who farmed the land and raised their animals. They were devout people with a simple faith. God and the Blessed Mother were very real in their lives. Lucia records that the first prayer she learned was the Hail Mary. Not very far from the village church were hamlets

[1] "Declaration to the Congress of Free Thought" quoted in Frère Michel de la Sainte Trinité, trans. John Collorafi, *The Whole Truth about Fatima: The Secret and the Church*, vol. 2 (Buffalo, NY: Immaculate Heart Publications, 1989), p. 314.

consisting of clusters of small homes. The most important one was Aljustrel, where the two families of the visionaries lived. Not far away was the hamlet Valinhos, which is where our Lady's apparition to the children in August took place. Just beyond Valinhos there was a path leading to a rocky hillside called Loca do Cabeco. It was in this place that the children saw the first and third apparitions of the Angel of Peace. The second appearance of the angel occurred at a well near Lucia's home in Aljustrel. The three shepherd children would often graze their flocks of sheep in the Cabeco. But the main grazing area was the Cova da Iria, a small pasture area about a mile and a half from Aljustrel that was owned by Lucia's parents. Five of the six apparitions of our Lady took place in the Cova.

Part II: Who Were the Three Little Visionaries?

Saint Paul tells us that "God chose what is foolish in the world to shame the wise, God chose what is weak in the world to shame the strong" (1 Cor 1:27). At Fatima, God chose three simple children to carry a message that would confound the sophisticated and arrogant anti-clerical thinkers of the world, men like the powerful Freemasons. Perhaps because of their innocence and simplicity, the children proved to be faithful messengers for our Lord and his Blessed Mother.

Lucia dos Santos

Lucia dos Santos was born in Aljustrel on March 22, 1907, to Antonio dos Santos and Maria Rosa. She was the youngest of seven children, having a brother and five sisters, one of whom died in infancy. She was also a cousin to Francisco and Jacinta Marto, the other two Fatima visionaries.

Lucia was the oldest of the three visionaries, being ten years old when the Blessed Mother appeared. Like Jacinta, Lucia could see and hear our Lady, but she was the only one who spoke to Mary. Little Francisco could see our Lady, but he could neither hear her nor speak with her.

Like the men of the area, Lucia's father took care of the farm. He raised crops in the Cova da Iria and looked after the family's livestock. After supper with his family, he would spend time with his friends in the local tavern. Both of Lucia's parents were religious. They observed the laws and feasts of the church and helped the poor and the sick. In addition to her duties caring for the home, Maria Rosa also taught Christian doctrine in the parish, and she made sure the family prayed the Rosary together.

With a dark complexion, black and shining eyes, and dark hair, Lucia had an attractive and lively disposition. She was especially fond of children, and they in turn loved her dearly. When the task of grazing the sheep fell to her as the youngest member of the family (as generally happened in all families), other boys and girls of the village often accompanied her with their flocks of sheep.

Lucia grew up in a home where the Catholic faith was lived daily. At the age of six she received her First Holy Communion. (In fact, Lucia was the only one of the three visionaries who had received First Holy Communion before the time of the three apparitions of the Angel of Peace.) Lucia's mother had taught her the catechism and, thinking she was ready to receive Communion, sent her with an older sister to classes preparing young people for the sacraments. The day before the First Communion Mass, the parish priest told Lucia to wait another year. When she tearfully pleaded with him, a visiting priest took her aside and questioned her. She knew the teachings of the Church so well that this priest asked the pastor to let her receive

First Holy Communion, which he did. Lucia described the profound effect her First Holy Communion had upon her:

> I felt as though transformed in God. It was almost one o'clock before the ceremonies were over... My mother came looking for me, quite distressed, thinking I might faint from weakness [due to the Communion fast from midnight at that time]. But I, filled to overflowing with the Bread of Angels, found it impossible to take any food whatsoever. After this, I lost the taste and attraction for the things of the world, and only felt at home in some solitary place where, all alone, I could recall the delights of my First Communion.[2]

Lucia received a special favor on the eve of her First Holy Communion that foreshadowed the singular mission she would fulfill. Right after she made her first confession, she prayed before the statue of Our Lady of the Rosary in her parish church. Lucia asked our Lady to keep her heart for God alone, and the statue seemed to smile at her and assure her that her prayer would be answered.

Francisco Marto

Francisco Marto was born in Aljustrel on June 11, 1908, in the home of his parents, Manuel Pedro "Ti" Marto and Olimpia de Jesus. At the time of our Lady's apparitions, Francisco was nine years old. He was a handsome boy with brown hair and dark eyes. In her memoirs, Lucia described him as passive, quiet and submissive by nature, so that he easily yielded to others and always lost at games because

[2] Lucia dos Santos, *Fatima in Lucia's Own Words: Sister Lucia's Memoirs*, ed. Fr. Louis Kondor, trans. Dominican Nuns of Perpetual Rosary (Fatima: Postulation Centre, 1976), p. 57.

he lacked a spirit of competition. He obeyed Lucia as if she had real authority over him. Before the apparitions of our Lady, young Francisco seemed not to care about anything. For example, if someone took something belonging to him, he would simply shrug off the injustice, "Let him have it. What do I care?" Lucia thought his greatest defect was this attitude of indifference. Yet, at other times Francisco could be a little bit mischievous.

Simple things, on the other hand, seemed to please Francisco. For example, he loved animals. He played with lizards and snakes, often bringing them home where they were quite unwelcome. He was especially fond of birds, and always saved some of his bread so he could feed them crumbs. He was also enchanted by the beauty of the sunrise and the sunset. What he loved the most, however, was to go to the mountains, sit on top of the highest rock, and there sing or play his flute. He especially enjoyed playing his flute for his sister Jacinta, who in turn loved to dance.

Francisco had some very admirable qualities. He had great compassion for sick people. He was always friendly and smiling, playing with all the other children. If another child did something he should not be doing, Francisco would not rebuke him. Rather, he simply moved aside and remained silent. In general, people felt good in his presence. Young Francisco was certainly not yet a saint, but God would prepare him to become very holy. Mother Teresa of Calcutta would often say: "God does not choose the qualified, but he qualifies the ones he chooses." During the apparitions, Francisco grew greatly in his desire to console our Lord and our Lady for the many offenses they suffered from our sins. He attained an exceptional love of suffering to make reparation for the sins of others, something which is difficult for most people and even more so for a young boy. He also experienced a burning desire to receive Jesus in Holy

Communion before his death, and this desire was fulfilled. Perhaps we can sum up Francisco's tremendous growth in the love of God by words he spoke regarding his love of Jesus and Mary:

> I loved seeing the Angel, but I loved still more seeing Our Lady. What I loved most of all was to see Our Lord in that light from Our Lady which penetrated our hearts. I love God so much! But he is very sad because of so many sins! We must never commit any sins again.[3]

Jacinta Marto

Little Jacinta was the youngest of the three visionaries, being only seven years old when our Lady appeared. Despite her tender age, she probably had the strongest character of the three. All one has to do is look at the famous picture of the three visionaries, showing Jacinta with her arm on her hip and a very determined look in her eyes, to know that she had a strong will and a mind of her own. In other words, she could be very stubborn. Interestingly, this was also true of Saint Therese of Lisieux as a little child. Future saints need a strong will to practice heroic virtue. Jacinta was practically the opposite of her brother Francisco. She had a very sensitive temperament. Possessive and assertive, she insisted on choosing her own games and partners and would pout at the slightest argument or opposition to her plans.

On the other hand, Lucia tells us in her memoirs that Jacinta had many endearing qualities. Before the apparitions of our Lady, she was a vivacious child and the very personification of enthusiasm. Above all, Jacinta loved to dance and sing. She could be sweet and gentle when she

[3] Ibid., p. 124.

wanted to be, and people found her lovable and attractive. Like her brother, she loved nature because it made her think about God. She also longed to receive Jesus in Holy Communion. She loved to hear about the Passion of Jesus and meditate on it, which often moved her to tears. Her love for God was so tender, she could not bear to hear anyone use his name in vain.

Lucia used to say that though Jacinta was the youngest of the visionaries, she seemed to have grasped our Lady's message, especially the meaning of suffering and sacrifice, most deeply of all. She was particularly moved by the vision of hell, which the visionaries saw during the appearance of our Lady on July 13. As a result, she did many penances and accepted her sufferings with patience, offering them all up for the salvation of souls. She did not want anyone ever to go to hell, but wanted everyone to go to heaven. We can sum up the burning zeal in the heart of little Jacinta by quoting her own words:

> I so love the Immaculate Heart of Mary! It is the heart of our dear Mother in heaven! . . . If I could only put into the hearts of all, the fire that is burning within my own heart, and that makes me love the Hearts of Jesus and Mary so very much![4]

We will have much more to say about Jacinta and the other visionaries of Fatima when we describe the apparitions of the Angel of Peace and of our Lady.

[4] Ibid., pp. 108 and 112.

3

THE FIRST AND SECOND
ANGEL APPARITIONS

The Angel of Peace Comes to Prepare the Way

T HROUGHOUT SALVATION HISTORY, God often prepared
his people for the graces and blessings he intended
to bestow upon them. For example, by preaching and by
performing miracles the prophets in the Old Testament prepared the hearts of the people to accept God's message of
reform. Saint John the Baptist, in the New Testament, prepared the way for Jesus to reveal himself as the long-
awaited Messiah. He told the people that the Messiah was
near, and that they should prepare to receive him by repent-
ing of their sins and by being baptized. During his own
public ministry, Jesus sent the twelve apostles and later
seventy-two other disciples to the various towns that he
intended to visit, so that the people would be ready to
welcome him and his call to conversion. Such preparations were necessary so that people would be disposed to
receive the significant graces the Lord wanted to give them.

God has sent not only men to prepare his people, but also
angels. The word *angel* means "messenger". There are many
instances of angels bearing messages in the Old Testament.

Abraham was visited by three angels who told him his wife would soon bear a son. Jacob wrestled with an angel who renamed him Israel. An angel guided Tobias and another instructed Elijah. In the New Testament, also, we see angels at work. Angels spoke to Joseph in his dreams. An angel told the Roman centurion Cornelius to send for Simon Peter, who would baptize him as the first Gentile Christian (Acts 10:3ff). An angel later freed Peter from jail. For the greatest message God ever gave his people, he sent the archangel Gabriel to the Blessed Virgin Mary to announce that he had chosen her to be the mother of his Divine Son (Lk 1:26–35).

At Fatima, an angel who called himself the Angel of Peace visited the visionaries to prepare them for what was to come. The children needed to be as prepared as possible for the mission they would receive from Jesus and Mary. The Mother of God would entrust to them a message of peace for the whole world. That peace would require prayer, sacrifice and suffering, all of which the children would need to experience in their own lives first before asking it of others. So God sent an angel three times to prepare the children for the coming of our Lady at Fatima. Let us look at each of the three angel apparitions, how they affected the children and what we can learn from them for our own lives.

First Apparition: Spring of 1916

Like most peasant children their age, the three visionaries did not keep track of dates in terms of days and months. When Lucia wrote her memoirs, she estimated the dates of the three angel apparitions. The first took place in the spring of 1916. Lucia, Francisco and Jacinta were together that day tending their families' flocks of sheep at the Cabeco, one of their favorite grazing spots. It had been raining earlier in the morning, but eventually the sky cleared. They ate their lunch and then prayed the Rosary together. Eager to play, the children often prayed as quickly as possible with their own shortened version of the Rosary, saying on each bead only the first two words of the Hail Mary or Our Father. After their prayers that day, as they were starting to play a game, a strong wind shook the tree tops. Lucia described in her memoirs what they saw: "a young man, about fourteen or fifteen years old, whiter than snow, transparent as crystal when the sun shines through it and of great beauty".[1] The children were astonished but said nothing to each other.

Then the angel spoke: "Do not be afraid. I am the Angel of Peace. Pray with me."[2] What a beautiful greeting from the angel! His words remind us of those spoken by angels on other occasions. At the Annunciation, when the archangel Gabriel had greeted our Lady as "full of grace", she was deeply troubled. The angel reassured her: "Do not be afraid, Mary, for you have found favor with God." When an angel of the Lord appeared to the shepherds on Christmas night to announce the birth of Jesus, he greeted them saying: "Be not afraid; for behold, I bring you good news. . . ." This angel also spoke of peace when he was joined by a heavenly host saying: "Glory to God in the highest, and on earth peace" (Lk 2:10, 14). This peace could only come from God through his Divine Son, the Prince of Peace. It was this same peace that a world engulfed in total war was yearning so desperately to receive.

An Invitation to Pray

The angel invited the children to pray with him and taught them a prayer they had never known before. First he knelt

[1] Ibid., p. 62.
[2] Ibid.

down and bowed until his forehead touched the ground. Interestingly, this is the posture of prayer that Muslims generally use. It is certainly one that expresses great reverence to God. The children were so moved that they knelt with their foreheads to the ground as well. A caution is needed here. Not everyone who reads this book is ready to pray in the same manner as the angel, namely, with one's forehead touching the ground. If we are not in adequate physical shape, we may have a hard time getting up! Or bowing so profoundly, we may get dizzy if too much of our blood rushes to our head! The important thing we can learn from the angel's example is to be reverent when we pray. Profoundly bowing before the Lord should not be interpreted as showing fear. Let us remember to Whom we are speaking: Almighty God. This means we should pray with respect for his infinite holiness and majesty, avoiding deliberate distractions, daydreaming, slouching, or any form of laziness or indifference. Rather, we should have a childlike trust in God's infinite goodness and mercy.

The Pardon Prayer

The angel then taught the children a beautiful prayer which is usually referred to as the Pardon Prayer:

> My God, I believe, I adore, I hope and I love You! I ask pardon of You for those who do not believe, do not adore, do not hope and do not love You.[3]

The angel repeated these words three times. Then he rose and said to the children, "Pray thus. The Hearts of Jesus

[3] Ibid. For the version of this prayer more commonly used in the United States, see Appendix A.

and Mary are attentive to the voice of your supplications." [4] Then the angel disappeared.

We have already seen how the angel's posture at prayer expressed a great sense of reverence for God's majesty. The content of the prayer he taught continues this theme. First the prayer outlines four fundamental actions we all must do in order to have a relationship with God: keep faith by believing, worship by adoring, trust by hoping and love by loving. Then the prayer asks God to pardon those who are neglecting these duties toward him. This prayer would prove to be for the children a powerful introduction to intercessory prayer for sinners. Praying for the salvation of souls is at the very center of Our Lady of Fatima's message. She would tell the children in her August 19, 1917, apparition: "Pray, pray very much, and make sacrifices for sinners; for many souls go to hell, because there are none to sacrifice themselves and to pray for them." [5]

Why Believing, Adoring, Hoping, Loving?

Like the present day, when our Lady was making her appearances in Fatima, many people were abandoning faith in God. They were trusting solely in their own intelligence and resources; as a result, their faith decreased greatly and grew cold. Yet faith is the very beginning of eternal life: we must believe in order to have God's life in us, as the Letter to the Hebrews reminds us: "My righteous one shall live by faith" (Heb 10:38). Since faith had grown weak, people were no longer adoring God. Instead, they were making idols of the riches of this world, the pleasures of the flesh and the exultation of their own egos. As a result of these distortions of

[4] Ibid.
[5] Ibid., p. 167.

life's purpose, coupled with the ongoing sorrow and suffering of World War I, many people were losing hope. They no longer trusted in God's help and promises; instead, they were falling into despair. Finally, the spiritual emptiness of the time diminished the greatest gift God gave his people, namely, his love. Jesus said that the time would come when sin would so abound that the love of many would grow cold. This was one such age. Prayer and sacrifice would be necessary to stir God's love into flame again!

When we pray the Pardon Prayer we are praying for faith, hope and charity to be renewed in the world. We need them in our own day as desperately as they were needed in 1917. If we heed the words of the Angel of Peace and pray the Pardon Prayer each day, or as often as we feel moved to do so, we have no idea how many souls will be brought closer to God. By praying for those who are not praying for themselves, we can hope that God will grant to those souls the graces to begin praying on their own. We can trust that Jesus and Mary will always be attentive to this prayer!

An Intense Experience of the Supernatural

The first apparition of the angel had an extraordinary impact on the children. Lucia described in her memoirs that as the angel left, the three children were enveloped in a supernatural atmosphere so intense that for a long time they were scarcely aware of their own existence.[6] They remained in the same posture for some time, continually repeating the prayer of the angel. They felt the presence of God so intimately that they did not attempt to speak to one another. This spiritual atmosphere carried over to the next day and

[6] Ibid., p. 151.

only gradually began to disappear. They were probably experiencing something like an ecstasy, during which a person receives a powerful presence of God in his soul. It is so strong that the use of the senses and even the ability to move are sharply limited.

Lucia would later contrast the apparitions by the angel with those by our Lady. Though both brought happiness and peace, during the apparitions of our Lady the children felt a joyful freedom and desire to speak to her, whereas during the angel's apparitions they experienced an overwhelming feeling that made them almost unable to speak. As a result, they did not speak about this experience among themselves. It was almost as if the very apparition itself imposed secrecy. Despite such a wonderful beginning, however, the children would need a reminder to pray the Pardon Prayer more ardently. This would come in the angel's second visit.

Second Angel Apparition: Summer of 1916

This second appearance of the angel took place at a well near the home of the Santos family. Lucia estimated the date to be in the summer because at that time of the year the children would take the sheep out to graze early in the morning and bring them back to their hamlet before noon, to the safety of a small barn that would provide shade from the blazing afternoon sun. During the siesta hours, the children remained in the shade under the trees near the well playing their games. On this occasion the angel appeared suddenly right beside the children. He had a gentle rebuke for them: "What are you doing?" [7] Those words must have made a very strong impression on the children because they responded very faithfully to the angel's second message: "Pray!

[7] Ibid.

Pray very much! The Hearts of Jesus and Mary have designs of mercy on you. Offer prayers and sacrifices constantly to the Most High." [8]

"Offer Prayers and Sacrifices Constantly"

The angel stressed the need for the children to pray even more than they had been doing. They responded very generously by praying the Pardon Prayer frequently. Learning to pray so faithfully takes years for the average person. With the extraordinary graces they were receiving, the children were learning to do this rapidly. The angel reminded them again that Jesus and Mary had plans for their lives. They needed to develop a strong prayer life to have the courage and generosity to respond to those plans.

In addition to prayer, the angel mentioned the need to offer sacrifices. When Lucia asked him how they were to make sacrifices, the angel answered:

> Make of everything you can a sacrifice, and offer it to God as an act of reparation for the sins by which He is offended, and in supplication for the conversion of sinners. You will thus draw down peace upon your country. I am its Angel Guardian, the Angel of Portugal. Above all, accept and bear with submission, the suffering which the Lord will send you. [9]

This statement of the angel contains some of the most important and basic elements of the Fatima message. We shall look at each of these elements.

Sacrifice—First, let us look at the meaning of the word *sacrifice*. A sacrifice is a giving up, or a surrendering, of something we hold dear or desire. Therefore, when the angel

[8] Ibid.
[9] Ibid., p. 152.

said to "make of everything you can a sacrifice", he was saying to use the many opportunities that come our way during the day to surrender our will, our preference, our desire, or our comfort, giving it to God, and possibly extending it to another person, as an offering of love. We deny ourselves in this way in order to give God a sign of our love for him. Everything we have comes from God's love for us. When we make sacrifices, we tell God we love him for himself, and not only for the good things he gives us. We also tell him we love him by obeying his commandment: "Love one another as I have loved you", i.e., with sacrificial love. Saint Therese of Lisieux would often say: "The food of real love is sacrifice!" Because sacrifice is a participation in God's own love, it expands the heart's capacity for love.

Reparation—The angel taught the children to offer their sacrifices to God in reparation for the sins by which he is offended. Reparation is an act of love to God to help make up for someone's failure or refusal to love him. In other words, when a person offers some good deed or act of self-denial as reparation to God, he is saying "God, I love you" in order to make up for an offense against him by which someone else said "God, I do not love you." When Christ offered his life on the Cross, he was making up for all the sins of mankind by his perfect obedience, out of love, to the Father. We are invited by Christ to share in his act of reparation by uniting our sufferings and sacrifices with his own to atone for the sins of the world.

Intercession for the Conversion of Sinners—The angel told the children that these same sacrifices were to be offered as a prayer or petition for the conversion of sinners. Just as these sacrifices would make reparation for sins, they would also obtain the conversion of those who committed those sins. We know from the Gospels that heaven rejoices more over one sinner who repents than over ninety-nine people who have no need to repent. In the spiritual life, as a person grows closer to God, the desire for the conversion of sinners also increases. Why? Because the more we love God, the more we must love those for whom he suffered and died and shed his precious Blood upon the Cross.

Bearing Sufferings Humbly—In a spirit of sacrifice, the children were to "accept and bear with submission, the suffering which the Lord will send." No one of sound mind likes to suffer. We do not endure pain very easily; in fact, it tests our patience and endurance. But suffering plays a very important role in our spiritual development. It is one of the most powerful, but difficult, graces one can receive from God, namely, to bear patiently, for the love of God, the trials and difficulties that come our way. This grace is usually given to persons who are coming close to God. He was drawing the little visionaries very close to himself. God allows suffering to purify us from sin, to help us resist temptations and to strengthen us in the practice of virtue. Furthermore, sufferings are often God's way of purifying our love, drawing us away from attachments to the temporary things of this world so that we can seek after the eternal things of heaven.

Our Lord himself willingly endured the sufferings of the Cross so that he might save us from our sins. Suffering by itself is not a good. God does not take any delight in seeing people suffer. Some people have the distorted notion that "God feels better if I feel worse." But our sufferings, when joined to the sufferings of Christ, become meritorious for obtaining graces for ourselves and others, especially the grace of conversion. To accept, then, the sufferings God sends us is a sign of our love for God and our trust in his divine providence. What was the children's reaction to the message of the angel regarding suffering? Lucia's summary of it is enlightening for all of us:

> These words were indelibly impressed upon our minds. They were like a light which made us understand who God is, how He loves us and desires to be loved, the value of sacrifice, how pleasing it is to Him, and how, on account of it, He grants the grace of conversion to sinners.[10]

The Fruit of Peace—The Angel of Peace told the children what would result if they offered sacrifices in reparation for sins and in supplication for sinners: "You will thus draw down peace upon your country." Saint Augustine defined peace as "the tranquility of order". When everything is in order, or the way it should be, we have peace. For example, if a person confessed his sins, received God's mercy and amended his life, he would experience peace. If a family reconciled their differences and divisions, they would have peace. If everyone in the Church accepted the teachings of the Magisterium and lived by them, there would be peace and unity within the Church. If nations put aside their rivalries and reconciled their differences, everything would be in order and there would be peace.

The children were certainly learning "who God is", as Lucia said. They were taking giant steps in their spiritual formation as the angel taught them. With this apparition the children were filled with a new enthusiasm for offering prayers and sacrifices. Their favorite sacrifice was to pray for hours on end kneeling with their foreheads touching the ground and repeating the prayer the angel had taught them. In his next apparition, the Angel of Portugal would bring the children a very special gift: Jesus in the Eucharist.

[10] Ibid.

4

The Third Angel Apparition

Eucharistic Adoration and Reparation

The Dream of Saint John Bosco

ONE OF THE GREATEST SAINTS OF THE nineteenth century was John Bosco, the founder of the religious community that bears his name (and that of Saint Francis de Sales), the Salesians of Don Bosco. He was very devoted to the Blessed Virgin Mary, especially under her title Help of Christians. From an early age he had prophetic dreams. In his most famous dream, he saw the Catholic Church represented as a great wooden ship. Surrounding the ship of the Church were smaller boats that represented the faithful who were loyal to the Holy Father. Opposing the ship of the Church was a huge enemy fleet whose ships had prows with sharp, spear-like points, which could pierce and destroy other ships. In addition, these enemy ships had cannons, rifles and other weapons, including books hostile to the teachings of the Church. While under enemy fire, the pope was guiding the ship of the Church. All of a sudden, two great columns emerged from the sea. At the top of the higher column was a very large Eucharistic Host and on the lower was a statue of the Blessed Virgin Mary. The pope realized that these two columns were given by God

for the safety of the Church, so he began to steer the ship
to safety between them. As the battle raged, a bullet fired
from one of the enemy ships hit the pope. He fell down,
but he did not die; the people raised him up.

The battle continued as the enemy ships relentlessly
attacked the ship of the Church, to stop it and sink it. Some
ships used writings and books as weapons; others used guns
and battering rams. Most of the time, their attempts were
useless, and their ammunition was simply wasted. However, if some formidable blows caused large and deep gashes
in the sides of the ship of the Church, gentle breezes from
the two columns would heal them immediately. Eventually,
many of the weapons on the enemy ships were exhausted
or destroyed, and some of the ships were shattered and sank
into the sea. The men who escaped their sinking ships
boarded the Church, where they attempted hand-to-hand
fighting, with fists and blows, as well as blasphemies and
curses. Toward the end of the battle, the pope was shot
again and this time was killed. A successor was soon elected
and this new pope routed the enemy fleet and guided the
ship of the Church safely between the two columns. Then,
without warning, the sea became extremely turbulent and
scattered the remaining enemy ships in every direction. In
the confusion, many of them collided with one another
and broke one another into pieces, and finally sank. The
ships of the faithful joined the ship of the Church and
anchored themselves safely against the columns. The battle
over, the Church was victorious, and the sea became calm.

When John Bosco explained his dream, he said that the
enemy ships were persecutions that would assail the Church.
In fact, he said that some of the most serious trials in the
long history of the Church were about to occur in the next
(twentieth) century. Compared to what would happen with
these terrible persecutions, all the suffering that had occurred

already in the Church's history would be almost insignificant. Finally, Saint John Bosco said that God was giving two means by which the Church could be saved: devotion to Jesus in the Most Blessed Sacrament and devotion to the Blessed Virgin Mary. It seems John Bosco's dream was partially fulfilled in the twentieth century, with the violent persecution of the Church by atheistic, anti-Catholic regimes and the attempted assassination of Pope John Paul II. There were more Catholic martyrs in the twentieth century than in any other period of Christian history.

Fatima: Linking Eucharistic Devotion and Marian Devotion

Eucharistic love and devotion, joined with love for and devotion to the Mother of God, have always formed the most solid defense of the Church against the attacks of her enemies. Whether they were the persecutions of the ancient Roman Empire, the Muslim conquests or the barbarian invasions, the Church has always found strength in Jesus and Mary. Fatima shows us this source of strength so clearly. The Mother of God herself came from heaven with a message of hope and a plan for victory. Before her appearance, a powerful lesson in Eucharistic devotion was given by the Angel of Peace during his third apparition. This apparition would instill in the young children a very ardent devotion to Jesus in the Most Blessed Sacrament.

Another link between the Blessed Sacrament and Our Lady of Fatima is the fact that our Lady's first appearance occurred on May 13, which at that time was the liturgical celebration of Our Lady of the Most Blessed Sacrament. Since heaven's choices are never made randomly, we must assume that Jesus was choosing to send his mother with a message of his love and peace on a feast day that reminds us of the awesome gift he had already given us: his precious Body and Blood in the Eucharist. Pope John Paul II often said, quoting from the Second Vatican Council, that the Eucharist was the source and the summit of the Christian life.

The Body and Blood with which Jesus feeds us in the Most Blessed Sacrament is the same flesh and blood given by his mother at the moment of his Incarnation. As Archbishop Fulton Sheen often said, next to Jesus, no one had more right than our Lady to say about the Eucharist that this is my Body and this is my Blood. We must ask our Lady to teach us how to love Jesus in the Most Blessed Sacrament.

The Angel of Peace Comes a Third Time

Lucia tells us that the third apparition of the angel occurred either in late September or early October of 1916. The children were again grazing their sheep at the Cabeco where the angel had appeared to them the first time. The angel's words at his second apparition made the children very faithful in praying the Pardon Prayer he had taught them, and on this occasion they were kneeling down with their heads to the ground, praying the prayer. After they had prayed it a number of times, an extraordinary light shone upon them. When they looked up, they saw the angel. He was holding in his left hand a chalice, and over it was a Eucharistic Host. Drops of Jesus' precious Blood were falling from the Host into the chalice. Leaving the chalice and Host suspended in the air, the angel knelt down beside the children. They all bowed profoundly before Jesus in the Blessed Sacrament with their foreheads to the ground. The angel then taught them another prayer:

Most Holy Trinity, Father, Son and Holy Spirit, I adore
You profoundly, and I offer You the most precious Body,
Blood, Soul and Divinity of Jesus Christ, present in all the
tabernacles of the world, in reparation for the outrages,
sacrileges and indifference with which He Himself is
offended. And through the infinite merits of His most Sacred
Heart, and the Immaculate Heart of Mary, I beg of You
the conversion of poor sinners.[1]

We want to look closely at this prayer and reflect on its
deep meaning. It is a prayer, like the Pardon Prayer, that
we would want to learn to pray daily, even frequently during the day. Let us, however, first see what happened to the
Eucharist and the children that day at the Cabeco. The angel
taught the children to repeat the prayer three times, just as
he had told them to do when praying the Pardon Prayer.
The angel then rose from where he was kneeling, took the
chalice and Host into his hands and offered the Eucharist as
Holy Communion to the children. Recall that only Lucia
had already made her First Holy Communion; Francisco
and Jacinta had not. Therefore, the angel gave the consecrated
Host to Lucia, while he allowed Francisco and Jacinta to
drink directly from the chalice. Everyone's First Holy Communion is memorable, but this was extraordinary! As he
gave Holy Communion to the children, the angel said to
them: "Take and drink the Body and Blood of Jesus Christ,
horribly outraged by ungrateful men. Make reparation for
their crimes and console your God."[2]
    After administering Holy Communion to the children,
the angel once again bowed down to the ground profoundly, repeating three times the prayer he had just taught

[1] Ibid. For a version of this prayer more commonly used in the United
States, see Appendix A.
[2] Ibid., p. 63.

them. Lucia tells us in her memoirs that the three vision-aries were so overwhelmed by a supernatural atmosphere that they too prostrated themselves and repeated the prayer three times. Lucia described the experience as so intense that the children seemed deprived of the use of their bodily senses, as they had been during the first angel apparition. We can only assume that the children were in a kind of ecstasy, which some people who have grown significantly in holiness have also experienced. Lucia also mentioned that their souls were filled with peace and happiness, which seemed to stay with them. At the same time, a great phys-ical exhaustion came over them. After praying as he did, the angel left the children. His mission was now over.

Catholic Eucharistic Devotion and the Third Angel Apparition

One thing we can learn from this apparition of the angel is the importance of our Catholic Eucharistic devotion. We have seen how the angel held aloft the Body and Blood of Christ for the children to adore. He himself bowed pro-foundly before the Lord's Eucharistic presence and taught the children to do the same. He then gave the Eucharistic Body and Blood of Jesus to the children. Eucharistic ado-ration and receiving Jesus in Holy Communion, along with attending the Holy Sacrifice of the Mass, are the essential elements of our Catholic devotion to Jesus in the Most Blessed Sacrament.

The Holy Sacrifice of the Mass

The Mass is the high point of our Eucharistic devotion because it is the unbloody renewal of the sacrifice of Jesus on the Cross. Jesus died once and for all to save us from our sins. He is now in glory, and he can never suffer or die again. But his death was the greatest act of love the world has ever seen; God died that his own creatures might live. Not all of Jesus' followers could have been at Calvary two thousand years ago to witness this greatest act of love; but by the Holy Sacrifice of the Mass, Jesus made it possible for the merits and graces of his sacrificial death to be present for all his followers everywhere on earth, even until the end of time. Thus we can speak about the infinite value of the Holy Sacrifice of the Mass.

Holy Communion

Holy Communion is also a very important part of our Eucharistic devotion as Catholics. We saw how the angel gave the children the Body and Blood of Christ. We also receive in Holy Communion the very Body, Blood, Soul and Divinity of Jesus. He lives in us and strengthens us to live our Christian lives faithfully every day. Just like the Jewish people had the manna in the desert to feed them during their long journey to the promised land of Israel, so we Christians have Jesus, the Bread of Life, to be our food for our journey to heaven. God allowed Francisco and Jacinta to receive Holy Communion from the angel even though they had not yet received their First Holy Communion in church. It was to strengthen them for the mission that he would give them that God wanted all three of the children to receive Jesus. Later on, during her July 13 apparition, our Lady would speak about the Communion of Reparation, which was to be an essential part of her request for the Five First Saturdays devotion. Our Lady wants us to stay close to her Divine Son in the Eucharist.

Eucharistic Adoration

Finally, Eucharistic adoration completes our devotion to our Lord in the Most Blessed Sacrament. Adoration includes the time we spend either in quiet or communal prayer before Jesus in the tabernacle or before Jesus exposed on the altar. Benediction of the Most Blessed Sacrament, which often concludes periods of adoration, is also a part of this devotion to the Eucharistic presence of the Lord. We need moments of adoration to speak heart-to-heart with our Eucharistic Lord so that we get to know him in a very personal way. Many people observe a Eucharistic holy hour. Archbishop Sheen, for example, was known for his daily practice of this devotion. Despite a very busy schedule, for sixty-two years he faithfully kept a promise he made in the seminary to make a daily holy hour because Jesus had asked for holy hours when he said to his apostles in the garden of Gethsemane: "Could you not watch and pray one hour with me?"(Mk 14:37–38). Archbishop Sheen generously responded to our Lord's request by promising to spend an hour with him each day. He said there are three main reasons for the Eucharistic holy hour: (1) our friendship with Jesus, (2) our transformation through God's grace and (3) our calling to make reparation and intercession for sinners. Let us look at each of these reasons separately.

First, our friendship with Jesus is based on the fact that he befriended us. Friends love to spend time together, and so we should love to spend time with Jesus, who is our greatest friend. We also like to give to our friends the things they ask of us. Since Jesus asked us for an hour, it is a sign of our love for him that we give him this time.

Second, holy hours will change us. We will be transformed by Jesus' love and grace that he pours forth into our hearts as we spend time with him. In addition, we can make known to him all our needs and concerns, whatever they might be. Jesus will lessen our cares and burdens, and pour his love, peace, and joy upon us. "Come to me, all who labor and are heavy laden, and I will give you rest. Take my yoke upon you, and learn from me; for I am gentle and lowly in heart, and you will find rest for your souls. For my yoke is easy, and my burden is light" (Mt 11:28–30). What better place to experience the peace of Christ than in Jesus' Eucharistic presence?

Third, Eucharistic adoration allows us to offer both reparation and intercession for sinners. The Angel of Peace had already talked to the children about these things in his second apparition. In his third visit, he stressed them again in the prayer that he taught them and in the instruction he gave them.

Offenses against the Eucharist

The Angel of Peace taught the children a prayer that focused them on the Holy Eucharist. We should say this prayer often, with reverence and careful attention to the important doctrinal points it expresses. It begins by adoring God as the Most Holy Trinity: the Father, the Son and the Holy Spirit. While saying this prayer, the angel and the children worshipped the Most Holy Trinity with great reverence, profoundly bowing their foreheads to the ground. We have already discussed the need for reverence, as well as childlike confidence, when we pray to Almighty God. The next part of the prayer offers Jesus to the Holy Trinity, because he is really present in the Blessed Sacrament in his Body, Blood, Soul and Divinity. The prayer offers the Eucharistic presence of Jesus in all the tabernacles of the world in reparation for outrages, sacrileges and indifference. Let us look at each.

Outrages

Outrages refer to serious acts of blasphemy and dishonor in regards to the Holy Eucharist. Unfortunately, there are satanic groups who profane the Eucharist, treating Jesus' Eucharistic presence with deliberate and horrific disdain. In countries where Catholics have been persecuted, churches have been damaged or destroyed while the Most Blessed Sacrament has been desecrated. Even in places where the Church is tolerated, consecrated Hosts have been found on the floors of churches after Mass was ended. Reparation for these offenses consists of acts of adoration, love and faith to make up for the dishonor shown to the Eucharistic presence of Jesus.

Sacrileges

Sacrileges generally occur when the faithful fail to give the Lord proper honor, especially when receiving him in Holy Communion. When speaking about receiving Jesus in Holy Communion, Saint Paul reminds us that it is important to receive our Eucharistic Lord worthily. He dealt with this question in his first letter to the Corinthians:

> For as often as you eat this bread and drink the chalice, you proclaim the Lord's death until He comes! Whoever, there-fore, eats the bread or drinks the cup of the Lord in an unworthy manner will be guilty of profaning the body and blood of the Lord. Let a man examine himself and so eat of the bread and drink of the cup. For any one who eats and drinks without discerning the body eats and drinks a judgment upon himself. That is why many of you are weak and ill, and some have died. (1 Cor 11:26–30)

In accordance with Saint Paul's teaching, the Catholic Church has always said that it is necessary to be in the state of grace to receive the Body and Blood of the Lord worthily. Should one knowingly and deliberately receive Holy Communion while conscious of mortal sin on his soul, he would be guilty of a sacrilege. Regular confession helps us to remain in the state of grace, so that we are always ready to receive the Lord worthily. Desiring to be always ready to receive Jesus can help us resist temptations to commit mortal sin. The story of Saint Maria Goretti is very inspiring. When a young man approached her and asked her to commit a sin of impurity, she refused, because the act would make her unworthy to receive Jesus in Holy Communion. When on another occasion he threatened her with violence, she remained steadfast. Though Maria lost her life, her purity saved not only her soul but that of her murderer. May her courageous example help all of us avoid mortal sin.

Pope John Paul II was very concerned that many Catholics were losing their sensitivity to sin. He remarked that it was good to see a lot of people going to Holy Communion, but where were these same people when it came to confession? He was afraid many were receiving unworthily. The angel's prayer provides a way to offer reparation for those who are receiving unworthily and to pray for their conversion.

Indifference

Acts of indifference include times when we do not show proper respect and care toward our Lord in the Eucharist. Allowing ourselves to be distracted during Mass and talking needlessly in church are examples of indifference. To this list we could add dressing inappropriately for church or sitting passively through the Mass. These behaviors reveal a lukewarm heart. They indicate that we need to become more ardent in our love of Jesus in this beautiful gift he gives of himself in the Most Blessed Sacrament. The visionaries ardently longed to receive Jesus in Holy Communion. They poured their hearts out to Jesus, whom they loved so much. They prayed the angel's prayer countless times, giving the Lord the love others refused to give him and obtaining the grace of conversion for them, that they might be saved.

The Angel's Instructions

By praying the angel's prayers often, the children were fulfilling his instructions. The Angel of Peace had said to them: "Console your God!" The fervent love of these little children was truly a gift to console God for the ingratitude, and even hatred, of so many.

Through the angel's three visits, the children were instructed in the ways of prayer; the importance of reparation, intercession and suffering; and the beauty and power of the Eucharist. Over the course of the next six months, the children put into practice all the angel had taught them. They were then ready to receive the first visit of their Blessed Mother.

5

THE MAY AND JUNE APPARITIONS OF OUR LADY OF FATIMA

A Beautiful Lady Came From Heaven

May 13, 1917

WE HAVE ALREADY DISCUSSED some of the background to the story of Our Lady of Fatima. World War I seemed like it would never end, so Pope Benedict XV called for a novena in honor of Our Lady, the Queen of Peace. On the eighth day of the novena, May 13, 1917, the Blessed Mother made her first of six appearances to Lucia, Francisco and Jacinta.

At the Cova da Iria

May 13 was a Sunday that year. The three little children went early to Mass. Then they took their flocks of sheep to the Cova da Iria (Cove of Irene or Cove of Peace) to graze them, while they themselves ate their lunches and said their prayers. It was a beautiful sunny day with blue skies. Then, while the children were playing their games, they saw what seemed to be a flash of lightning. They thought a thunderstorm was brewing so they decided to head home. Hurrying with their flocks, they saw another flash. They had gone a few steps more when before them, on a small holmoak tree, they saw a lady dressed in white. Here is the way Lucia described her:

> She was more brilliant than the sun, and radiated light more clear and intense than a crystal glass filled with sparkling water, when the rays of the burning sun shine through it.[1]

Lucia later added other details of our Lady's appearance. She looked about seventeen years old. She wore a mantle and a tunic that seemed to be made of light. Around her neck was a cord with a little ball of light. There was a star toward the bottom of her tunic. In her hands were beads of a rosary which shone like stars, with the crucifix the most radiant of all.

What an impression this apparition must have made on the young children! It is interesting to note that light accompanied both the Angel of Peace and our Lady in their appearances to the children. In Scripture, light is often a symbol of God and his Kingdom, as opposed to the kingdom of darkness of Satan and his followers. Light was the first gift God created: "Let there be light" (Gn 1:3). Jesus called himself the light of the world (Jn 9:5). Jesus sent his own mother and the Angel of Peace to give the children the light of his truth and love so that they in turn would help to spread this light throughout the world.

Lucia's Conversation with Our Lady

Our Lady sensed the initial apprehension on the part of the young visionaries. So, she hastened to calm them: "Do not be afraid. I will do you no harm."[2] Like the Angel of Peace,

[1] Ibid., p. 156.
[2] Ibid., p. 158.

our Lady's first concern was that the children not be afraid. She knew how overwhelming the brilliant light would be to the children, especially since this was her first appearance to them. The children, however, quickly became used to the light around our Lady and felt at ease in her presence. Lucia then spoke on behalf of all three of the visionaries. As already noted, all three children saw our Lady, but only Lucia and Jacinta could hear her; Lucia was the only one who actually spoke to our Lady.

Talk about Heaven

Feeling joy and confidence in her presence, Lucia asked the Blessed Mother a question: "Where are you from?" Our Lady answered very simply: "I am from heaven." Lucia then asked a second question: "What do you want of me?" Our Lady answered that she wanted the children to return there on the thirteenth of each month for the next six months, and at the very same hour. "Later on I will tell you who I am and what I want. Afterwards I will return here yet a seventh time." [3] Lucia then asked if each of the three visionaries would go to heaven. The Lady said they would, but Francisco would first need to say many rosaries. As our Lady said these words, she looked at Francisco with a glance of compassion mingled with a little sadness.

Purgatory Is Real

Then Lucia asked about two young women who had recently died. They were friends who had stayed at her house while one of her older sisters taught them how to

[3] Ibid. The "seventh time" refers to the apparition to Sister Lucia on June 16, 1921.

weave. Lucia asked our Lady: "Is Maria Neves already in heaven?" Our Lady answered: "Yes, she is." Maria was about sixteen years old when she died. Then Lucia asked about Amelia, who had been between the ages of eighteen and twenty. Our Lady's answer was startling: "She will be in purgatory until the end of the world." It was later learned that Amelia died in circumstances involving immoral behavior. Only God knows why she would be in purgatory until the end of the world. To be in purgatory, she must have been sincerely sorry for her sins when she died; however, she probably did not have sufficient time before her death to make satisfaction for all the temporal punishment due to these sins.[4] The fate of Amelia is a powerful reminder to practice the virtues of a Christian life and to do penance now, while we have the chance, so that when we die we may go as quickly as possible to heaven.

The Mission to Suffer

Our Blessed Lady next asked the visionaries a very important question. We might even say it is at the heart of her first apparition.

Are you willing to offer yourselves to God and bear all the sufferings He wills to send you, as an act of reparation for

[4] There are two kinds of punishments God in his justice imposes for sin: eternal and temporal. When a person dies with unrepented mortal sin on his soul, he incurs eternal punishment (that is eternal separation from God in hell). Because of the redeeming sacrifice of Christ, God mercifully removes our eternal punishment when we repent of our sins. However, sin damages us, and we must do penance during our lifetime on earth (that is, satisfaction for our temporal punishments) in order to repair the harm we have done. After death, any temporal punishments left unsatisfied by our voluntary penance will be endured in purgatory until we are ready to enter the presence of God.

the sins by which He is offended, and of supplication for the conversion of sinners?[5]

When God calls someone to a mission in his plan of salvation, he never forces him to accept it. He always asks for his free, loving and generous consent. When the archangel Gabriel presented God's message to our Lady at the Annunciation, he invited her to accept freely God's will. Our Lady's loving answer, "Behold, I am the handmaid of the Lord; let it be to me according to your word", brought about the greatest event in human history. At the moment Mary gave her free, loving consent, the Second Person of the Blessed Trinity became man. In a similar way, our Lady desired the children to give their free, loving consent to God's plan in their own lives. With great enthusiasm, the children responded: "Yes, we are willing." We can see in their joyful consent how the children had learned to offer prayers, make sacrifices and endure patiently any sufferings God sent to them because of the teaching they had received from the Angel of Portugal. The children had been prepared well for what our Lady was asking of them.

After the children placed their lives at the disposal of God's plan, our Lady told them suffering would come: "Then you are going to have much to suffer, but the grace of God will be your comfort."[6] We shall soon see how much the children were to suffer for the love of Christ and our Lady in order that many souls may be saved.

A Beautiful Light Penetrates the Children's Souls

After our Lady had accepted the generous consent of the children to suffer and promised them God's comfort, a

[5] *Lucia's Memoirs*, p. 158.
[6] Ibid.

wonderful thing happened. A light from our Lady enveloped the children and consoled them greatly. Here is how Lucia described what happened:

> Our Lady opened her hands for the first time, communicating to us a light so intense that, as it streamed from her hands, its rays penetrated our hearts and the innermost depths of our souls, making us see ourselves in God, Who was that light, more clearly than we see ourselves in the best of mirrors. Then, moved by an interior impulse that was also communicated to us, we fell on our knees, repeating in our hearts:
> "O most Holy Trinity, I adore you! My God, my God, I love You in the most Blessed Sacrament!" [7]

Request for the Daily Rosary

The children remained kneeling for a few moments in the marvelous light that enveloped them. Then our Lady made another request of them: "Pray the Rosary every day to obtain peace for the world, and the end of the war." [8] The children, in their innocence and simplicity and living far from the fields of battle, would have understood little about the harsh realities of the war. However, our Lady's request that they daily pray the Rosary for peace was the only request she repeated in all six of her apparitions to the three visionaries. How powerful this prayer must be if it can obtain peace for the world. We, too, need to put into practice our Lady's request to pray the Rosary daily for peace in our time and an end to the culture of death so prevalent today.

[7] Ibid.
[8] Ibid., p. 160.

The First Apparition Ends, but the Suffering Begins

Lucia said that our Lady then began to rise very serenely in the direction of the east until she disappeared in the immense distance. The light that surrounded her seemed to open a way for her amidst the stars. Lucia said it was like heaven opened for her.

The serenity caused by Mary's presence was soon lost after her absence. Lucia practically begged her two younger cousins not to mention anything to anyone about the vision of our Lady. She had an intuition that people would not welcome such news. She was quite right, especially regarding her own family. Her younger cousins promised they would say nothing. Jacinta, however, in her innocence and great joy could not restrain herself from telling her mother everything about "the beautiful Lady from heaven". Her mother, Olimpia, thought Jacinta's story was simply a childish fancy. Her brothers and sisters laughed at the story and even made fun of their little sister. Her father, Ti Marto, a prudent man, believed his little daughter because she had never lied and because her brother Francisco confirmed her story. Furthermore, he believed that if our Lady had appeared at other times, why could she not appear to Lucia, Francisco and Jacinta? Because of his attitude, Ti Marto became the first believer in the Fatima apparitions.

It was to be quite different for Lucia. Her mother, Maria Rosa, strongly disbelieved her. She thought Lucia was the instigator of a fraud, if not of a blasphemy. Complicating things further, the family had recently suffered a number of difficulties. Maria was afraid that people would become more angry at her family if her youngest daughter was fabricating a hoax. As a result of their mother's attitude, the whole family turned against Lucia. Even friends and neighbors began to turn against her, making fun of her and mocking her. As she wrote in her memoirs, "My mother and my sisters persisted in their contemptuous attitude, and this cut me to the heart, and was indeed as hurtful to me as insults." [9] Lucia's whole world seemed to be caving in on her. The sufferings our Lady had mentioned came quickly.

When Lucia's mother could not get her to recant her story, she brought her daughter to see the parish priest, Father Manuel Ferreira. His approach was cautious and prudent. He listened to Lucia's story very carefully. He was not convinced that she had seen a heavenly vision, but he advised Maria Rosa to wait and see what would happen in the months ahead. He also told her not to stop Lucia and the others from returning to the Cova. Needless to say, Maria Rosa was disappointed with Father Ferreira's response. She wanted him to condemn the "vision" as an illusion or even the devil's trick. Time would tell he did the right thing.

Though her mother did not keep her from the Cova, Lucia became so saddened and discouraged by all the disbelief and ridicule she was receiving that she herself actually began to feel that she should not return to the Cova in June. Even the pleading of her cousins Francisco and Jacinta could not convince her otherwise. But when the time for the June apparition actually came, she felt herself so drawn back to the Cova that she simply could not stay away. All three of the visionaries were present when our Lady arrived on June 13.

June 13, 1917—Our Lady's Second Apparition

In Portugal June 13 is a day of great celebration. It is the feast of one of the great patrons of Portugal, Saint Anthony (1195–1231), one of the most popular saints in the Catholic

[9] Ibid., pp. 66–67.

Church. To most of the world, he is known as Saint Anthony of Padua, the city in Italy where he died. But the Portuguese people call him Saint Anthony of Lisbon because he was born in Lisbon, Portugal. There has been an ongoing dispute between the Portuguese and the Italians over what his name should be. When Pope John Paul II visited Portugal, he told a large crowd that their native saint was not Saint Anthony of Padua. The people cheered! Then the Pope said that he was not Saint Anthony of Lisbon either, and the people were stunned to silence. Finally, the Pope said that their saint was Saint Anthony of the whole world, and the people cheered loudly!

June 13, 1917, was a day of added celebration in Fatima because the parish church was named after Saint Anthony. Most of the people went to the church celebration, but the three little visionaries made their way to the Cova da Iria for their appointed meeting at noon with the beautiful Lady from heaven. Some people accompanied them from their village to the apparition site, where a small group of people were already waiting for them. In all about fifty people gathered together at the Cova. They even joined the three children in praying the Rosary as they awaited the coming of our Lady. After finishing the Rosary, the children saw a light coming toward them, and suddenly our Lady was present on the holmoak tree like she had been in May.

Lucia's Conversation with Our Lady

Simple Requests of Our Lady—Lucia began with her usual question: "What do you want of me?" Our Lady responded with a short list of requests, some of which she had already made in May. First, she told Lucia to come back with Francisco and Jacinta on July 13. Then our Lady repeated another of her requests from May, to pray the Rosary every day.

Mary's third request was new: she told Lucia to learn to read. As we will see, it was Lucia's mission to spread our Lady's message from Fatima to the whole world. It was most important, then, for Lucia to learn to read and write. She learned quite successfully. Eventually, she even mastered the use of the computer. Our Lady then finished her remarks by saying: "Later I will tell you what I want." [10] In her July apparition our Lady would make known other requests.

Lucia Asks for Healing—Lucia then requested a cure for a sick person. Our Lady responded, "If he is converted he will be cured during the year." We do not know the person Lucia had in mind or what the specific healing was that she asked for. We do know that these requests for healings and other significant blessings and graces increased as the crowds at the Cova grew over the months. Our Lady's response reminds us that a true and living faith was required by our Lord when he worked many of his miraculous healings in the Gospels. For example, he asked two blind men who wanted to receive their sight, "Do you believe that I am able to do this?" When they responded that they believed, he said, "According to your faith be it done to you" (Mt 9:28–30), and they recovered their sight. On the other hand, Matthew tells us that Jesus could not work many miracles in his native town of Nazareth because of their lack of faith in him (Mt 13:57–58).

Saint Augustine tells us that God does not answer prayers for one of three reasons. The person is asking for "wrong things" (e.g., money, worldly possessions, occasions of sin, etc., all of which could hinder the person's eternal salvation); he is asking while "living wrongly" (e.g., living a sinful life, giving no thought to how he is offending God);

[10] Ibid., p. 160.

or, he is "asking in the wrong way" (e.g., asking without trust or belief that God can help him, or asking without perseverance in his requests). Our Lady spoke of a sick person's need for conversion. The person in question could have needed to change in any one of the ways Augustine mentions or in all three of them. Our Lady's words are an important reminder to all of us that when we ask God for blessings, and especially for a healing, we need to be properly disposed.

Lucia's Request to Go to Heaven—As we already saw in our Lady's first apparition, Lucia asked if the children would go to heaven. This time Lucia asked on behalf of all three visionaries if the Lady would take them there. Our Lady's answer reveals an important part of God's plan:

> Yes, I will take Jacinta and Francisco soon. But you are to stay here some time longer. Jesus wishes to make use of you to make me known and loved. He wants to establish in the world devotion to my Immaculate Heart.[11]

These words of our Lady must have caused great joy and sorrow at the same time. They brought joy to Jacinta and Francisco because they longed so much to go to heaven, but for Lucia, our Lady's words brought sorrow. She would have to stay long after her little cousins went to heaven and spread our Lady's message to the whole world. Just as Jesus had chosen Saint Faustina to be the "apostle" and "secretary" for devotion to Divine Mercy, so in a similar way he chose Lucia to be an apostle and secretary for devotion to the Immaculate Heart of Mary. However, our Lady made promises to those who would embrace devotion to her under this title: promises of salvation and of being specially loved

[11] Ibid., p. 161.

by God. One who would experience the special love of the Immaculate Heart was Lucia herself. When she asked our Lady if she would be alone after her cousins went to heaven, our Lady replied:

> No, my daughter. Are you suffering a great deal? Don't lose heart. I will never forsake you. My Immaculate Heart will be your refuge and the way that will lead you to God.[12]

Lucia lived nearly eighty-seven more years from the time God entrusted this mission to her. All through those many years, she remained faithful to the task of spreading devotion to the Immaculate Heart of Mary.

The Apparition Ends with a Heavenly Light

As soon as our Lady finished speaking, she opened her hands and communicated to the children an immense light that enveloped them, as happened at the end of the first apparition. In this light the children saw themselves submerged in God. Jacinta and Francisco appeared to be in a part of the light that was rising to heaven, while Lucia was in a light spreading over the earth. This vision confirmed what our Lady had just told the children about their future. Finally, the children saw the heart of our Lady surrounded with piercing thorns, which represented the offenses committed against her. These were the sins that needed reparation, and the children were eager to offer it.

[12] Ibid.

6

THE JULY APPARITION: PART I

The First Secret—The Vision of Hell

An Important Message with Three Parts

WITHOUT DOUBT THE APPEARANCES of our Lady in July and October of 1917 were the most powerful and important of all the Fatima apparitions. In July our Lady gave the children the core of her message, which blended many serious warnings with a promise of hope in the ultimate victory of her Immaculate Heart. In October our Lady provided the miraculous sign by which people would know that the apparitions to the children were real.

In one of his many statements about Our Lady of Fatima, Pope John Paul II said that she summed up the whole twentieth century. In her July apparition, she made reference to some of the most momentous events and movements that shaped the modern world. She spoke of the end of World War I, but warned of another greater war that would happen if people did not heed her call to prayer, penance and amendment of life. She warned of the menace of Communism that would arise in Russia and spread its evil teachings throughout the world, provoking wars and other calamities, especially persecutions of the Catholic Church. She also warned of famines that would affect various parts of the world, such as eastern Europe in the 1930s.

When Lucia later described the July apparition of our Lady, she divided the message into three parts, which she called "secrets". She explained the first two secrets in one of her memoirs on August 31, 1941, and she made some additions to this text on December 8, 1941. She wrote about the Third Secret under the date of January 3, 1944. She stated that she did so "by order of His Excellency, the Bishop of Leiria,[1] and the Most Holy Mother". This separate manuscript was placed into a sealed envelope, which was initially kept in the custody of Bishop da Silva of Leiria. On April 4, 1957, the unopened envelope was placed in the secret archives of the Holy Office at the Vatican. This extreme confidentiality led to a great deal of speculation and conjecture about the contents of the Third Secret, which were finally revealed by Pope John Paul II at the Mass of Beatification of Francisco and Jacinta Marto in the Cova da Iria on May 13, 2000. This chapter will deal with the First Secret, while the Second and Third secrets will follow in the next two chapters.

A Crowd Accompanies the Children

By the time our Lady appeared on July 13, word of the apparitions had spread throughout Portugal. Many people believed the children were telling the truth, but there were also many who doubted the children, some because of their atheistic beliefs and others because they thought the visions were from the devil. In spite of it all, a crowd of about four thousand people were present in the Cova for the July 13

[1] Dom Jose Alves Correia da Silva, bishop of Leiria, the diocese that includes Fatima, 1920–1957.

visit of our Lady. Many of them were praying the Rosary before she arrived; as in the previous apparitions, our Lady appeared above the holmoak tree.

Lucia Puts Questions to Our Lady

As the apparition began, Lucia brought up three concerns to our Lady. The first was her usual question: "What do you want of me?" In her answer our Lady repeated things she had already told the children: to return on the thirteenth of the month and to pray the Rosary daily. Again, our Lady stressed the power and importance of the Rosary to obtain world peace, but she added two new phrases: "in honor of Our Lady of the Rosary ... because only she can help you." [2] Lucia would later reveal that Jesus told her he had placed the peace of the world into the hands and heart of his mother! Jesus therefore desires us to achieve peace in the world with our Lady's help and intercession.

Lucia's second concern arose from the scepticism of her family, especially of her mother, and from the ridicule she was receiving from people who did not believe in the apparitions. "I would like to ask you to tell us who you are, and to work a miracle so that everybody will believe that you are appearing to us." [3] In her May apparition, our Lady had said to the children only that "later on" she would tell them who she is. This time she told them when: In October she would both reveal her identity and perform a miracle to help people believe the apparitions are real.

Finally, Lucia requested favors for various people. As the number of people grew at the apparition site, as well as at the homes of the visionaries, the number of requests for

---

[2] *Lucia's Memoirs*, p. 161.
[3] Ibid.

both spiritual and material favors increased. Lucia did not remember all the favors she asked for on this occasion, but she did remember our Lady telling her it would be "necessary for such people to pray the Rosary in order to obtain the graces" [4] they were requesting.

The Vision of Hell and Prayers to Save Sinners

The little shepherd children then had what is probably the most frightening experience anyone could ever undergo—a vision of hell. Why Jesus and Mary allowed this and what the effects of it were will be looked at very carefully. Before doing that, it is important to point out that our Lady prepared the children with a heartfelt plea on behalf of those of her spiritual children who were in danger of being eternally lost from God:

> Sacrifice yourselves for sinners, and say many times, especially whenever you make any sacrifice: O Jesus, it is for love of You, for the conversion of sinners, and in reparation for the sins committed against the Immaculate Heart of Mary. [5]

These words of our Lady found a ready place in the minds and hearts of the three little visionaries. They had already been given the message of sacrifice, reparation and the salvation of sinners by the Angel of Peace. They understood, despite their tender years, the desire of God to share his work of redemption with them. They were already generous in making sacrifices, and our Lady's words only made them more so. Each part of the prayer she taught them is significant.

[4] Ibid.
[5] Ibid., p. 162.

"O Jesus, It Is for Love of You"—The main purpose of everything we do should be the love of Jesus. God wants us to love him with all our mind, heart, soul and body! This petition helps us to fulfill this desire. Furthermore, when we pray it as the visionaries did, our zeal for the greater glory of God will grow rapidly.

"For the Conversion of Sinners"—The children knew very well that Jesus had suffered and died for the conversion of sinners. Mary, in her turn, spiritually shared in Jesus' suffering and death. Their love for our Lord and our Blessed Mother moved them deeply to share in the redemptive mission. This concern for the salvation of others is a sign of closeness to God. Saint Francis of Assisi used to say that nothing should take precedence over the work of saving souls for whom Jesus shed his Precious Blood. Saint Therese of Lisieux said that she was about fourteen years old when God gave her a great desire to save souls. One of the first situations in which she would practice her zeal was to pray and offer sacrifices for the conversion of a hardened criminal who had killed three people. He was facing the death sentence, but remained unrepentant. Saint Therese asked God to give him sorrow for his sins so that he might be saved. Even if he did not go to confession, Therese asked God to give her some sign that he was sorry. Moments before he was executed, the criminal reached out, took hold of a crucifix near him and kissed it! Therese saw that as a sign that God had accepted her prayers and sacrifices for his conversion. She went on to convert many other sinners by her hidden prayers and sacrifices. Our Lady of Fatima is asking us to do the same.

"In Reparation for the Sins Committed against the Immaculate Heart of Mary"—This was a new intention for which the children were to offer reparation. At the end

of the June 13 apparition, the children had seen the Immaculate Heart of Mary surrounded by a crown of thorns. They
understood that these thorns represented the outrageous sins
of those who offend our Lady. The prayer our Lady taught
them asks for reparation for these blasphemies.

The Vision of Hell

As our Lady was finishing the prayer, she opened her hands
as she had done in her two previous apparitions. Rays of
light once again came from her hands, but what the children saw was far different from what they had seen the first
two times. Here is Lucia's description of the First Secret—
the vision of hell:

> The rays of light seemed to penetrate the earth, and we
> saw as it were a sea of fire. Plunged in this fire were demons
> and souls in human form, like transparent burning embers,
> all blackened or burnished bronze, floating about in the con-
> flagration, now raised into the air by the flames that issued
> from within themselves together with great clouds of smoke,
> now falling back on every side like sparks in huge fires,
> without weight or equilibrium, amid shrieks and groans of
> pain and despair, which horrified us and made us tremble
> with fear.... The demons could be distinguished by their
> terrifying and repellent likeness to frightful and unknown
> animals, black and transparent like burning coals. Terrified
> and as if to plead for succour, we looked up at Our Lady,
> who said to us, so kindly and so sadly: "You have seen hell
> where the souls of poor sinners go. To save them, God wishes
> to establish in the world devotion to my Immaculate Heart.
> If what I say to you is done, many souls will be saved and
> there will be peace." [6]

[6] Ibid.

One can only imagine the impact this vision of hell must have had on the little children. Lucia said later that if our Lady had not already told them that they were going to heaven, they might have died of fright. Witnesses at the Cova at the time, though not knowing what the children saw, said that after the July apparition their faces showed signs of fear, terror and shock.

Why a Vision of Hell?

The first question that comes to mind is why did Jesus and Mary allow the children to see such a terrifying vision of hell? This question is very important because it brings us to the heart of why our Lady appeared. She came to lead men back to God, who has been so grievously offended by their sins.

Hell Is Real

Hell is not a pleasant topic. Many writers do not like to write about it, many preachers do not like to preach about it, and many people do not like to hear about it. Hell is so disturbing that people do not even want to consider it as a possibility; they prefer, instead, to live as if hell did not exist. It is interesting that when religious surveys are conducted and questions of heaven and hell are asked, the results are quite different. When asked if they believe in hell, many people say no because they believe life cannot be any worse than it is now. Also, many people do not want to face the fact that they could end up in hell. When these same people are asked if they believe in heaven, many of them say yes because they hope in a life better than what they have now.

The children did not need to see the vision of hell for their own sakes; they had already been assured by our Lady that they would be going to heaven and they were living good and holy lives pleasing to God. They were given the vision of hell to remind *us* that hell is real. That in turn reminds us that we must live our lives in such a way that we stay close to God. Simply denying that there is a hell does not make it go away. Saint Padre Pio was hearing the confession of a man who was leading a very bad life. Padre Pio warned him that if he didn't change his immoral living, he would end up in hell. The man answered Padre Pio: "I don't believe in hell!" Padre Pio immediately retorted, "You will when you get there!" Of course, that will be too late. We must make our salvation our main purpose in life. As Jesus said, "For what does it profit a man, to gain the whole world and forfeit his life? For what can a man give in return for his life?" (Mk 8:36–37).

Fear of Hell Can Motivate Someone to Turn from Sin

There are many people who are so self-centered and enslaved by sinful habits that they do not even think of turning to God. That would require unselfish love, and such people do not have that kind of love. However, out of their self-love and self-concern, they could be affected by the thought that they might have to spend eternity in great suffering. As a result, such fear (called "servile fear" or "fear of punishment") could actually move them to turn away from sin and start them on the road to God. Such a person would eventually need to develop true contrition, which is remorse for having offended God, who is all good and deserving of all our love.

Even some great saints needed the fear of hell to start them on the journey to holiness. One such person was

Saint Teresa of Jesus (Avila), one of the greatest women in
the history of the Catholic Church. She had entered the
Carmelite Order around age twenty, and in about four years
she had reached the beginning of mystical prayer. Teresa
was a rather attractive woman, with a sharp wit and great
insights into the spiritual life. These attributes made her a
favorite of the wealthy women who often came to the monastery to chit-chat about spiritual things. Unfortunately, she
began to spend a great deal of her time each day in the
parlor instead of with the Lord in prayer. This went on for
about nineteen years. She tried various times to return to a
serious prayer life, but she would always fall back into hours
in the parlor.

When her father died, his confessor came to the convent
to speak with Sister Teresa. When he realized the kind of
life she was living, with such serious inattention to prayer,
he told her that she could easily lose her soul if she continued to neglect the most important part of her contemplative
life. Added to that counsel was a dream she had of a narrow
shaft filled with snakes, spiders, and scorpions—all of which
she hated. Teresa understood that this horrible place was in
hell and that it was being prepared for her because she had
abandoned her responsibilities as a religious. The image had
such a powerful effect that she not only returned to more
frequent and ardent prayer, but also desired to live a fervent
Carmelite life according to its stricter primitive observance.
Thus, she became the great reformer of the Carmelite nuns.
Fear was necessary for her in the beginning so that she could
attain a truly great love in the end.

It Is Important to Reflect on the End of Our Earthly Lives

Pope John Paul II often recommended that the faithful meditate on what are called the "four last things": (1) death—we

all are going to die someday; (2) judgment—each one of us will then be judged by Jesus on whether our actions have been good or evil, and whether or not we cooperated with his grace during our stay on earth; (3) heaven—the place and condition of perfect and eternal joy, love and peace with God in his Kingdom; and (4) hell—the place and state of eternal punishment created for the angels who rebelled against God and those human beings who die resisting God's mercy.

What are the sufferings of hell? Briefly, there are four main sufferings. (1) The loss of God and his love for all eternity—this pain is the greatest suffering because we were made to possess God's love. Those in heaven will forever have God's love; those in hell, however, will never be able to love God or be loved by him because they refused God's love and forgiveness during their earthly lives. The loss of God is like having an infinite hunger that can never be satisfied. (2) The pain of fire—the children saw how terrible this suffering was for those condemned to hell. On earth we have such a difficult time putting up with even the smallest suffering. In hell this suffering will never end. (3) The reproach of conscience—sometimes we read of people who cannot live with the thought of the evil things they have done in their lifetime. The souls in hell will constantly reproach themselves for the evil they did which has caused them to be separated from God and to suffer so much, (4) The vision of the devil—before his fall into sin Lucifer, was a beautiful angel; but after he rebelled, he became totally disfigured. As beautiful as he was before his fall, that is how ugly he is now. Saint Catherine of Siena once saw the devil for a moment; she was so repulsed by him that she pleaded with God to give her any other suffering but spare her from seeing the devil again! The torments of hell are so terrible that Jesus said it would be better to lose an eye, a hand or a foot if it causes a person to sin than to keep one's body intact but end up in hell.

The Devil Is Real and Dangerous

Many people do not believe in the existence of evil spirits. It has often been said that the devil's greatest deceit is to make people think he does not exist. This way, people will do nothing to guard against his temptations. The devil has basically two titles. First, he is called the "deceiver". In this role he presents himself as a friend who wants to make us an offer. But as Adam and Eve discovered, you never make a deal with Satan and win. His second title is the "accuser". In this role he presents himself as our adversary, condemning us mercilessly for the sins we have committed and telling us that there is no hope of forgiveness. All we have left then is despair!

It is very, very important to remember that the devil can never do any harm to us, whether physical or spiritual, that God does not allow him to do. Mainly the devil tries to lead us away from God through sin. After we have fallen into sin, he tries to convince us that we are beyond the help of God's grace, that we have burned our bridges behind us. Sometimes God allows him to cause some obstacles to hinder our work, especially when we are working for the salvation of souls. One obstacle is confusion. For example, he tried to make Lucia think that the apparitions of our Lady were not from God and that by claiming they were, she would be punished by God. Another time, God permitted the devil to appear to Francisco to try to scare him. He called on the help of the Blessed Mother and she came. Sometimes the devil tries to make us afraid in order to discourage us from praying, doing works of charity, and the like. If we feel upset by the devil, we need to pray with trust and confidence for the protection of Jesus, Mary and

Joseph. We should also say every day the prayer to Saint Michael the Archangel to defend us in spiritual battle against the devil. As the Bible says: "Resist the devil and he will flee from you" (Jas 4:7).

Hell as an Incentive for the Salvation of Souls

A final reason we can give for why the children saw the vision of hell may very well be the most important one as far as they were concerned. The overwhelming experience of seeing hell, plus the sorrow with which our Lady spoke about it and her desire that many souls be saved, motivated the children to work unceasingly for the salvation of souls, no matter what the cost. In all the ways they had already learned from our Lady and the Angel of Peace—sacrifices, prayers and sufferings humbly and patiently accepted—the children constantly offered whatever they could so that no one would be lost! After the vision of hell, Our Lady taught the children another special prayer. She asked that it be recited at the end of each decade, or mystery, of the Rosary. It is usually referred to as the "decade prayer":

> O my Jesus, forgive us, save us from the fire of hell. Lead all souls to heaven, especially those who are most in need.[7]

Zeal for the salvation of souls is a characteristic of great holiness. We do not want to go to heaven alone; we want to bring with us as many others as possible. Jesus wants us to cooperate with him and with our Lady in the salvation of souls by our prayer, sacrifice and good Christian example. For the children, no sacrifice would be too great to make.

[7] Ibid., p. 166. For a version of this prayer more commonly used in the United States, see Appendix A.

Lucia wrote that the vision of hell profoundly affected all three of the visionaries, but that Jacinta, the youngest of them, seemed to be especially moved.

> The vision of hell filled her with horror to such a degree, that every penance and mortification was nothing in her eyes, if it could only prevent souls from going there... Jacinta often sat thoughtfully on the ground or on a rock and exclaimed:
>
> "Oh, Hell! Hell! How sorry I am for the souls who go to hell! And the people down there, burning alive, like wood in the fire!" Then, shuddering, she knelt down with her hands joined, and recited the prayer that Our Lady had taught us.[8]

The vision of hell had such an impact on Jacinta that she wished everyone could see it and be persuaded to stop sinning. Though so young, Jacinta showed an ardent love for souls and a tremendous capacity for sacrificing for others. For example, she often gave up food for those who ate too much. Even when sick, she went to a weekday Mass for those who failed to go on Sunday.

The final and most telling example of little Jacinta's zeal for souls came at the end of her brief life on earth. Our Lady appeared to her and her brother when they were suffering from influenza. Our Lady told her she would take Francisco to heaven soon, but asked her if she wanted to remain longer on earth to convert more sinners.[9] Jacinta agreed to stay and suffer longer. Francisco died on April 4, 1919, six months after he and his sister fell ill. Jacinta lingered until February 20, 1920, when she died in a Lisbon hospital.

[8] Ibid., p. 105.
[9] Ibid., p. 42.

7

The July Apparition: Part II

The Second Secret—War, Communism and the Immaculate Heart of Mary

It was on May 13, the eighth day of Pope Benedict XV's novena to our Lady for peace in the world, that she made her first appearance at Fatima. During that apparition our Lady requested of the children that they pray the Rosary for peace every day. During her third apparition in July, she spoke more about peace and war and the importance of devotion to her Immaculate Heart.

World War I and a Message of Peace

World War I began in the summer of 1914 and lasted until November 11, 1918, when an armistice was signed and the guns finally fell silent. It was the deadliest war the world had ever seen, killing about twenty million people. When the war began, it was largely a European conflict between the Allies (France, Great Britain and Russia) and the Central Powers (Austria-Hungary and Germany). It became a world war because gradually, willingly or by force of events, nearly every nation in the world became involved. Germany declared war

on Portugal in 1916 in retaliation for heeding a British request
to intern German ships in Portuguese ports. Small as Portugal
was both in size and population, it committed many soldiers
to the war effort. The United States, after a period of neutrality, entered the war in April 1917 on the side of the Allies.

Benedict XV was elected pope in early September 1914.
He maintained strict neutrality between the warring fac-
tions and attempted to serve as a mediator. He urged the
belligerent powers to observe the law of God and to make
justice and charity the foundation of society; but, since the
causes of this war were rooted in governments and peoples
turning away from God and rejecting Christian ideals, the
Pope's pleas and attempts to reconcile went unheeded. Fueled
by great ambition for material wealth and by extreme forms
of proud and aggressive nationalism, any spirit of cooper-
ation among nations was almost nonexistent, while the role
of the Church in human affairs was disregarded. Protestant
countries took offense at papal interference, and even Catholic Italy joined the Allies on the condition that the Pope
would have nothing to say about the terms of peace. As it
turned out, the treaty at the end of the war was harsh and
oppressive to the Central Powers and laid the groundwork
for an even more terrible conflict.

The devastation being caused by the war prompted Benedict XV to say that it was the "suicide of civilized Europe".
Though his diplomatic efforts were rejected, the Pope did
all that he could to alleviate the human misery resulting
from the war. He helped those civilians being deported,
living in occupied areas and suffering from the severe food
shortages that spread as the war dragged on. He negotiated exchanges of wounded prisoners of war and pleaded
for better treatment of the men detained in POW camps.

In the Second Secret of her July apparition, our Lady
announced to the visionaries what the world had been

desperately waiting to hear: "The war is going to end . . ."
What joy these words must have brought! So much suffering had been caused by the war, not only for the soldiers who were actively engaged in the fighting, but also
for the civilian populations that suffered the unavoidable
evils of war—the loss of loved ones, harsh treatment by
enemy forces and the constant threat of hunger and want.

Pray, Especially the Rosary

Our Lady said that lasting peace could only come about if
certain conditions were met. One of them, as we have already
seen, was prayer, especially the Rosary. Her request for prayer
for world peace raises an important question for us to consider: Why are our prayers needed? Remember Saint Augustine's words: "God made us without us, but he will not
save us without us." We must do our part: we must choose
to offer our prayers and sacrifices for the gift of peace in
the world. In some way, God has made himself dependent
on our prayers and sacrifices. Strictly speaking, he doesn't
need them, but he wants them. Like Saint Padre Pio said of
his sufferings in regard to the salvation of souls: "Jesus wants
my sufferings; Jesus needs my sufferings." The same is true
of our prayers.

Put My Message into Practice

Our Lady added another condition for peace. Let us go
back for a moment to the First Secret on July 13. The visionaries saw hell where unrepentant sinners go. As the vision
of hell was ending, our Lady told them that God desires to
establish devotion to her Immaculate Heart as a way to save
souls from hell. She then added this important message:

If what I say to you is done, many souls will be saved and there will be peace. The war is going to end; but if people do not cease offending God, a worse one will break out during the pontificate of Pius XI. When you see a night illumined by an unknown light, know that this is the great sign given you by God that he is about to punish the world for its crimes, by means of war, famine, and persecutions of the Church and of the Holy Father.[1]

Peace in the world must begin with peace in the human heart. If the heart of each person possesses peace, then that peace can be shared with the family, the local parish community, the neighborhood, the nation, the entire Church and ultimately the whole world. Peace, whether personal or worldwide, is ultimately a gift from the Lord. Jesus gave this gift to his disciples at the Last Supper when he said: "Peace I leave with you; my peace I give to you; not as the world gives do I give to you." (Jn 14:27). Saint Paul describes what this gift of the Lord's peace does for us: "And the peace of God, which passes all understanding, will keep your hearts and your minds in Christ Jesus" (Phil 4:7). If our minds are at peace it means we are not distressed by disturbing thoughts or fantasies, by distorted values, ambitions or worldly standards of success. This peace helps us to know who we are and why we choose to live the way we do. The peace of God keeps us focused on reality, and God is the greatest Reality! If our hearts are at peace, we are not agitated or anxious over things we cannot control such as the past or the future. Rather we live the present moment with great trust that everything is in God's hands. The person with God's peace knows that everything in this world and everything in our personal lives are guided by God's divine wisdom and providence.

[1] Ibid., p. 162.

In Dante's *Divine Comedy* is the famous statement: "In his will is our peace." When we do God's will by keeping his commandments, our lives are rightly ordered and we have God's peace in our hearts. Sin is the rejection of right order because by sinning we act contrary to God's will. Our Lady told Lucia that if we do what she tells us, which is what God wants from us, then there will be peace. At the same time, since what our Lady has asked us to do is also for the salvation of souls, then many souls will be saved in the process.

A Worse War Will Come

Little Jacinta received many private apparitions from our Blessed Lady. On one occasion our Lady told her: "War is a punishment for sin." In the July apparition, our Lady warned that unless people stopped offending God a worse war would break out during the pontificate of Pius XI. Of course, this "worse war" was World War II. We have seen that about twenty million people died in World War I; in World War II about fifty million people were killed, and there were many more atrocities visited upon civilians. Sister Lucia wrote that the mass murder of Jews was a main reason World War II was worse than World War I.

> In what sense would it be worse? In the sense that it would be an atheistic war that attempted to exterminate Judaism, which gave the world Jesus Christ, Our Lady, the Apostles, who transmitted the Word of God and the gift of faith, hope, and charity. The Jews are God's elect people, whom he chose from the beginning: "Salvation is from the Jews." [2]

[2] From a text written by Sr. Lucia in 1955, which she began to revise in 2000, quoted in Cardinal Tarcisio Bertone, *The Last Secret of Fatima: My Conversations with Sister Lucia*, trans. Adrian J. Walker (New York: Doubleday, 2008), p. 135. (Hereafter, *The Last Secret.*)

In addition to the Nazi concentration camps, there were fire bombings of cities and two atomic explosions in Japan. To think such suffering could have been avoided if people had heeded the Blessed Mother's message and done penance for their sins.

Very Important Today

Our Lady's warning is as meaningful now as it was in 1917. We know that the superpowers of the world have huge stockpiles of horrible weapons. May God forbid that these weapons of mass destruction ever be used. And they will not be, if we do what our Blessed Lady has told us to do. She has the plan for peace, so we do not have to invent another one. We only have to put her plan into practice.

A Great Sign Was Given

After mentioning that a worse war would happen if people did not stop offending God, our Lady said it would be preceded by an unknown light in the night sky. This sign occurred between January 25 and 26, 1938. It consisted of an extraordinary aurora borealis that illuminated the night skies of Europe and parts of America for almost five hours. Lucia, a nun at the time, regarded it as the God-given sign that the next world war was near.

Some critics have raised an objection to our Lady's prophecy. She said that the war would begin during the pontificate of Pope Pius XI, who died on February 10, 1939, whereas war was not declared on Germany by England and France until after it invaded Poland on September 1, 1939. However, the fighting began earlier than that. In 1937, Japan invaded Manchuria; a year later, it invaded Russia. In addition, Germany annexed Austria and occupied it with troops on March 12, 1938 and according to Sister Lucia, this act of aggression began the Second World War in Europe. In September that same year, Germany moved into the Sudetenland.

An Evil in Russia—Communism

In addition to another world war, our Lady mentioned other punishments that God would send if his people would not reform their lives. She spoke also of famine, other wars and persecutions. The latter two she especially attributed to Communism, which took hold of Russia in 1917. Let us look at our Lady's words:

> I shall come to ask for the consecration of Russia to my Immaculate Heart, and the Communion of Reparation on the First Saturdays. If my requests are heeded, Russia will be converted, and there will be peace; if not, she will spread her errors throughout the world, causing wars and persecutions of the Church. The good will be martyred, the Holy Father will have much to suffer, various nations will be annihilated.[3]

Russia is a country with a long history of Christianity. The Russian Orthodox Church traces its origins to the apostle Andrew, who brought the gospel to Kiev by way of the Black Sea. Russian Christians were under the spiritual leadership of Kiev and Constantinople, but after political power moved from Kiev to Moscow, and Constantinople fell to the Ottoman Turks in 1453, Moscow assumed a greater leadership role over Christians in eastern Europe. In 1589, Moscow became a patriarchate, making the Russian Orthodox Church an autonomous, national church with the czar

---

[3] *Lucia's Memoirs*, p. 162.

as its protector. The Russian people possessed such a deep religious piety that the country was called Holy Russia. As in western Europe, the closeness of church and state in Russia led to problems. However, unlike the Roman Church, the Russian Church did not undergo a Reformation and the subsequent political movements that loosened the link between ecclesiastical and civil authority. There was much that was good and much that was evil in Russia in the period leading up to the twentieth century. The great Russian writer Fyodor Dostoevsky (d. 1881) compared Russia to the Gerasene demoniac (Lk 8:26ff), saying Russia was full of devils in his time but one day would sit peacefully at the feet of Christ.

In the early twentieth century, Russia was in grave difficulty. The church needed distance from the monarchy in order to be reformed, but this was neglected. The czar at the time, Nicholas II, was a pious man but weak and irresolute. He took command of Russia's troops in World War I, and Russia suffered terrible losses. By the end of the war, more than three million Russian soldiers and civilians had died. This death toll, the highest in the war, coupled with harsh living and working conditions, radicalized some segments of the population. There were riots in the cities, and the stage was set for revolution. In early 1917 the Czar was deposed; later he and his family were executed. The Bolsheviks took power the following October, bringing in the rule of Communism.

Under the leadership of Vladimir Lenin, the Bolsheviks adopted the philosophy of Karl Marx. Rejecting God, this philosophy also rejected the God-given freedom and dignity of each human person and gave supreme power to the state to restructure society in order to remake man. Marx called religion "the opium of the people" because he believed it numbed them to the pain of injustice and prevented them from violently overthrowing their oppressors. Hence, the Bolsheviks set out to destroy the Russian Orthodox Church. They nationalized all of its property, turning churches into barns, factories, military barracks, etc. Dozens of bishops and thousands of priests were executed, while thousands more were imprisoned or deported. The Communists set up a "red" church as a schismatic division in the Orthodox Church, infiltrating the clergy with members of the secret police. They then tried to destroy all Christian practices. Sunday religious services were abolished in all but the officially sanctioned churches, and holy days were replaced by civic holidays. Religious instruction was outlawed, and materialism and atheism were taught to the young in schools and in Communist organizations. The rank and file faithful were terrorized into affecting hostility or indifference toward religion. The traditional family was no longer respected as the fundamental building block of society, but regarded as a source of oppression and a rival to the authority of the state.

After the death of Lenin, another man took power. His real name was Iosif Vissarionovich Dzhugashvili, but when he assumed full command of Communist Russia he proudly renamed himself *Stalin*, which means "man of steel". At one time he had been in the seminary. He did not really want to be a priest, but his mother wished that for him. The experience embittered him toward religion, and his persecution of the Church was even worse than that of Lenin. He destroyed more churches and killed or imprisoned many more clergy, religious and laymen. He imposed harsh penalties on those who continued to practice their faith, and he demanded that workers renounce God in order to be given jobs.

With Russia as its base, the Communists began spreading their ideology throughout the world, as Our Lady of Fatima had prophesied. Just prior to World War II, Spain was plunged into bloody civil strife. After the Second World War, Russia took control of many of its neighbors, including the Baltic states, eastern Germany, Poland, the Balkans, and the peoples bordering the Black and Caspian seas. As our Lady had predicted, entire nations were annihilated. Meanwhile, revolution brought Communists to power in China, and then to Cuba. The era known as the Cold War was underway, and conflicts between Communist revolutionaries financed by Russia or China and governments that wished to remain under the protection and influence of the United States erupted all over the globe. The Communists called these conflicts "wars of liberation", but wherever they got the upper hand, they brutally oppressed their rivals and harshly persecuted the Church. During the first fifty years of Communist ascendancy, there were more Christian martyrs than there were in all the previous years of Christian history combined!

A Promise of Hope—"In the End My Immaculate Heart Will Triumph"

Our Lady had warned that these wars and persecutions would result if people did not change their sinful ways. Her warning is still relevant for us now because sin continues to cause social upheaval and violence. The struggle against evil in the world is still going on. Many of the social problems we face today can be traced to the growing secularism in our society, which is related to the anti-Christian ideology that took root in Russia and then spread around the world. Materialism, with its rejection of God, the freedom to worship him and the traditional family, is the basis of the aggressive secularism we are experiencing. Despite the gains made by this movement, Mary's promise of her triumph is like a beacon of hope in the midst of the spiritual and moral darkness of our age.

We have not yet experienced her triumph, but we have every reason to trust that Mary will be faithful to her words. We must remember, however, that for the triumph to be realized, we have to do our part. This is why our Lady told the Fatima visionaries that she would return at a future time and repeat the two requests that would be necessary for her triumph to occur.

Communion of Reparation and Consecration of Russia

Our Lady did return to Lucia to explain her requests for a Communion of Reparation and the consecration of Russia to her Immaculate Heart to prevent the terrible tragedies of war, famine and persecution. She first returned on December 10, 1925, when Lucia was a postulant with the Dorothean Sisters at a convent in Pontevedra, Spain. We shall explain this appearance and the Communion of Reparation requested by our Lady in greater detail in a later chapter. For now let us simply say that our Lady and the Christ Child appeared to Lucia in her room at the convent and requested the Five First Saturdays devotion. Jesus and Mary asked that on the first Saturdays of five consecutive months we go to confession, receive Holy Communion, say a Rosary and then meditate for fifteen minutes on the mysteries of the Rosary. All of these are to be done with the intention of making reparation to the Immaculate Heart of Mary for the many sins and blasphemies by which she is offended. Mary promised that she will assist at the moment of death, with all the graces necessary for salvation, every person who makes this devotion. The Christ Child stressed, however, that we should not make this devotion only once, but make it over and over again. Our Lord and his holy mother want and even need our ongoing prayers and sacrifices for the conversion of sinners and the promotion of world peace.

Our Lady appeared again to Lucia when she was a Dorothean sister living in Tuy, Spain. On June 13, 1929, Sister Lucia was making a holy hour of reparation in the convent chapel just before midnight. There she saw a magnificent vision of the Most Holy Trinity and our Blessed Lady. We will look at the details of this apparition later. But for now it is important to mention our Lady's request on that occasion:

> The moment has come in which God asks the Holy Father, in union with all the Bishops of the world, to make the consecration of Russia to my Immaculate Heart, promising to save it by this means.[4]

Unfortunately, various factors contributed to delaying the consecration of Russia to Mary's Immaculate Heart. This delay allowed Russia to spread her errors around the world, causing the great evils our Lady had warned us about. We will look at this request very carefully, and trace its history and final fulfillment by Pope John Paul II.

The Triumph Will Come!

We now return to the Second Secret of the July apparition, in which our Lady promised that she will be victorious. Here are her words:

> In the end, my Immaculate Heart will triumph. The Holy Father will consecrate Russia to me, and she will be converted, and a period of peace will be granted to the world. In Portugal, the dogma of the Faith will always be preserved.[5]

[4] Ibid., p. 200.
[5] Ibid., p. 162.

At this point our Lady again asked the children to conclude each decade of the Rosary with the special prayer she
had already taught them to save souls from hell. The children had seen a vision of hell earlier in this July apparition.
And our Lady took the opportunity to emphasize once again
the importance of the mission to save souls. Let us keep in
mind that Mary's heart is not only immaculate, but also
sorrowful. It is immaculate because God spared her from all
sin, even original sin, and filled her from the moment of
her conception with a superabundance of grace. But it is
also sorrowful because she shared in the sufferings of her
son. She witnessed with anguish of heart the shedding of
every drop of his Precious Blood for the remission of sins.
Jesus wants all to be saved, and so does our Blessed Mother.

8

THE JULY APPARITION: PART III

*The Third Secret—Penance and the
Sufferings of the Church*

I T IS WITHOUT EXAGGERATION to say that no part of the
Fatima message has received as much attention as the
Third Secret of the July 13 apparition. As we have already
seen, the First Secret was the vision of hell, and the Second Secret was our Lady's warnings about World War II
and the evils of Communism. The Third Secret was a vision
of events that primarily have occurred during the Second
World War and the Cold War. There is an interesting contrast between the first two secrets and the third. In the
first two parts of the July apparition, our Lady spoke. In
the third part, she did not speak at all, rather the children
saw a series of images that unfolded before them.

The Third Secret of the July apparition was publicly
announced at the Beatification Mass for Francisco and Jacinta
that Pope John Paul II offered in the Cova da Iria on May 13,
2000. During the Mass, Cardinal Angelo Sodano, then Vatican secretary of state, read a statement by the Holy Father
that contained the Third Secret. Cardinal Sodano said that
the children saw a "prophetic vision", which must be understood as symbolic:

[The] text contains a prophetic vision similar to those found in Sacred Scripture, which do not describe photographically the details of future events, but synthesize and compress against a single background facts which extend through time in an unspecified succession and duration. As a result, the text must be interpreted *in a symbolic key*.[1]

We will now examine the various images the children saw and offer the Church's official interpretation of them.

Part I: The Angel with the Flaming Sword

The first thing the visionaries saw was an angel with a flaming sword. Here is how Sister Lucia described him:

[A]t the left of Our Lady and a little above, we saw an Angel with a flaming sword in his left hand; flashing, it gave out flames that looked as though they would set the world on fire; but they died out in contact with the splendour that Our Lady radiated towards him from her right hand: pointing to the earth with his right hand, the Angel cried out in a loud voice: "<u>Penance</u>, <u>Penance</u>, <u>Penance</u>!"[2]

Who Is the Angel?

No specific angel is named, but we can see this angel as a symbol of God's punishment about to come upon the world for its sins. A flaming sword that could set the world on fire could indicate a tremendous war. Cardinal Joseph Ratzinger (now Pope Benedict XVI), as prefect of the Congregation for the Doctrine of the Faith, issued a "Theological

---

[1] Congregation for the Doctrine of the Faith, *The Message of Fatima*, accessed May 24, 2010, http://www.vatican.va/roman_curia/congregations/cfaith/documents/rc_con_cfaith_doc_20000626_message-fatima_en.html. (Hereafter *Message of Fatima*.)

[2] Ibid.

Commentary" to help us understand the meaning of the Third Secret. Here is his comment on the angel:

> The angel with the flaming sword on the left of the Mother of God recalls similar images in the Book of Revelation. This represents the threat of judgment which looms over the world. Today the prospect that the world might be reduced to ashes by a sea of fire no longer seems pure fantasy: man himself, with his inventions, has forged the flaming sword.[3]

In one of his talks years ago, Archbishop Sheen said that the United States and the Soviet Union with their nuclear arsenals had enough explosive power to destroy every person on earth. Today many more countries have nuclear weapons. Imagine how much more explosive power exists in the world now. We are therefore always in danger of a nuclear holocaust.

Our Lady Intervenes

Sister Lucia said that the splendor radiating from our Lady's right hand extinguished the flames from the angel's sword. Our Lady's intervention, therefore, is powerful enough to stop the chastisement of war. Throughout history Mary has intervened to save Christians from defeat at the hands of an often far superior enemy. Her special weapon in these cases has been the Rosary.

The Battle of Lepanto (October 7, 1571)—At the Battle of Lepanto, the Christian fleet was greatly outnumbered by the Muslim fleet. The pope at the time, Saint Pius V, ordered the Christians of Rome to pray the Rosary continuously on the day of the battle. When the flagship of the Christians carrying a picture of our Lady moved forward just as

---

[3] Ibid. For the full text of "Theological Commentary", see Appendix E.

the Christian fleet was about to be surrounded and annihilated, the wind turned against the Muslims, and the Christians destroyed more than ninety percent of the enemy ships.
The commanding Christian officer, Don John of Austria,
sent this summary of the battle to the Pope: "We came! We
saw! But Mary conquered!"

Austria (1955)—Another example of Mary's intervention
occurred in Austria after World War II, when the Russians
held large portions of Austria and had plans to gain control
of the entire country. Father Petrus Pavlicek prayed to our
Blessed Lady, asking for her help to save his country from
Communist control. Inspired to begin a nationwide prayer
campaign, he formed groups that prayed the Rosary and
fasted for the same intention. (He was simply following what
our Lady asked for at Fatima!) The people persevered in
prayer. When all seemed lost, suddenly, miraculously, the
Communists gave up control of the country and moved
their army out of Austria. Not a bullet was fired.

The Nedelin Disaster (October 24, 1960)—Five years later,
the Soviet Union was working on a new intercontinental
ballistic missile called the R-16. It was bigger than any missile the Americans had, and so was capable of carrying a
more destructive nuclear warhead. Headed by the com-
mander of Soviet nuclear missile forces, Marshal Mitrofan
Nedelin, this project was considered a top priority by the
Soviet leaders. When Russian Premier Nikita Khrushchev
addressed the United Nations on October 12, 1960, a del-
egate from the Philippines accused the Russians of colo-
nialism. In response, Khrushchev took off his shoe and angrily
banged on the podium, saying in reference to the capitalist
countries, "We will bury you." He knew that the final test
of the R-16 was scheduled for October 24, and he was
confident that it would intimidate Russia's rivals.

Prior to Khrushchev's speech, Bishop Joao Pereira Venan-
cio of Leiria had sent a letter to all the bishops of the world
urgently asking them to pray and do penance in reparation
for offenses against the Hearts of Jesus and Mary and for
the conversion of Russia. He also invited the people of Portugal to come to the shrine of Fatima on October 12 and
13, 1960, to pray for these same blessings. Did the Bishop
know of the new Soviet rocket and of its scheduled test?
Even if he did not, he knew prayers were needed, as did
the approximately forty-eight thousand pilgrims who prayed
at the shrine on October 12 and the three to four hundred
thousand pilgrims who prayed the following day. They
endured pouring rain to answer the call to prayer. The bishops of Portugal, along with tens of thousands of pilgrims,
even spent the entire night in adoration.

Eleven days later, when the Soviets were to fire their R-16
for its final test, many top military officers, scientists and
politicians gathered to witness this event. Something went
wrong, however, and the rocket never left the launch pad.
After the work crew waited for twenty minutes in their
bunkers, Nedelin gave the order to approach the rocket. As
more than a hundred people were working on the rocket,
someone accidentally ignited the second stage engines of
the missile. A huge explosion resulted, killing more than
one hundred people, many of them engineers and military
men. The story was suppressed in the Soviet media; it was
even falsely reported that Marshal Nedelin, who perished
in the accident, died in a plane crash. Could there be a
connection between the outpouring of prayer and the failure of the R-16?

The Cuban Missile Crisis (October 1962)—In 1962 the
Cuban and Soviet governments began building in Cuba
nuclear missile bases with weapons that could destroy cities

in the United States. When the U.S. government got photographic proof that the bases were being built, tensions between the United States and the Soviet Union escalated into what could easily have turned into a nuclear war. President John F. Kennedy's advisors recommended an attack on Cuba, but the President decided instead to place a naval blockade around Cuba and demand the Soviets remove the weapons. He then informed the public of the situation on October 22. At first the Russians showed no intention of backing down, and Americans wondered nervously if our confrontation of the Soviets would result in a nuclear war. During these tension-filled days, many American Catholics turned to the Rosary and invoked the intercession of our Blessed Mother. On October 26, Soviet President Nikita Khrushchev wrote Kennedy that he would remove the missiles if the United States promised not to invade Cuba. As a Catholic who lived through the Cuban Missile Crisis, I believe the many prayers to our Lady helped bring about a peaceful resolution to the conflict.

"Penance, Penance, Penance"

In the vision of the flaming sword, the angel pointed to the earth with his right hand and cried out in a loud voice: "Penance, Penance, Penance!" The angel's call to penance reminds us that God intervenes in the world when we do penance. What is the meaning of penance? We can see it in the Greek word *metanoia*, which means "change of heart" or "conversion". This conversion is a real turning away from sin and toward God. When we are truly sorry for our sins, we try to conquer our bad habits and control our disordered passions. We willingly give up all those occasions of sin—the persons, places and things that lead us to offend God. As we saw in the Pardon Prayer that the Angel of Peace taught to the children, the purpose of penance is to help us believe, adore, trust and love God. In his "Theological Commentary", Cardinal Ratzinger focused on this:

> "To save souls" has emerged as the key word of the first and second parts of the "secret", and the key word of this third part is the threefold cry: "Penance, Penance, Penance!" The beginning of the Gospel comes to mind: "Repent and believe the Good News" (Mk 1:15). To understand the signs of the times means to accept the urgency of penance—of conversion—of faith. This is the correct response to this moment of history, characterized by the grave perils outlined in the images that follow. Allow me to add here a personal recollection: in a conversation with me Sister Lucia said that it appeared ever more clearly to her that the purpose of all the apparitions was to help people to grow more and more in faith, hope and love—everything else was intended to lead to this.[4]

Penance, willingly embraced by us and achieved by the grace of God, is our contribution to God's work of redemption. As noted earlier, Saint Augustine said: "God made us without us, but he will not save us without us." We must choose in freedom and love to do what God wants us to do! In this way we will please the Lord. Cardinal Ratzinger stressed the importance of our freedom:

> [T]he future is not in fact unchangeably set, and the image which the children saw is in no way a film preview of a future in which nothing can be changed. Indeed, the whole point of the vision is to bring freedom onto the scene and to steer freedom in a positive direction. The purpose of the vision is not to show a film of an irrevocably fixed future.

[4] *Message of Fatima.*

Its meaning is exactly the opposite: it is meant to mobilize the forces of change in the right direction.[5]

Part II: The People Climbing the Mountain

This second part of the Third Secret is quite different from what went before. The children find themselves enveloped in a divine light much like they had experienced during the first two apparitions of our Lady. By means of that light they see a number of people making their way up a steep mountain at the top of which is a big cross. Here is Sister Lucia's description, taken from the Vatican translation of her handwritten account:

> And we saw in an immense light that is God (something similar to how people appear in a mirror when they pass in front of it) a Bishop dressed in White (we had the impression that it was the Holy Father). Other Bishops, Priests, men and women Religious going up a steep mountain, at the top of which there was a big Cross of rough-hewn trunks as of a cork-tree with the bark; before reaching there the Holy Father passed through a big city half in ruins and half trembling with halting step, afflicted with pain and sorrow, he prayed for the souls of the corpses he met on his way; having reached the top of the mountain, on his knees at the foot of the big Cross he was killed by a group of soldiers who fired bullets and arrows at him, and in the same way there died one after another the other Bishops, Priests, men and women Religious and various laypeople of different ranks and positions.[6]

In his "Theological Commentary", Cardinal Ratzinger explained the symbols of the steep mountain, the great city

[5] Ibid.
[6] Ibid.

half reduced to ruins, and the large rough-hewn cross. He said that the mountain and the city symbolize the arena of human history. Human activity is both an arduous ascent and an expression of creativity and community; on the other hand, the city can become a place of death and destruction because men can destroy what they have built up. At the summit of the mountain stands the cross, which Ratzinger saw as the Cross of Christ, "the goal and guide of history". The Cross both stands for and transforms human misery into the means of salvation. It is therefore a sign of hope.

The Bishop Dressed in White

Leading the procession of people coming up the mountain is the pope. He is described as trembling and in great pain and sorrow as he passes ruins and corpses. "The Church's path is thus described as a *Via Crucis* [Way of the Cross]," wrote Cardinal Ratzinger, "as a journey through a time of violence, destruction and persecution." [7] The entire twentieth century is represented in these images, he added, and through it all, the pope had a special role. Ratzinger saw in the image of the pope all the popes of the twentieth century, beginning with Saint Pius X and ending with Pope John Paul II. They all shared the sufferings of the century as they strove to lead the Church, but Pope John Paul II had a particular destiny:

> In the vision, the Pope too is killed along with the martyrs. When, after the attempted assassination on 13 May 1981, the Holy Father had the text of the third part of the "secret" brought to him, was it not inevitable that he should see in it his own fate? He had been very close to death, and he himself explained his survival in the following words: ". . . it

[7] Ibid.

was a mother's hand that guided the bullet's path and in his throes the Pope halted at the threshold of death" (13 May 1994). That here "a mother's hand" had deflected the fateful bullet only shows once more that there is no immutable destiny, that faith and prayer are forces which can influence history and that in the end prayer is more powerful than bullets, and faith more powerful than armies.[8]

The "mother's hand" the Pope credited with saving him was that of Our Lady of Fatima. He had been shot on her feast day, May 13, and on the first anniversary of the assassination attempt he went to her shrine in Fatima in order to thank her for sparing his life, placing the bullet that had struck him upon her altar. It was later placed in her statue's crown.

The doctors who cared for the fallen Pope reported that he had come very near to death. By the time he had arrived at Gemelli hospital in Rome, he had lost six pints of blood, and his blood pressure was falling rapidly. As the Pope was taken to an operating room, he lost consciousness, and his secretary gave him the last rites. Five hours of surgery were needed to close wounds in his colon and remove twenty-two inches of damaged intestine. If the bullet had not missed vital organs and major arteries, it is very likely the Holy Father would not have survived. "The pope's life was saved in extremis" wrote Cardinal Bertone, "It was as if he had died and then been snatched back from the very jaws of death."[9]

Other Bishops, Priests, Religious and Laity

In the vision seen by the children, many others were following the pope as he was climbing the mountain to the

[8] Ibid.
[9] *The Last Secret*, p. 51.

foot of the huge cross on the top. They included bishops, priests, men and women religious and laity of different ranks and positions. Just as the Holy Father was killed in the vision, so were all of those who followed after him. These were men and women who died as martyrs because of their love for Christ and the Church. We have already seen the tremendous number of martyrs in Russia. There were countless others who sacrificed their lives as well. Cardinal Ratzinger offered this reflection on these heroic souls:

> In the vision we can recognize the last century as a century of martyrs, a century of suffering and persecution for the Church, a century of World Wars and the many local wars which filled the last fifty years and have inflicted unprecedented forms of cruelty. In the "mirror" of this vision we see passing before us the witnesses of the faith decade by decade.[10]

Part III: The Blood of the Martyrs

The Third Secret ends with a focus on the blood of the martyrs of the twentieth century of which we have just spoken. Here are Sister Lucia's words:

> Beneath the two arms of the Cross there were two Angels each with a crystal aspersorium in his hand, in which they gathered up the blood of the Martyrs and with it sprinkled the souls that were making their way to God.[11]

This brief description by Sister Lucia of the final image the children saw in the July apparition helps us to understand the sufferings of martyrs as witnesses of the faith.

[10] *Message of Fatima.*
[11] Ibid.

Sacred Scripture says that the death of the just is precious in the eyes of the Lord, and so is their blood shed for love of him. There is also an important saying in the Church that goes all the way back to the earliest Christian martyrs during the ancient Roman persecutions: "The blood of the martyrs is the seed of the Church." Where men and women have such courageous and generous love that they lay down their lives for the love of Christ and their neighbor in witness to their faith, great graces are poured forth upon the whole Church. It was believed that the merits of the sufferings and deaths of the first martyrs won the graces that brought about the conversion of the pagan Roman Empire and later of the various barbarians who invaded Europe.

The children saw the souls of those who were journeying toward God being sprinkled by the blood of the martyrs mingled with the blood of Christ from the Cross hanging above them, suggesting that the merits of the martyrs of the twentieth century were supplying strength to the Church entering the twenty-first century. Cardinal Ratzinger in his "Theological Commentary" noted:

> As from Christ's death, from his wounded side, the Church was born, so the death of the witnesses is fruitful for the future life of the Church. Therefore, the vision of the third part of the "secret", so distressing at first, concludes with an image of hope: no suffering is in vain, and it is a suffering Church, a Church of martyrs, which becomes a signpost for man in his search for God. The loving arms of God welcome not only those who suffer like Lazarus, who found great solace there and mysteriously represents Christ, who wished to become for us the poor Lazarus. There is something more: from the suffering of the witnesses there comes a purifying and renewing power, because their suffering is the actualization of the suffering of Christ himself

and a communication in the here and now of its saving
effect.[12]

Beatification and Canonization of the Martyrs

Let us conclude with two final thoughts from the life of
Pope John Paul II that seem to flow from this part of the
Third Secret of Fatima. The first is related to the many
canonizations and beatifications that Pope John Paul II carried out during his pontificate. It is said that he canonized
and beatified more men and women than had been done
by all the previous popes put together. During his pontificate
four hundred eighty men and women were named saints.
Many of these were martyrs; some of them even formed
large groups of martyrs from various countries. We only
have to think of the martyred priests from Mexico, the many
martyrs from Korea, Vietnam and China, the martyr vic-
tims of the Spanish Civil War, those martyred by the Nazis
and the Communists in Europe and those murdered by religious extremists in the Muslim countries. In many of these
places today the Church is still persecuted, and so we still
have martyrs witnessing to Christ. No doubt Pope John
Paul II gave us these many saints and blesseds to inspire us
to have courage to live our faith today no matter what the
cost. At the same time, they are now our advocates in heaven
where they intercede for us continually before the throne
of Almighty God.

The New Springtime

As the third millennium approached, Pope John Paul II often
spoke of a "new springtime" in the Church. He saw it,

[12] Ibid.

first of all, as the fruit of the Second Vatican Council's authentic calls for renewal. He said of the Council that it was the greatest spiritual experience in the Roman Catholic Church since Pentecost. He also said that when Pope John XXIII called the Council, it was only "the dawn", but now it is "the day". Secondly, he saw this "new springtime" as the fruit of the many martyrs, whose merits will bring about a great renewal of the Church in the twenty-first century. Unfortunately certain unforeseen factors hindered this new springtime from emerging clearly in Pope John Paul II's lifetime. We can recognize two such factors in the United States: the clerical sex scandals, which have harmed the Church's missions worldwide and the terrorist attack on September 11, 2001, which resulted in the American invasions of Iraq and Afghanistan. But we can believe that Pope John Paul II knew the new springtime would eventually come, as would Our Lady of Fatima's promise that in the end Russia would be converted and her Immaculate Heart would triumph!

9

THE AUGUST APPARITION

Our Lady's Coming Is Delayed

I N THE NINETEENTH AND TWENTIETH CENTURIES, Free-masonry was gaining political power and ascendancy in many countries in Europe and Latin America. Its followers were fiercely anti-Catholic and especially anti-clerical. They came to power in Portugal with the assassination of the king, Dom Carlos, and his son Dom Felipe on February 1, 1908. When another son, Dom Manuel II, became king, he was overthrown by a revolution of Freemasons in 1910. As we have seen, once they were in power, they persecuted the Church, especially priests and religious. They even expelled the Cardinal Patriarch of Lisbon. As they seized control of the government and passed a severely anti-religious law in 1911, the leader of the Masons, Alfonso Costa, boasted that in two generations Catholicism would be eliminated in Portugal.

Imprisonment

The little village of Aljustrel and the area around it were under the control of the administrative council of the city of Vila Nova de Ourem, or simply Ourem. The council was headed by a fiercely anti-clerical man named Arturo de

Oliveira Santos, a fallen-away Catholic and a leading Freemason. Word of the apparitions at Fatima was spreading rapidly throughout Portugal. Many people were coming to the Cova for a variety of reasons. Some came out of curiosity, others to scorn and ridicule, while many of the faithful came believing. The crowds grew: there were an estimated four thousand people at the July 13 apparition. Even the Portuguese newspapers were beginning to carry articles about the claimed apparitions and the little shepherd children. However, because journalists tended to be anti-religious, they began to criticize the authorities for negligence and ineffectiveness in not putting a stop to what they considered "childish fantasies" or "religious fanaticism" or "clerical deceptions". As administrator of the area, Santos took these criticisms as being aimed at himself.

After the July apparition of our Lady, people became even more interested in the events at Fatima. After the apparition, the children told everyone that our Lady had confided a secret to them and that she had also told them there would be a great miracle in October to prove that she was really appearing at the Cova da Iria. We can only imagine how talk of a secret from heaven and of a spectacular miracle spread and aroused even more curiosity among believers and non-believers alike. Interest in what was going on at Fatima was growing all over Portugal and even beyond its borders. With all of this excitement being stirred, Administrator Santos felt moved to stop the spread of this religious "hoax". He decided to do everything he could to discredit the children and to stop the people from going to the apparition site in the Cova.

Pressure on the Families

How did the families of the visionaries react to the secret? Lucia's family took no interest in the secret, since they did not believe in the apparitions to begin with, though Lucia's father was more sympathetic toward her than were her mother and siblings. Francisco and Jacinta's father, who believed in the apparitions all along, said that if the children received a secret, they must keep it. Father Ferreira, the pastor of the church at Fatima, questioned the children after each apparition. He tried in different ways to get the children to reveal the secret, but he was unsuccessful. In the end he realized he could not force the children to reveal a secret confided to them by our Lady.

Administrator Santos, however, was determined to pry it out of them. First he arranged to meet with the three shepherd children and their parents at the administrative council headquarters in Ourem. Lucia's father, Antonio, accompanied her, but Ti Marto went alone because he would not allow his little children to walk so far: Ourem was about nine miles from Fatima. From Lucia's memoirs we can see that the children thought she would be forced to choose between fidelity to the Lady and death:

> As we [Lucia and her father] were passing by my uncle's house, my father had to wait a few minutes for my uncle. I ran to say goodbye to Jacinta who was still in bed. Doubtful as to whether we would ever see one another again, I threw my arms around her. Bursting into tears, the poor child sobbed:
>
> "If they kill you, tell them that Francisco and I are just the same as you, and that we want to die too. I'm going right now to the well [where the Angel of Peace appeared the second time] with Francisco, and we'll pray hard for you." [1]

While Lucia was being interrogated by Santos, he tried to pressure her to reveal the secret. He also wanted her to declare

[1] *Lucia's Memoirs*, p. 35.

that the apparitions were a hoax, and to promise that she would never go back to the Cova da Iria. He threatened to have her killed if she did not comply, but it was all in vain. Santos then threatened civil penalties against the parents of the visionaries if they did not stop the children from going to the Cova.

The Administrator's Deceit

On August 13, the date for our Lady's next apparition, Santos and a priest from a nearby parish went to the homes of the visionaries. Santos claimed he wanted to witness the apparition so that like Saint Thomas, "seeing he would believe". He then suggested he take the children to their own pastor, Father Ferreira, so that he could question them again. After that meeting, he said, he would take them to the Cova da Iria in his own horse-drawn wagon. Not suspecting deceit, the children went with Santos. At first the wagon went in the right direction; but when it arrived at the juncture with the main road, Santos suddenly changed course and sped on in the direction of Ourem. Once in the city, Santos took the children to his own home. His wife was a good Catholic, but she had to practice her faith secretly to keep it from her husband. She treated the children kindly and gave them a nice lunch. Afterward the children went to the city hall, where they were questioned about the secret. That night they slept at Santos' home.

The Children in Jail

The next day, to terrorize the children as much as he could, Santos locked the children up in the jail with a group of prisoners who were thieves. What was their imprisonment like? In her memoirs, Lucia recorded a few very striking incidents of that experience.

Heroic Courage to Suffer—First of all, the children exhibited a great willingness to suffer and to offer their sufferings to Jesus and Mary for the salvation of souls.

> When, some time later, we were put in prison, what made Jacinta suffer most, was to feel that [our] parents had abandoned [us]. With tears streaming down her cheeks, she would say: "Neither your parents nor mine have come to see us. They don't bother about us anymore!"
>
> "Don't cry," said Francisco, "we can offer this to Jesus for sinners." Then, raising his eyes and hands to heaven, he made the offering: "Oh my Jesus, this is for love of you, and for the conversion of sinners." Jacinta added: "And also for the Holy Father, and in reparation for the sins committed against the Immaculate Heart of Mary." [2]

Death Rather than Reveal Our Lady's Secret—In spite of their intense feelings of fear and abandonment, the children showed tremendous courage.

> The prisoners who were present ... sought to console us: "But all you have to do," they said, "is to tell the Administrator the secret! What does it matter whether the Lady wants you to or not!"
>
> "Never!" was Jacinta's vigorous reply, "I'd rather die!"

A Powerful Prison Rosary—The presence of the innocent children must have softened the hearts of some of the men, for they joined in praying the Rosary:

> Jacinta took off a medal that she was wearing around her neck, and asked a prisoner to hang it up for her on a nail in the wall. Kneeling before this medal, we began to pray.

[2] Ibid., pp. 35–36.

The prisoners prayed with us, that is, if they knew how to pray, but at least they were down on their knees. . . . While we were saying the Rosary in prison, [Francisco] noticed that one of the prisoners was on his knees with his cap still on his head. Francisco went up to him and said, "If you wish to pray, you should take your cap off." Right away, the poor man handed it to him and he went over and put it on the bench on top of his own.[3]

A Joyful Dance in Prison—Praying together changed the atmosphere of the prison, and one of the thieves began to play his concertina, while the others began to sing.

They asked us if we knew how to dance. We said we knew the "fandango" and the "vira". Jacinta's partner was a poor thief who, finding her so tiny, picked her up and went on dancing with her in his arms! We only hope that our Lady has had pity on his soul and converted him![4]

Despite how much Jacinta loved dancing, she later gave it up as a sacrifice to our Lord.

A Cruel and Terrifying Ordeal for the Children—In her very first appearance to the little children, our Lady had asked them if they were willing to bear all the sufferings God would send them in reparation for sins and for the conversion of sinners. When they willingly said yes, our Lady told them that they would have "much to suffer". But she also assured them that the grace of God would be their comfort. One of their greatest sufferings occurred during their imprisonment. After the children were brought from the cell where they had been kept with the thieves, Administrator Santos questioned them about what our Lady had told them. He wanted them to reveal the secret and

[3] Ibid., pp. 36, 128.
[4] Ibid., p. 37.

then declare that they had made up the whole story about the apparitions. But the children would not give in. With a courage far beyond their years, they said they would rather die than reveal the secret that our Lady confided to them. Becoming angry, the Administrator sternly warned the children that it was a serious crime to withhold information from the government about such an important matter, and he threatened to throw them alive into a vat of boiling oil. Though so young, the visionaries met their trial head-on with the confidence of the martyrs who preferred to lose their lives rather than to offend their God. Even the Administrator was amazed by their courage. In one last attempt to weaken their resolve, Santos questioned each child separately, beginning with the youngest, Jacinta. He demanded she reveal the secret and when she refused, he called over one of the guards and asked if the cauldron of oil was boiling. The guard answered it was ready and led little Jacinta out of the room, apparently to her death as a martyr. Then Santos tried to intimidate Francisco, and when he chose martyrdom rather than reveal our Lady's secret, he was led out of the room. Finally, Lucia, all alone, was questioned whether she would reveal the secret. When she steadfastly refused and desired rather to die and go to heaven, she too was led away. To their surprise, the three children met together, alive and well. They were no doubt disappointed that they did not die and go to heaven, which they each desired so much to do.

The Children Are Set Free

In the meantime, a great crowd of people had gathered in the Cova at noon on August 13, the scheduled date for our Lady's next appearance. When the children did not arrive at the proper time, people began to wonder what had happened. They did not know about the plot of the Administrator. Witnesses at the apparition site testified that they seemed to sense some of the signs that were present when our Lady had last appeared, but when the children failed to arrive, they left disappointed and confused.

Finally, on August 15, the Solemnity of the Assumption of the Blessed Virgin Mary into Heaven, Santos had the three children driven back to Fatima and left on the steps of the parish rectory. A crowd of people were coming from Mass at the time. When they saw the children at the rectory and the car that had delivered them, they were ready to take their anger out on the driver. They also thought Father Ferreira was involved with the abduction since they had seen the children at the rectory before their disappearance. Tempers were flaring, and the people would have harmed the Pastor had Ti Marto not intervened. Because the people respected him, he was able to calm them down, saying that God had allowed this ordeal to happen to the visionaries.

Lucia's Greatest Torment

The children's imprisonment and interrogation were harrowing experiences, but Lucia's greatest source of suffering was the apparent callousness of her own family. Her mother, especially, thought Lucia had invented the story of the Lady's appearances, and she had already tried everything she could think of—caresses, threats and beatings—to make her admit that she was lying. The first time Administrator Santos ordered Lucia and her father to appear before him, her mother happily sent her off to Ourem, hoping the frightening tactics of the Administrator would make her come to her senses. Lucia could not help but compare her parents' behavior with that shown by her aunt and uncle, who refused to send Jacinta and Francisco to Ourem, fearing the journey would be too hard on them. "What hurt me most was the indifference shown me by my parents," Lucia wrote in her memoirs.[5] When Lucia returned home after her imprisonment, her parents showed her no signs of welcome or even of relief that she was alive and well. They simply sent her to the pasture with the sheep, as if nothing had happened. Her cousins, on the other hand, were kept at home with their parents, who sent an older son to shepherd the animals in their place. Though deeply hurt by her parents' lack of affection, "[b]y a special grace from Our Lord," wrote Lucia, "I never experienced the slightest thought or feeling of resentment." Rather, she accepted this source of suffering as a form of penance, seeing "the hand of God in it".[6]

Our Lady's Apparition on August 19

As the saying goes, "God may not come when we expect him, but he is never late!" The adage can certainly be applied to our Lady's rescheduled August apparition. Back at home, the children had resumed their task of caring for their family's sheep. It was Sunday, August 19, when Lucia, Francisco and his brother John were grazing their flocks at a little place called Valinhos. It was about a ten-minute walk from their hamlet of Aljustrel and near the site where the Angel of Peace made two of his appearances. All of a sudden, around four o'clock in the afternoon, Lucia sensed that our Lady was about to appear. The brightness of the sun faded and the air grew cooler, and they saw the flash of light which they called lightning. Jacinta was not with them, and

[5] Ibid., p. 72.
[6] Ibid., p. 74.

Lucia was afraid that she would miss our Lady's apparition. Lucia asked John to run home and get Jacinta, but he did not want to go. Finally, Lucia had to bribe him by giving him a couple of pennies for his errand. The moment Jacinta arrived, our Lady appeared standing upon a holmoak tree. It was to be the only apparition of Our Lady of Fatima that did not happen in the Cova da Iria.

Our Lady's visit was not a long one. Once she appeared, Lucia began the conversation with her usual question: "What do you want of me?" Our Lady responded as she usually did:

> I want you to continue going to the Cova da Iria on the 13th, and to continue praying the Rosary every day. In the last month [October], I will perform a miracle so that all may believe.[7]

There is no doubt about our Lady's insistence on the Rosary for peace in the world and for the salvation of souls. About Our Lady's repeated promise to perform a miracle, when Lucia spoke to her pastor, Father Marques, on August 21, she told him that our Lady had said in reference to their imprisonment by the civil authorities: "Had they not taken you to Ourem, the miracle would have been greater." We have already seen how a lack of faith can diminish God's miraculous power. Here we see that opposition to his plan also can have a similar effect.

What About the Money Left at the Cova?

Lucia's conversation with our Lady continued. She asked: "What are we to do with the offerings of money that people leave at the Cova da Iria?" Our Lady answered:

[7] Ibid., p. 166.

Have two litters [used to carry statues] made. One is to be carried by you and Jacinta and two other girls dressed in white; the other one is to be carried by Francisco and three other boys. The money from the litters is for the "festa" of Our Lady of the Rosary, and what is left over will help towards the construction of a chapel that is to be built here.[8]

The Feast of Our Lady of the Rosary is celebrated on October 7. The litters would be used to carry statues in the procession during the celebration of that feast day. The money provided by donations would allow for some beautiful litters to be made. In addition, whatever money was left over after paying for the litters would be used for the construction of a chapel that our Lady foretold would be built in the Cova someday. These two simple requests of our Lady are self-explanatory, but they deserve further reflection.

The majority of the people coming to the Cova were poor peasants. They had a simple but lively faith in God, and they clearly recognized that all of their blessings were God's gifts to them. As part of their gratitude to God, they would offer him some of the fruits of their harvest, each according to his means. Those who had money would make donations just as we are accustomed to making offerings at Sunday Mass as part of our support of the Church. Our Lady's answer clearly shows her approval of these simple acts of thanksgiving. After all, gratitude is one of the primary responsibilities we have toward Almighty God for his goodness to us. At the same time, her answer stresses that each person has an obligation to take part in supporting the works of the Church to the degree his means allow.

[8] Ibid.

The use of the litters has expanded beyond what the little visionaries could have ever imagined or expected. Years later, when an archbishop asked Sister Lucia about other uses of the litters specified by our Lady, she said they were a prophetic sign pointing to the pilgrim statues of Our Lady of Fatima that go around the world. These images of Our Lady of Fatima are used to spread her message, which she came to bring to all of mankind. The traveling images of Mary, called the pilgrim virgin statues, are bringing hope, peace and love to people all over the world who are searching for these blessings. Like her visitation to Elizabeth, Mary still journeys throughout the world spreading the light of Christ, which radiates from her Immaculate Heart. The archbishop replied to Sister Lucia that our Lady's litters also signified those used in the daily processions around the grounds of the Cova, where now stands the Chapel of the Apparitions. In the procession on Sunday, Jesus in the most Blessed Sacrament is carried while the people pray and sing in his honor. The other days of the week, there is always the procession of Our Lady of Fatima.

Our Lady's Plea for Prayer and Sacrifice

The August conversation with our Lady ended with Lucia asking her to cure some sick people. Her response was simple: "Some I will cure during the year." We have already seen how our Lady answered Lucia's requests for healings in previous apparitions. She had promised there would be a number of them, but She had also said it was necessary for some people to reform their lives and return to God, while others needed to pray especially the Rosary. Lucia recorded that our Lady's face suddenly became sad as she said:

Pray, pray very much, and make sacrifices for sinners; for many souls go to hell, because there are none to sacrifice themselves and to pray for them.[9]

Thus, this apparition ended with a theme our Lady had already expressed. As a mother deeply concerned for the salvation of all her children, she pleaded for the two things that will help bring many souls to heaven, namely, our prayers and our sacrifices for their conversion. The three little visionaries had already taken to heart our Lady's request for sacrifice and prayer. In her memoirs, Lucia described the children's almsgiving and fasting:

We had agreed that whenever we met any poor children like these, we would give them our lunch. They were only too happy to receive such an alms, and they took good care to meet us; they used to wait for us along the road. We no sooner saw them then Jacinta ran to give them all the food we had for that day, as happy as if she had no need of it herself. On days like that, our only nourishment consisted of pine nuts, and little berries ... as well as blackberries, mushrooms, and some other things we found on the roots of pine trees.... If there was fruit available on the land belonging to our parents, we used to eat that.[10]

Our Lady knew only too well the price of the salvation of souls, for she had seen her divine Son suffer and die on the Cross, shedding the very last drops of his precious blood. This was the price that Jesus and Mary paid for souls, and she does not want any of it to be wasted! Let us heed our Mother's plea, like Lucia, Francisco and Jacinta.

[9] Ibid., p. 167.
[10] Ibid., pp. 31–32.

THE SEPTEMBER APPARITION

Preparations for the Great Miracle to Come

A Large Crowd

THE CHILDREN'S IMPRISONMENT IN AUGUST created such a stir that interest in the events at the Cova da Iria increased tremendously. As a result, an estimated twenty-five thousand people arrived there on September 13 for our Lady's apparition. The crowd was so thick it was difficult for the children to make their way to the Cova. Lucia vividly described her experience in her memoirs:

> As the hour approached, I set out with Jacinta and Francisco, but owing to the crowds around us we could only advance with difficulty. The roads were packed with people, and everyone wanted to see us and speak to us. . . . Some climbed up to the tops of trees and walls to see us go by and shouted down to us. Saying yes to some, giving a hand to others and helping them up from the dusty ground, we managed to move forward, thanks to some gentlemen who went ahead and opened a passage for us through the multitude.[1]

[1] Ibid.

The People Offer Petitions

We might say that the demands of the crowd were part of the price for the popularity, or at least the notoriety, that the children received because of the apparitions of our Lady. Lucia compared their experience to that of Jesus when he went through the crowds who pressed upon him to receive healings and other favors:

> They threw themselves on their knees before us, begging us to place their petitions before Our Lady. Others who could not get close to us shouted from a distance: "For the love of God, ask Our Lady to cure my son who is a cripple!" Yet another cried out: "And to cure mine who is blind! ... To cure mine who is deaf! ... To bring back my husband, my son, who has gone to war! ... To convert a sinner! ... To give me back my health as I have tuberculosis!" and so on. All the afflictions of poor humanity were assembled there.[2]

We know that not everyone who went to the Cova came as a true believer. We know there were those who came simply out of curiosity, much like drivers of cars who are "rubbernecking" at scenes of accidents hoping to see something. Others came disbelieving, simply wanting to scoff at what they considered a grand deception in the name of religion. But many devout people came in faith-filled expectation. Lucia said of these:

> I give thanks to God, offering Him the faith of our good Portuguese people, and I think: "If these people so humbled themselves before three poor children, just because they were mercifully granted the grace to speak to the Mother

[2] Ibid., p. 167.

of God, what would they not do if they saw Our Lord
Himself in person before them?" [3]

Our Lady Arrives

With some difficulty the children finally reached the Cova
at the spot where our Lady had been appearing. They began
to say the Rosary with the people when suddenly they
saw the flash of light that always preceded our Lady's coming. Then she appeared above the holmoak tree. The brief
conversation between our Lady and the visionaries began
with Lucia's usual question, "What do you want of me?"
Our Lady then gave her usual response: "Continue to pray
the Rosary in order to obtain the end of the war!" [4]

Our Lady's continuous insistence on the need for the
Rosary to obtain world peace should make a lasting impression on all of us. Her repeated admonition is reminiscent
of a story told about Saint John the apostle when he was
an old man. He had a group of his own disciples who
were always with him. Each day they would ask him, "Tell
us something of Jesus." And every day he would give them
the same answer: "My little children, love one another!"
Finally, one of the disciples said to Saint John: "You spent
three years with our Lord as his disciple. You later wrote
the fourth Gospel. You have so much to tell us, but when
we ask you to do so, you always tell us the same thing!
Can't you tell us something different?" John answered: "To
love one another is the commandment of Christ; when
you have done that, you have done everything!" If we are
careful to carry out Mary's request to pray the Rosary every
day for peace in the world and for the conversion of

[3] Ibid.
[4] Ibid., p. 168.

sinners, it will likely follow that we will carry out everything else she asks of us.

Reference to the Mysteries of the Rosary?

During her September apparition, our Lady foretold a
sequence of appearances that the children would see in October along with the promised miracle that would convince
the people that our Lady had been appearing in the Cova:

> In October Our Lord will come, as well as Our Lady of
> Dolours [sorrows] and Our Lady of Mount Carmel. St.
> Joseph will appear with the Child Jesus to bless the world.[5]

These images are rich in meaning and have an unmistake-
able relation to the mysteries of the Rosary. They can be
seen as a call to holiness in every phase and experience of
human life. We will look at their meaning more fully when
we discuss the October 13 apparition, but for now let us
reflect upon their relationship with the mysteries of the
Rosary in order to deepen our commitment to this devotion that our Lady has requested of us.

The Joyful Mysteries—In October when the children see
Saint Joseph with the Child Jesus blessing the world, our
Lady is with them, not in her usual appearance as Our Lady
of Fatima, but dressed in white with a blue mantle. This
vision of the Holy Family relates to the joyful mysteries of
the Rosary, which allow us to focus on the true meaning
and dignity of marriage and family life. A central part of
the message of Fatima is a call to renew Christian family
life.

[5] Ibid.

The Luminous Mysteries—When Jesus is next seen by the children in October he is in the fullness of his manhood, which corresponds to the new luminous mysteries given to us by Pope John Paul II. These mysteries focus on Jesus' public ministry and fill a gap in the reflections on Jesus' life in the mysteries of the Rosary. Previously we moved from the joyful mysteries of his childhood to the sorrowful mysteries of his Passion and death without any reflection on the events that took place in between. The baptism of our Lord, his miracle at Cana, his proclamation of the Kingdom, the Transfiguration and the institution of the Eucharist all reveal for us who Jesus really is. These mysteries allow for us to meditate on Jesus' identity as the Son of God before moving to the mysteries that focus our attention on his Passion and death.

The Sorrowful Mysteries—The October appearance of the Blessed Virgin as Our Lady of Sorrows reminds us of our need to carry our cross daily. We have seen our Lady's urgent plea for prayer and a willingness to suffer for others. In the sorrowful mysteries we see that our Lady herself willingly shared in the sufferings of her son. These mysteries give us the courage we need to endure the struggles of the Christian life and lift them up for the salvation of souls.

The Glorious Mysteries—The story of our Christian faith does not end with a sealed tomb. That tomb was only necessary so that Christ might come forth from it in glory. He conquered sin by dying on the Cross; he rose again from the dead to conquer death itself. The glorious mysteries give us the hope we need to continue our earthly struggle so that we may win a heavenly crown. Hope gives us courage (because we know we can overcome all obstacles by the power of the risen Christ), perseverance (because we know Christ has gone ahead of us to prepare a place for us in his Kingdom where we long to be) and joy (because we know that someday by God's grace we will possess the eternal joys of heaven for which we were made).

We may ask how the image of Our Lady of Mount Carmel can point us in the direction of the glorious mysteries of the Rosary. In the Old Testament, the prophet Elijah remained faithful to God at a time when many children of Israel had adopted the worship of Baal, a pagan deity whose rites included the sacrifice of human infants. Because of Elijah's faith, God was able to perform on Mount Carmel a miracle that discredited the prophets of Baal and proved he alone is the Lord. This miracle caused many lost children of Israel to repent of their idolatry and return to the one, true God. (See 1 Kings 18.) As Our Lady of Mount Carmel, Mary can be seen as the faithful daughter of Israel whose obedience to the Lord allows her to share in his victory over Satan and the many forms of idolatry that lead souls away from God. In praying the glorious mysteries for the conversion of sinners, as Our Lady of Fatima has asked, we can help rescue souls from the snares of false gods.

Our Lady Speaks to the Children About Their Penances

Like the good and kind mother she is, our Lady gave the children words of praise and encouragement about their penances. But she also added a word of caution so that the children would not hurt themselves:

> God is pleased with your sacrifices. He does not want you to sleep with the rope on [tied around your waist], but only to wear it during the daytime.[6]

[6] Ibid.

We have seen the generosity of the children in making their sacrifices of reparation to God. Their zeal was truly heroic, to a degree characteristic of saints! But sometimes in our zeal we can do things that are not sufficiently balanced against a harmful extreme. Such seems to have been the case with one of the penances the children had chosen to practice. Here is how Lucia explained the origin of the penance of wearing the rope around their waists:

> As we were walking along the road with our sheep, I found a piece of rope that had fallen off a cart. I picked it up and, just for fun, I tied it around my arm. Before long, I noticed that the rope was hurting me. "Look, this hurts!" I said to my cousins: "We could tie it around our waists and offer this sacrifice to God." [7]

Sometimes in living the spiritual life, people who do not have a spiritual director can make decisions that a prudent and experienced guide would have cautioned against. In a way, this is what happened to the three little shepherd children. Lucia suggested this practice to her little cousins and they quickly accepted it. They cut up the rope between the three of them, and each took a part of it. But this practice of penance caused the little ones terrible suffering. Sometimes it was because the rope was either too thick or too rough, and at other times it was because they tied it so tightly. Many times it prevented them at night from getting the sleep they needed. Jacinta, particularly, suffered a great deal because of the discomfort, so much so that she could hardly hold back her tears. Whenever Lucia would tell her to remove the rope, Jacinta would say that she wanted to offer the sacrifice to our Lord in reparation for the offenses against him and for the conversion of sinners. Obviously,

[7] Ibid., p. 115.

when the children heard that God did not want them to sleep with the rope around their waists, they immediately stopped the practice. They knew that obedience to God was the greatest sacrifice they could offer. Furthermore, it would not be pleasing to God if they offered him an act of penance that was done in disobedience to him.

We can learn certain important lessons from this experience of the children. First, we must always be prudent in choosing acts of penance. Some people can do certain acts of penance while others cannot. For example, some people can fast without doing any harm to their health, while other people would be injured if they tried to fast. Perhaps these latter would do better simply to give up things they like as their sacrifices. Secondly, if we are doing bodily penances, we must also be sure we are trying to practice virtues in our hearts. For example, it would be a contradiction to fast from certain foods while refusing to forgive someone who has hurt me or failing to make an effort to overcome my tendency to become angry or annoyed. This is where the Pharisees in the Gospels failed; they fasted twice a week, but lacked love of neighbor and the readiness to forgive in their hearts. Worse still would be people who practiced exterior penances while deliberately continuing sinful practices in their lives. Sorrow for our sins is one of the most pleasing and effective penances we can offer the Lord, as we see in the psalm King David prayed after his fall into serious sin: "The sacrifice acceptable to God is a broken spirit; a broken contrite heart, O God, you will not despise" (Psalm 51:19).

Lucia Offers Petitions to Our Lady

The conversation with our Lady ended like it had during other apparitions, with Lucia offering petitions to our Lady. As we saw, just a short time before the apparition began, many people pressed against the children and anxiously poured out their petitions for our Lady's intercession. These needs no doubt touched the hearts of the children very deeply.

As our Lady departed, Lucia cried out in great simplicity: "If you want to see our Lady, look there!" She pointed toward the east. Many people later testified that they had seen something like a luminous cloud moving toward the east. Most were convinced that they had not seen our Lady herself, but perhaps a kind of "vehicle" which brought our Lady from heaven and returned her there again after the apparition.

For the first time, during the September apparition there were many priests present in the crowd of onlookers at the Cova. Some of them later gave favorable testimony, which contributed to the official approval of Fatima's apparitions by a canonical commission appointed by Bishop da Silva of Leiria to study the evidence.

With the ending of the September 13 apparition, the stage was set for October and the promised miracle that would convince the multitudes that our Lady was truly appearing at the Cova and giving a message of great importance for the world. The waiting, however, would not be easy for Lucia, Francisco and Jacinta.

THE OCTOBER APPARITION

The Day the Sun Danced at Fatima

Great Tension and Turmoil Preceded
the October Apparition

OCTOBER 13, 1917, promised to bring one of the greatest manifestations of God's power in the history of
the Catholic Church. A spectacular miracle was to occur,
but not without being preceded by enormous opposition.
Opposition to divine intervention has often happened in
the drama of salvation history. After Jesus was baptized
by John in the Jordan River, he was led into the desert
by the Holy Spirit to fast and pray for forty days and
be tempted by the devil (Lk 4:1–2). Whenever the Holy
Spirit begins to work in the Church, the evil spirit—the
devil—immediately moves to counteract what he does. Our
Lady, according to Saint Maximilian Kolbe, is the greatest
instrument of the Holy Spirit. So when she promised great
graces for her October 13 apparition, the devil stirred
up as much trouble as he could before that date. Some of
the difficulties came from those at a distance; others were
caused by neighbors and even family members of the
visionaries.

The Secular Press and Anti-Clerical Government

We have already seen how the local administrator, Arturo Santos, had failed to force the children either to reveal our Lady's secret or to deny the apparitions. Other antagonistic politicians, however, were already gloating over how events would go in October. Self-assured and arrogant, they were convinced that nothing miraculous was ever going to happen. Then, they figured, the three little shepherd children would be persecuted, and religion would be held up to ridicule. In league with these anti-religious politicians, the secular press throughout Portugal carried out a bitter campaign of mockery to discredit the apparitions. The liberal and sophisticated intellectuals of the day could not accept that religion had anything worthwhile to contribute to a world seemingly governed by science and human reason alone. Of course faith and science do not need to be in conflict, as this simple story illustrates: An old man was sitting on a train in France saying his Rosary. At a certain stop a university student got onto the train and sat near the old man. When the student noticed the Rosary, he began to ridicule the old man. "Put that Rosary away! We don't need prayer anymore! We're not dependent on God! We can run the world on our own; today we have science to control our own destiny!" The old man just sat there silently, continuing to pray his Rosary. When he got up to leave the train, he reached into his pocket, took out a business card and gave it to the student. We can only imagine the surprise and shock on the face of the young man when he read the card: "Dr. Louis Pasteur—Academy of Science—Paris, France". (Pasteur died in 1895.) Genuine scientists who have open minds and hearts know that there are limits to science, but there are no limits to God.

Neighbors and Family

Politicians and journalists were not the only ones upset with the children. In Aljustrel where the children lived, the majority of their neighbors were sceptical about the apparitions and hostile toward the children and their families. Jesus said that prophets are not without honor except in their native land and indeed in their own homes (Mt 13:57). Perhaps this disrespect is due to a certain jealousy: "Why wasn't our Lady appearing to me?" Or maybe the neighbors were fed up with the crowds that must have been overrunning their little hamlet, destroying their routines, and even their fields, looking for the visionaries. Other people, including priests and family members, were trying to persuade the children to admit that they had made up the whole story about the apparitions of our Lady. Still others were threatening the children, saying: "If the children have lied and nothing happens at the Cova, then..." A devout woman named Dona Maria lo Carmo Menezes had taken the three children to her home to give them a rest. When she saw the number of people who came looking for them, she was overwhelmed and remarked: "My children, if the miracle that you predict does not take place, these people are capable of burning you alive." With great confidence in our Lady's love and promise, the children responded: "We are not afraid, because our Lady does not deceive us. She told us that there would be a great miracle so that everyone would have to believe." [1]

Harder by far to deal with was the continuing disbelief and criticism coming from Lucia's own family members, especially her mother. Her negative attitude toward the

[1] Luiz Sergio Solimeo, *Fatima: A Message More Urgent Than Ever* (Spring Grove, PA: The American Society for the Defense of Tradition, Family and Property, 2008), pp. 78–79.

apparitions had turned the whole family against young Lucia. The mother was already angry over the damage done at the Cova by the crowds who were continuously trampling over this plot of land used to grow crops for the family and to graze their flock of sheep. Furthermore, the family was concerned about the disgrace they would suffer if everyone's expectations were left unfulfilled. Though disbelieving, Lucia's mother was prepared to suffer her daughter's fate if the people turned against her. On October 12,

> Maria Rosa jumped out of bed and went to wake her daughter saying, "Lucia, we had better go to confession. Everyone says that we shall probably be killed tomorrow in the Cova da Iria. If the lady doesn't do the miracle the people will attack us, so we had better go to confession and be properly prepared for death." [2]

Lucia was willing to go with her mother to confession, but not because she was afraid of dying. "I'm absolutely certain that the Lady will do all that she promised," she said. The next day, Lucia's mother went with her daughter to the place of the apparitions, saying, "If my child is going to die, I want to die with her!" [3]

The Day Long-Awaited Finally Came

Crowds of people had been coming for days to the Cova da Iria to witness a spectacular miracle. They would not be disappointed. Estimates of the crowd ranged from forty thousand to eighty thousand in the Cova itself. Another twenty thousand were watching from about twenty-five miles around. The rain had been coming down for more than a

[2] John de Marchi, I.M.C., *Fatima: From the Beginning*, trans I. M. Kingsbury (Fatima: Edições Missões Consolata, 2006), p. 128. (Hereafter, *From the Beginning*.)
[3] Ibid., p. 133.

day, and everyone was drenched. There was mud all over. The rain would continue right up to the moment the apparition began. Here is how Lucia described the beginning of the events of that day:

> We left home quite early, expecting that we would be delayed along the way. Masses of people thronged the roads. The rain fell in torrents. . . .
>
> On the way, the scenes of the previous month, still more numerous and moving, were repeated. Not even the muddy roads could prevent these people from kneeling in the most humble and suppliant of attitudes. We reached the holmoak in the Cova da Iria. Once there, moved by an interior impulse, I asked the people to shut their umbrellas and say the Rosary.[4]

Lucia's Conversation with Our Lady

At last the children saw the flash of light, and our Lady appeared on the holmoak. Lucia then began her conversation in this last apparition with our Lady with her usual question: "What do you want of me?" Our Lady's response gave a couple of specific answers to questions that Lucia had been asking all along:

> I want to tell you that a chapel is to be built here in my honour. I am the Lady of the Rosary. Continue always to pray the Rosary every day. The war is going to end, and the soldiers will soon return to their homes.[5]

"Build a Chapel Here"—By her apparitions at the Cova da Iria, our Lady has made it a holy place. Fatima is like the sacred places in the Holy Land hallowed by Jesus, Mary,

[4] *Lucia's Memoirs*, p. 168.
[5] Ibid., p. 172.

Joseph and the many saints who have lived and died there. These sites are now places of pilgrimage, where the faithful can go and be renewed by prayer and acts of piety. People feel a closeness to God in these holy places. The shrine in Fatima is also a place of pilgrimage for millions of people every year; and to accommodate these pilgrims she knew would come, our Lady asked that a chapel be built there.

Our Lady has asked for chapels before. She told Saint Bernadette that she desired a chapel at Lourdes, so that the people could come and pray to her there, and also bathe in the miraculous waters. Our Lady of Guadalupe told Saint Juan Diego to give a message to his bishop about a chapel in her honor on Tepeyac Hill in Mexico City. Here is how she put her request:

> I ardently desire a temple [church] be built here for me where I will show and offer all my love, my compassion, my help and protection to the people. I am your merciful Mother, the Mother of all who live united in this land, and of all of mankind, of all those who love me, of those who cry to me, of those who have confidence in me. Here I will hear their weeping and their sorrows, and will remedy and alleviate their sufferings, necessities and misfortunes.[6]

The first chapel at the Cova da Iria was constructed in 1920. On October 13, 1921, the first Mass was celebrated in this Chapel of the Apparitions. Unfortunately, on March 6, 1922, anti-religious extremists destroyed the chapel with dynamite. A few years later, another chapel was begun to replace it, and in 1928, the first stone for the new sanctuary was laid. This second Chapel of the Apparitions was erected on the spot of the little holmoak on which our Lady had appeared. Later a magnificent basilica in honor of the mysteries of the

[6] David Michael Lindsey, *The Woman and the Dragon: Apparitions of Mary* (Gretna, LA: Pelican Publishing Company, 2000), p. 64.

Rosary was built nearby. The bodies of the three visionaries—Lucia, Francisco and Jacinta—were moved to the basilica. On the shrine grounds there is also a chapel of perpetual adoration of the Most Blessed Sacrament, where pilgrims can adore Jesus throughout the day and night. Our Lady's request for a chapel has certainly been fulfilled.

"I Am the Lady of the Rosary"—During our Lady's apparition on July 13, Lucia had asked her: "Tell us who you are." She responded that she would tell them in October. In the meantime the children referred to her as "the beautiful Lady who came from heaven". After telling the children about the chapel, Mary revealed her true identity: "I am the Lady of the Rosary." We have seen all along in the different apparitions how much our Lady emphasized the praying of that beautiful prayer. Let us simply recall Saint Padre Pio's words: "Is there any prayer more beautiful than the prayer our Lady herself taught us? . . . than the Rosary? Always pray the Rosary!" Our Lady told the children of the Rosary's power to end wars, bring world peace and convert sinners. Everyone who wants to fulfill our Lady's requests at Fatima must make the resolution to pray the Rosary every day. Remember, Mary wants our prayers; Mary needs our prayers for the triumph of her Immaculate Heart.

"The War Is Going to End"—Our Lady had already told the children in July that the war was going to end. She repeated this in October and added that the soldiers would soon return to their homes. World War I ended a year later, with the signing of an armistice on November 11, 1918, but our Lady made it abundantly clear that peace in the world depended on the way we live our Christian lives and make reparation for our sins. Penitence is what holds back the hand of God from punishing the world by war.

Lucia Presents the People's Petitions

Once again Lucia placed before our Lady petitions for the sick, and once again our Lady said that those who seek blessings from God must ask for forgiveness for their sins and reform their lives. There is an old saying that certainly applies here: "God listens to those who listen to him." Sometimes illnesses are the result of sin. So, to cure these illnesses, we must remove the sins that caused them in the first place. We must remember that not all afflictions are direct punishments for sin. As in the case of Job in the Old Testament, God sometimes allows trials and afflictions to test those who love him and to purify their love. During the miracle of the sun, which occurred during the October apparition, many people did experience miraculous healings of various kinds. There were the blind who received their sight, the crippled who were able to walk and many others who received blessings, both physical and spiritual.

"Do Not Offend the Lord Our God Anymore"

While touching upon the need for repentance for those who seek God's blessings, our Lady expressed what might be her most heartfelt plea:

> Looking very sad, Our Lady said: "Do not offend the Lord our God anymore, because He is already so much offended." [7]

One can almost sense the sadness with which this plea came directly from our Lady's heart. No one knows the meaning of sin more than our Blessed Lady. Of all God's creatures, no one's heart is as filled with God's love as the heart of Mary. So she understands the gravity of offending

[7] *Lucia's Memoirs*, p. 168.

God who is all-good and worthy of all our love. To see God offended by our sins is an enormous suffering for one so filled with his love. In addition, she understands the price that love paid for sin—the death of her son on the Cross. He was scourged, crowned with thorns, mocked and spat upon. Nails were driven into his hands and feet, and his heart was pierced by a spear. This is what sin means to our Lady!

Two Simultaneous Apparitions

Lucia described in her memoirs what happened next, when our Lady was about to leave:

> Then, opening her hands, she made them reflect on the sun, and as she ascended, the reflection of her own light continued to be projected on the sun itself. Here. . . . is the reason why I cried out to the people to look at the sun. My aim was not to call their attention to the sun, because I was not even aware of their presence. I was moved to do so under the guidance of an interior impulse.[8]

Once the October apparition began, the three children were oblivious of everything around them, even the great crowd of people. They were no doubt in a kind of ecstatic state resulting from their being in the presence of the Mother of God, as they had experienced on previous occasions. Lucia's spontaneous words to the people made the great crowd turn their attention to the sun, and they witnessed the great miracle of the sun dancing at Fatima. What the three little visionaries saw was quite a different apparition:

> After our Lady had disappeared into the immense distance of the firmament, we beheld St. Joseph with the Child Jesus

[8] Ibid., p. 170.

and Our Lady robed in white with a blue mantle, beside
the sun. St. Joseph and the Child Jesus appeared to bless
the world, for they traced the Sign of the Cross with their
hands. When a little later, this apparition disappeared, I saw
Our Lord and Our Lady; it seemed to me that it was Our
Lady of Dolours [Sorrows]. Our Lord appeared to bless the
world in the same manner as St. Joseph had done. This
apparition also vanished, and I saw Our Lady once more,
this time resembling Our Lady of Carmel.[9]

Our Lady had promised this threefold appearance of the
Holy Family in her September apparition. We saw how these
appearances can be related to the mysteries of the Rosary.
Here let us focus on a very important teaching that comes
especially from the joyful mysteries of the Rosary.

The Message of Fatima and the Need to Strengthen Family Life

The appearance of the Holy Family emphasized the importance of the Fatima message for strengthening Christian family life. God knew the many problems and attacks that would
afflict Christian families in the future. None of these are
new, but never before have they been so deliberately pro-
moted and so widespread: divorce, infidelity, cohabitation,
abortion, illegitimacy, all kinds of sexual and substance abuse,
neglect, anger and violence. Add to these the assault on
marriage and parenthood by modern technologies such as
artificial birth control and in vitro fertilization. Then there
is the pressure to redefine marriage itself, as we see in the
push to equate same-sex relationships with matrimony.

All of these are tragic signs that society is turning more
and more away from God. As a result of sin increasing in
the world, and even in the Church, as Pope Benedict XVI

[9] Ibid.

often points out, there is growing religious indifference and secularism undermining respect for the sanctity of human life and the stability of the traditional family. Many Catholics do not pray, do not go to Mass regularly or receive the Sacrament of Penance sufficiently throughout the year. We need to heed our Lady's call to return to the Lord. The family is the basic building block of society. This holds true for religious society, the Church, as well as for civil society, the state. As the family goes, so goes society. If the fundamental building block of all society disintegrates, then the whole social structure will eventually collapse.

Saint Joseph's Importance and the Message of Fatima

It is interesting to point out that Saint Joseph is the only saint to appear at Fatima with our Lady. He represents the roles of husband and father, which sorely need to be strengthened today. Saint Joseph was certainly a faithful and loving husband to our Blessed Lady. His holiness must have been extraordinary since God prepared him to be the earthly spouse of our Lady and the earthly father of Jesus. As we know Joseph and Mary did not consummate their marriage physically, but they were true husband and wife. We see the tenderness and care of Saint Joseph when he refused to condemn our Lady publicly after he came to realize that she was with child (Mt 1:18ff). Instead of acting impulsively or condemning her rashly, he prayed over the situation and trusted in God's guidance. The Lord rewarded him with the revelation that the Child was conceived by the Holy Spirit.

Saint Joseph is a powerful model for the traditional roles of fatherhood, namely, provider and protector. He provided the necessities of life for the Holy Family through his work as a carpenter. We may assume that he taught his

trade to Jesus, because people from his own town of Nazareth asked of Jesus: "Is this not the carpenter, the Son of
Mary?" Joseph protected the Christ Child and the Blessed
Virgin Mary when Herod ordered the slaughter of baby
boys in Bethlehem. Warned in a dream of the danger, Joseph
arose in the middle of the night and took Mary and Jesus
into Egypt for safety (Mt 2:13–14). After Herod's death,
Joseph took the Holy Family back to Israel, but for their
safety he went to Nazareth instead of Bethlehem. Because
of his great care and protection for Jesus and Mary, Saint
Joseph has been given the title of "Protector of the Universal Church". This title comes to mind as we meditate
on the image of Saint Joseph and the Christ Child blessing
the world. We need the protection and intercession of this
great saint in our struggle against the demonic forces that
even today are attempting to destroy the Mystical Body of
Christ, the Church.

The Great Miracle of the Sun

Unless we had been present at the Cova on October 13,
1917, we really cannot grasp the tremendous impact of the
spectacular miracle the people witnessed that day. It certainly was one of the most incredible events in history, as it
defies any human explanation. First of all, the miracle
involved the sun, which no human person can control or
influence in any way. Secondly, it was witnessed by approximately seventy-five thousand people. There were about fifty-
five thousand people right in the area of the Cova da Iria.
Then there were another estimated twenty thousand people who saw the miracle of the sun from as far as twenty-
five miles away. Finally, the miracle had been predicted three
months before it happened. After the first apparition by our
Lady on May 13, the people began asking for a sign that she

was truly appearing at the Cova. During her July apparition, our Lady said to the children that in October she would tell them who she was and what she wanted of them. She would also perform a miracle for all to see and believe.

As a result of our Lady's promise, the crowds were enormous that day. The number of people present was important because for that reason the phenomenon they witnessed could not then be dismissed as a simple case of mass hysteria. Among the people who came were not only the faithful who believed, but also the curious, sceptics and atheists. Not everyone present that day believed he had seen a miracle. Believing in something or someone is ultimately an act of the will. Many people, for example, who saw Jesus raise Lazarus from the dead did believe in Jesus, but others did not. These latter simply went to the Pharisees and reported what Jesus had done (Jn 11:45–46). On the day the sun danced, many who came believing in the apparitions were strengthened in their faith. Some who were sceptical had their doubts removed, many of the curious went away believers. Of those who did not believe, perhaps some simply refused to do so, despite what they witnessed. Perhaps they did not want to see what others saw.

The Witnesses Speak of What They Saw

Many people who saw the great miracle have shared what they experienced. Here are a few of the many testimonies from witnesses who were actually at the Cova da Iria.

Mary Allen—We know very little about this woman, except that she was an eye-witness of the miracle of the sun.

> As we approached the hillside upon which the appearances were supposed to have taken place, I saw a sea of people. (Some newspapers said there were 70,000 people there.) I

didn't count, but it was more people than I have ever seen in my life, even to this day.... We had just arrived there when suddenly my attention was drawn by a sudden bright light from the heavens, lighting up the whole countryside. Suddenly the rain ceased, the clouds separated and I saw a large sun, brighter than the sun, yet I could look at it without hurting my eyes, as if it were only the moon. This sun began to get larger and larger, brighter and brighter until the whole heavens seemed more brilliantly lighted than I have ever seen it. Then the sun started spinning and shooting streams of light, which changed it to all colors of the rainbow... At the same time, it started getting bigger and bigger in the sky as though it were headed directly for us, as though it were falling on the earth. Everyone was frightened. We all thought it was the end of the world. Everyone threw themselves on their knees praying and screaming the Act of Contrition. Suddenly the sun stopped spinning and returned to its place in the sky. Everyone started shouting: "Miracle! This is a miracle!" Just then I noticed that both the ground and my clothes were bone dry. Everyone seemed to rush forward to see the children. Unfortunately I was only able to see them at a distance![10]

Ti Marto, father of Francisco and Jacinta—believed the children's stories of the apparitions from the beginning. He knew that his children did not tell lies and that our Lady could appear to them. This "first believer" in Fatima told the following:

We looked easily at the sun, which for some reason did not blind us. It seemed to flicker on and off, first one way, then another. It cast its rays in many directions and painted everything in different colors—the trees, the people, the air and the ground. But what was most extraordinary, I thought, was that the sun did not hurt our eyes. Everything was still

[10] "The Message of Fatima: Part III", *Soul*, Winter 2009, p. 7.

and quiet, and everyone was looking up. Then at a certain moment, the sun appeared to stop spinning. It then began to move and to dance in the sky until it seemed to detach itself from its place and fall upon us. It was a terrible moment.[11]

Maria Carreira—was given the title *Maria de Capelinha* ("Mary of the little chapel") because she spent so much time in the Cova and dedicated herself to caring for the chapel, especially decorating it with flowers. She was one of the earliest and most faithful believers in the apparitions. She related that

> [T]he sun turned everything to different colors—yellow, blue and white. Then it shook and trembled. It looked like a wheel of fire that was going to fall on the people. They began to cry out, "We shall all be killed!" Others called to Our Lady to save them. They recited acts of contrition. One woman began to confess her sins aloud, advertising that she had done this and that... When at last the sun stopped leaping and moving, we all breathed our relief. We were still alive, and the miracle which the children had foretold, had been seen by everyone.[12]

Alfredo da Silva Santos—was a professional man from Lisbon. By his own admission, he seems to have been sceptical about the apparitions, or at least not an ardent believer. What he experienced on October 13 touched him deeply.

> We made our arrangements, and went in three motorcars on the early morning of the 13th. There was a thick mist, and the car which went in front mistook the way so that we were all lost for a time and only arrived at the Cova da Iria at midday by the sun. It was absolutely full of people, but for my part I felt devoid of any religious feeling. When

[11] *From the Beginning*, pp. 135–36.
[12] Ibid., p. 136.

Lucia called out: "Look at the sun!", the whole multitude repeated: "Attention to the sun!" It was a day of incessant drizzle but a few moments before the miracle it stopped raining. I can hardly find words to describe what followed. The sun began to move, and at a certain moment appeared to be detached from the sky and about to hurtle upon us like a wheel of flame. My wife—we had been married only a short time—fainted, and I was too upset to attend to her, and my brother-in-law ... supported her on his arm. I fell on my knees, oblivious of everything, and when I got up I don't know what I said. I think I began to cry out like the others. An old man with a white beard began to attack the atheists aloud, and challenged them to say whether or not something supernatural had occurred.[13]

O Seculo—was a pro-government, anti-clerical newspaper with a large circulation not only in Lisbon, but also in the surrounding provinces. Reporter Avelino de Almeida had written negative articles about the apparitions, which ironically helped to publicize the promised miracle. Here is an excerpt from Almeida's O Seculo article about the miracle of the sun.

From the road, where the vehicles were parked and where hundreds of people who had not dared to brave the mud were congregated, one could see the immense multitude turn toward the sun, which appeared free from clouds and in its zenith. It looked like a plaque of dull silver, and it was possible to look at it without the least discomfort. It might have been an eclipse which was taking place. But at that moment a great shout went up, and one could hear the spectators nearest at hand shouting: "A miracle! A miracle!". . . . Before the astonished eyes of the crowd, whose aspect was biblical as they stood bareheaded, eagerly searching the sky, the sun trembled, made sudden incredible movements outside

[13] Ibid., p. 140.

all cosmic laws—the sun "danced" according to the typical expression of the people. . . . Standing on the step of an omnibus was an old man. With his face turned to the sun, he recited the Creed in a loud voice. I asked who he was; I saw him afterwards going up to those around him who still had their hats on, and vehemently imploring them to uncover their heads before such an extraordinary demonstration of the existence of God. . . . People then began to ask each other what they had seen. The great majority admitted to having seen the trembling and the dancing of the sun; others affirmed that they saw the face of the Blessed Virgin; others, again, swore that the sun whirled on itself like a giant wheel and that it lowered itself to the earth as if to burn it in its rays. Some said they saw it change colors successively. . .[14]

Father Ignacio Lorenco—gave a very interesting and important account. He was a witness to the miracle of the sun from the village of Alburitel, eleven miles from the Cova.

I was only nine years old at the time, and I went to the local village school. At about midday we were surprised by the shouts and cries of some men and women who were passing in front of the school. The teacher, a good, pious woman, though nervous and impressionable, was the first to run into the road, with the children after her. . . . Outside, the people were shouting and weeping and pointing to the sun, ignoring the agitated questions of the schoolmistress. It was a great Miracle, which one could see quite distinctly from the top of the hill where my village was situated—the Miracle of the Sun, accompanied by all the extraordinary phenomena.

I feel incapable of describing what I saw and felt. I looked fixedly at the sun, which seemed pale and did not hurt the eyes. Looking like a ball of snow revolving on itself, it suddenly seemed to come down in a zigzag [motion], menacing

14 Ibid., p. 137.

the earth. Terrified, I ran and hid myself among the people, who were weeping and expecting the end of the world at any moment. Near us was an unbeliever who had spent the morning mocking at the simpletons who had gone off to Fatima "just to see an ordinary girl." He now seemed to be paralyzed, his eyes fixed on the sun. Afterwards he trembled from head to foot and lifting up his arms fell on his knees in the mud, crying out to Our Lady.

Meanwhile the people continued to cry out and to weep, asking God to pardon their sins. We all ran to the two chapels in the village, which were soon filled to overflowing. During those long moments of the solar prodigy, objects around us turned all the colors of the rainbow. We saw ourselves blue, yellow, red, etc. All the strange phenomena increased the fears of the people. After about 10 minutes the sun, now dull and pallid, returned to its place. When the people realized that the danger was over, there was an explosion of joy, and everyone joined in thanksgiving and praise to Our Lady.[15]

The Impact of the Miracle

Our Lady had kept her promise to perform a miracle that would allow everyone to believe. The faith of many witnesses grew stronger and more ardent. Unfortunately, the hearts of some others only became harder in disbelief. The evidence, as we have seen in these testimonies, is convincing, but hearing eye-witness accounts does not necessarily assure believing. We can say of this great miracle of the sun what was said of the miraculous happenings at Lourdes: "For those with faith, no explanation is necessary. For those without faith, no explanation is possible."

[15] Ibid., p. 141.

12

JACINTA AND FRANCISCO

The Little Ones Are Taken to Heaven

W E HAVE SEEN THE STORY of Fatima in terms of the three apparitions of the Angel of Peace and the six apparitions of our Lady to Lucia, Francisco and Jacinta. Though so young they received a message of enormous importance for the world. What happened to the three little visionaries after the last apparition with the great miracle of the sun? In this chapter we will focus on the lives of Francisco and Jacinta, for they were not to remain in this world very long. We will look at the life of Lucia in another chapter.

After the apparitions ended, the mission of Francisco and Jacinta consisted of putting into practice all our Lady taught them about prayer, sacrifice, suffering and reparation. But as our Lady had told Lucia, her mission would involve more than these disciplines and would continue for some time. In fact, it lasted for another eighty-seven years. We will come back to Lucia later in this book. Let us first look at what happened to Francisco and Jacinta.

Francisco Marto—June 11, 1908–April 4, 1919

Francisco died within two years after the apparitions ended, after having contracted influenza in the terrible epidemic that would take the lives of about twenty million people all over the world. Little Jacinta came down with the sickness first, in October 1918, and Francisco contracted it shortly afterward.

Francisco had learned to be very generous in making sacrifices and quite courageous in suffering. When the children were imprisoned at Ourem, he was willing to die by being boiled in oil rather than reveal the secret our Lady had given them. His willingness to die flowed from his longing for heaven, which our Lady promised he would soon enter. When people asked him what he wanted to be when he grew up, he would simply answer that he wanted to go to heaven. Here is an example of a little dialogue with some ladies who questioned him about what he wanted to be when he grew up:

> "Do you want to be a carpenter?"
>   "No, madam."
>   "A soldier?"
>   "No, madam."
>   "Surely you would like to be a doctor?"
>   "No, not that either."
>   "Then I know what you would like to be ... a priest! Then you could say Mass and preach..."
>   "No, madam, I don't want to be a priest either."
>   "Well, then, what do you want to be?"
>   "I don't want to be anything. I want to die and go to heaven...." [1]

Francisco's father, who was listening to this conversation, told the women that heaven was his son's heart's desire.

Francisco's Sufferings

In her memoirs, Lucia wrote about Francisco's desire to make reparation for sinners throughout his final illness. He

[1] *From the Beginning*, p. 171.

began experiencing flu symptoms on the way to school, but he preferred praying in church to returning home:

> I noticed, as we left the house, that Francisco was walking very slowly. "What's the matter?" I asked him. "You seem unable to walk."
>
> "I have such a bad headache and I feel as though I'm going to fall."
>
> "Then don't come. Stay at home!"
>
> "I don't want to. I'd rather stay in the church with the Hidden Jesus, while you go to school." [2]

Lucia added that when Francisco visited a church he liked to pray behind the altar at the foot of the tabernacle. He liked to be hidden as he prayed close to Jesus. Many people testified that they had received great graces after having asked Francisco to pray for them.

The visits from our Lady had given Francisco a desire for solitude and prayer. Before his final illness, when the children would graze their sheep, he would separate himself from Jacinta and Lucia in order to meditate on all that our Lady had told the children and to pray. He told Lucia and Jacinta:

> I loved seeing the angel, and I loved seeing Our Lady even better, but what I liked best of all was seeing Our Lord in that light which Our Lady put into our hearts. I love God so much, but he is so sad because of all the sins. We mustn't commit even the tiniest sin! [3]

As Francisco's illness intensified, he became more heroic in his suffering. Here is how Lucia described it:

[2] *Lucia's Memoirs*, p. 141.
[3] *From the Beginning*, p. 172.

While he was ill, Francisco always appeared joyful and content. I asked him sometimes: "Are you suffering a lot, Francisco?"

"Quite a lot, but never mind! I am suffering to console our Lord, and afterwards, within a short time, I am going to heaven!"[4]

Preparing for Our Lady to Come and Take Him to Heaven

As his death neared, Francisco continued to offer his suffering for the conversion of sinners and in reparation to the Hearts of Jesus and Mary for all the offenses committed against them. He prepared for his coming death with great care by requesting confession and Holy Communion, and he asked Lucia to pray that he would be able to receive these sacraments. In order to make a good confession, Francisco asked Lucia and Jacinta to remind him of sins they had seen him commit. They could only remember some small sins. When Francisco heard what they had to say, he said: "I have already confessed those, but I'll do so again. Maybe it is because of these sins that I committed that Our Lord is so sad!"[5] Once he had made a good confession, he wanted to receive the "Hidden Jesus" in Holy Communion. Remember that Francisco had never received his First Holy Communion formally in church. But during the third apparition of the Angel of Peace, he drank the Precious Blood of Jesus from the chalice the angel administered to him. At last on his deathbed he was allowed to receive Jesus in the Sacred Host. It was his Viaticum, which is the last Holy Communion a person

---

[4] *Lucia's Memoirs*, p. 143.
[5] Ibid., p. 144.

receives so as to have Jesus accompany him on his journey to heaven.

On the night before he died, Lucia came to see Francisco. Here is her final conversation with him:

> "Goodbye, Francisco! If you go to heaven tonight, don't forget me when you get there, do you hear me?"
>
> "No, I won't forget. Be sure of that." Then seizing my right hand, he held it tightly for a long time, looking at me with tears in his eyes. "Do you want anything more?" I asked him, with tears running down my cheeks too. "No," he answered, in a low voice. . . .
>
> "Goodbye, then, Francisco! Till we meet in heaven, goodbye!" [6]

On the morning of his last day on earth, April 4, 1919, Francisco asked pardon of his family for all his faults. Then little Jacinta, with tears in her eyes, came to say goodbye to her brother with these words: "Give my love to Our Lord and Our Lady and tell them I'll suffer as much as they want, to convert sinners and to make up to the Immaculate Heart of Mary." [7] Finally, at ten o'clock in the morning, Francisco said to his mother: "Mother, look at that lovely light by the door!" [8] It was the sign our Lady was coming to take her little Francisco to heaven. Now he would be forever with "his beautiful Lady".

After his funeral Mass, Francisco's body was buried in the cemetery of the parish church of St. Anthony in Fatima. On March 12, 1952, his remains were transferred to a side chapel in the basilica built at the site of the Cova da Iria.

[6] Ibid., p. 145.
[7] *From the Beginning*, p. 185.
[8] Ibid.

Jacinta Marto—March 11, 1910–February 20, 1920

Jacinta had a very charming personality. People who knew her, loved her. She was especially fond of her cousin Lucia, even jealous of her time and attention. When she was not available, Jacinta felt lonely and sad. Because of her desire to be with Lucia, Jacinta's mother allowed her and her brother Francisco to pasture their sheep with Lucia and her flock. Jacinta loved the sheep; they became her friends, and she gave them names. She even tried to carry a little lamb home on her shoulders after she had seen a picture of the Good Shepherd. She loved the things of nature. She would call the sun "our Lady's lamp" and the stars were "the angels' lanterns". After the apparitions of our Lady, and particularly after the vision of hell, Jacinta's naturally lively personality became subdued and very serious.

Jacinta was only seven years old at the time of the apparitions. She could see the angel and our Lady and also hear everything they said, but she never spoke to them. We have already seen that before the apparitions, little Jacinta could be stubborn and self-centered. At the same time, she was intelligent and very sensitive. So despite her being the youngest of the three visionaries, Lucia said that the message of our Lady seemed to have made the greatest impact on her. Jacinta was especially moved by the seriousness of sin, how it offends and separates us from God. The vision of hell affected her so much that she did not want anyone to ever go there. She wished that everyone could see a vision of hell so that no one would ever end up there. With incredible generosity for one so young, Jacinta offered herself completely for the salvation of souls. We will see how her spirit of sacrifice reached heroic proportions.

Examples of Jacinta's Sacrificing Spirit

Lucia recorded Jacinta's great desire to save souls by her willingness to offer significant sacrifices. One very hot day the children were suffering terribly from thirst.

> A little old woman gave me not only a pitcher of water, but also some bread, which I accepted gratefully. I ran to share it with my little companions, and then offered the pitcher to Francisco, and told him to take a drink. "I don't want to," he replied. "I want to suffer for the conversion of sinners."
>
> "You have a drink, Jacinta!"
>
> "But I want to offer the sacrifice for sinners too!" Then I poured the water into a hollow in the rock, so that the sheep could drink it, and went to return the pitcher to its owner. The heat was getting more and more intense. The shrill singing of the crickets and grasshoppers, coupled with the croaking of the frogs in the neighboring pond, made an uproar that was almost unbearable. Jacinta, frail as she was, and weakened still more by the lack of food and drink, said to me with that simplicity which was natural to her: "Tell the crickets and the frogs to keep quiet! I have such a terrible headache." Then Francisco asked her: "Don't you want to suffer this for sinners?" The poor child, clasping her head between her two little hands, replied: "Yes, I do. Let them sing!" [9]

Jacinta also willingly suffered trials that God permitted from other people. People would mock her, and even neighbors would insult her. She was called a liar and a fraud and was even beaten. She also had to put up with endless exhausting interrogations, including those from priests who were sceptical of the events at the Cova. At the same time, Jacinta's holiness was growing. Many people, especially after the

[9] *Lucia's Memoirs*, p. 32.

last apparition of our Lady, sought her intercession, and many received favors through her prayers.

Jacinta's Special Love for the Holy Father

Jacinta was privileged to have two visions of the Holy Father. In one vision she saw the pope suffering deeply:

> I saw the Holy Father in a very big house, kneeling by a table, with his head buried in his hands, and he was weeping. Outside the house, there were many people. Some of them were throwing stones, others were cursing and using bad language. Poor Holy Father, we must pray very much for him.[10]

Another time, when the children were praying outdoors, Jacinta stood up and asked Lucia:

> Can't you see all those highways and roads and fields full of people, who are crying with hunger and have nothing to eat? And the Holy Father in a church praying before the Immaculate Heart of Mary? And so many people praying with him?[11]

Remember that our Lady in her third apparition had foretold that with the spread of Communism, the Church would be persecuted and the Holy Father would have much to suffer. After these visions the children, but especially Jacinta, always kept the pope in their prayers and sacrifices. In our own love and loyalty for the Church, we should do likewise. His task and responsibilities are enormous. He certainly shares the passion of Christ as "the servant of the servants of God". An example of this comes from the talks of Archbishop Sheen, who personally knew a number of

[10] Ibid., p. 108.
[11] Ibid., p. 109.

the popes. Pope Paul VI once told Archbishop Sheen that he read his mail at midnight, just before going to bed. The Pope said that in nine out of every ten letters, there was a thorn. Perhaps it was a bishop writing to the Holy Father about persecutions, or scandals or lack of vocations in his diocese. Pope Paul VI said that when he lay his head on the pillow after reading all those letters, he felt it was like placing his head on a crown of thorns. No one can truly understand the tremendous burden the Holy Father carries for the love of Christ and the love of his people. Like Jacinta, let us pray often for the Holy Father.

Jacinta Prepares for Her Coming Death

Jacinta had become very generous in her willingness to suffer for the love of the Hearts of Jesus and Mary, and for the salvation of souls. She would be even more heroic as her death approached. As we have seen, Jacinta contracted influenza in October 1918. When her brother Francisco became ill with the same disease, she felt more concerned for him than for herself. For example, whenever Lucia went to visit her, Jacinta told her to see Francisco first, saying she would make a sacrifice of being alone. One of her greatest sufferings was to see her brother dying, and after he died she missed him greatly. We can only imagine the bond that was formed between this little brother and sister because of their having seen our Lady together. A little incident illustrates this suffering. When Lucia went to see Jacinta in the time of her illness, she said the girl remained a long time in deep thought. When Lucia asked her what she was thinking about, she answered with tears in her eyes: "About Francisco. I'd give anything to see him again!" [12]

[12] Ibid., p. 43.

Suffering in Two Hospitals—Suffering Alone!

Jacinta told Lucia that our Lady had appeared to her and
Francisco and told them that she would take Francisco to
heaven soon. Then our Lady asked Jacinta if she wanted to
stay on earth longer to suffer for the conversion of sinners.
When Jacinta said yes, our Lady told her she would be going
to a hospital where she would have much to suffer for the
salvation of souls. At the time, Jacinta had bronchial pneumonia. Later on an abscess formed which caused her great
physical pain, and she was sent to a hospital in Ourem. The
child knew she would suffer there a great deal, but she feared
most being alone. Before she left for Ourem, she told Lucia
that she would offer her sufferings for the conversion of
sinners and for the Holy Father. After her stay of almost
two months in the hospital, she returned home with a large
open wound in her chest and tuberculosis consuming her
body.

In January 1920, Jacinta went to another hospital, and as
before our Lady prepared her for this ordeal:

> [Our Lady] told me that I am going to Lisbon, to another
> hospital, that I will not see you again, nor my parents either,
> and after suffering a great deal, I shall die alone. But she
> said I must not be afraid, since she herself is coming to take
> me to heaven.[13]

At first, Jacinta went to a Catholic orphanage where she
was able to attend Mass and receive Holy Communion,
which brought her much happiness, but she did not stay
very long.[14] She was moved to another hospital, where she
made her final offering to Jesus and Mary for the salvation

[13] Ibid., p. 45.
[14] *From the Beginning*, p. 197.

of souls. A little while before leaving for Lisbon, Jacinta told Lucia that she would soon go to heaven:

> You must stay to tell people that God wants to establish in the world devotion to the Immaculate Heart of Mary. When you have to say this don't hide, but tell everybody that God gives us His grace through the Immaculate Heart and that people must ask it through her and that the Sacred Heart of Jesus wants the Immaculate Heart of Mary by His side. They must ask peace through the Immaculate Heart because God has given it to her. I wish I could put into everybody the fire that I have here in my heart which makes me love the Sacred Heart of Jesus and the Immaculate Heart of Mary so much![15]

While in the hospital in Lisbon, our Lady visited Jacinta three times, and revealed many things to the little visionary. Though we have touched on some of these messages earlier, they bear repeating: that war is a punishment for sin; that many fashions would come that would offend our Lord very much; that many marriages are not of God; that priests must be very pure, concentrate on their mission to the Church and souls, and be obedient to the pope and their lawful superiors; and finally that more souls go to hell because of sins of impurity than any other. Our Lady also mentioned the importance of respecting priests and doing penance.[16]

Jacinta knew that her going to the hospital was not for a cure, but to suffer more. Since our Lady had told her before she entered the hospital that she was going to die, she objected to surgical treatment. The doctors, however,

[15] Ibid., p. 192.

[16] World Apostolate of Fatima, *Spiritual Guide for the Salvation of Souls and World Peace* (Washington, NJ: World Apostolate of Fatima, U.S.A., 2008), p. 92.

performed a successful operation, but she only grew worse. Jacinta accepted all of her sufferings with a burning desire to make reparation for sinners and to pray for their conversion. Our Lady visited Jacinta four days before her death and comforted her. "Now I'm much better," the girl said. "Our Lady said that she would soon come to fetch me and that she would take away the pain." [17] The remarkable life of this saintly child came to an end the evening of February 20, 1920, when her beloved Lady returned to take her soul to heaven.

After her funeral Mass, Jacinta was buried in a cemetery in Ourem. In 1935, her body was moved to the parish cemetery of Saint Anthony in Fatima, where she was buried near her brother Francisco. On March 1, 1951, her coffin was exhumed and opened, and her body was found to be preserved. She was then placed in a side chapel of the basilica at the Cova da Iria.

Both Francisco Marto and his sister Jacinta were beatified at a solemn Mass in the shrine of the Cova da Iria by Pope John Paul II on May 13, 2000. Sister Lucia, then a Carmelite nun in Coimbra, Portugal, attended the Mass of beatification for her two little cousins.

[17] *From the Beginning*, p. 203.

13

THE APPARITIONS AT PONTEVEDRA, SPAIN

Our Lady Asks for the Five First Saturdays Devotion

THE SIX MAJOR APPARITIONS of our Lady of Fatima at the Cova da Iria had ended with the great "dance of the sun". Francisco and Jacinta had faithfully and generously fulfilled their mission and gone to their reward in heaven. Lucia alone remained to finish the task entrusted to her by Jesus and his Blessed Mother, namely, to establish in the world devotion to the Immaculate Heart of Mary. In order to do this, our Lady told Lucia to learn how to read and write; she would need these skills to spread the messages our Lady intended to give the world through her.

Our Lady Comes to Ask for the "Communion of Reparation"

The next chapter in the Fatima story was a series of three private revelations Lucia received in prayer. These mystical experiences were connected with our Lady's words on July 13 about another world war and the evil of Communism, which she said would begin in Russia and spread its errors

147

around the world, causing wars, and persecutions of the
Church and of the Holy Father. To prevent these evils from
happening, our Lady said she would come back again and
ask for two things: the Communion of Reparation and the
consecration of Russia to her Immaculate Heart. On December 10, 1925, the first of these promises was fulfilled; the
other promise would await a later date.

First Apparition at Pontevedra, Spain—
December 10, 1925

When our Lady returned in 1925, Lucia was a postulant in
the Congregation of the Dorothean Sisters. She was living
in a convent of the community in Pontevedra, Spain. In a
written account Sister Lucia produced for her spiritual director at the time, Father P. Aparicio, S.J., we find her description of the three apparitions of Mary requesting the
Communion of Reparation. At the request of her spiritual
director, Sister Lucia wrote in the third person. Here is her
description of the first apparition:

> On December 10, 1925, the most holy Virgin appeared to
> her, and by her side, elevated on a luminous cloud, was
> [the Christ] child. The most holy Virgin rested her hand
> on [Sister Lucia's] shoulder, and as she did so, she showed
> her a heart encircled by thorns, which she was holding in
> her other hand. At the same time, the [Christ] Child said:
> "Have compassion on the Heart of your most holy Mother,
> covered with thorns, with which ungrateful men pierce it
> at every moment, and there is no one to make an act of
> reparation to remove them." Then the most holy Virgin
> said: "Look, my daughter, at my Heart, surrounded with
> thorns with which ungrateful man pierce me at every
> moment by their blasphemies and ingratitude. You at least
> try to console me and say that I promise to assist at the

hour of death, with the graces necessary for salvation, all those who, on the first Saturday of five consecutive months, shall confess [their sins], receive Holy Communion, recite five decades of the Rosary, and keep me company for fifteen minutes while meditating on the fifteen mysteries of the Rosary, with the intention of making reparation to me." [1]

Lucia had seen a vision of the sorrowful heart of Mary before. During our Lady's apparition on June 13, 1917, in an immense light that descended upon the visionaries from her hands, the children saw a similar crown of thorns, representing the sins by which our Lady was offended, piercing her heart. Sister Lucia described the vision in her memoirs:

In front of the palm of Our Lady's right hand was a heart encircled by thorns which pierced it. We understood that this was the Immaculate Heart of Mary, outraged by the sins of humanity, and seeking reparation. [2]

The most striking thing about the first apparition to Sister Lucia at Pontevedra, is the Christ Child, who requested reparation for the sins of blasphemy and ingratitude by which our Lady's heart is continuously offended. We see in these words of Jesus the great compassionate love he has for his holy mother, especially for the great sorrows she endured for love of him throughout his life, and particularly during his bitter Passion and death. Our Lord wants his mother honored for all she suffered for him and with him. After all, she had no sins of her own. She suffered with Jesus to atone for our sins.

A Belgian mystic named Bertha Pettit, who lived at the time of the Fatima events, received private revelations from

---

[1] *Lucia's Memoirs*, p. 195. There are now twenty mysteries of the Rosary since Pope John Paul II's addition of the five luminous mysteries.

[2] Ibid., p. 161.

the Sacred Heart of Jesus and the Immaculate Heart of Mary. During one of these revelations, our Lord told Bertha that his mother's heart had two qualities: immaculate and sorrowful. He told her that "immaculate" referred to everything he did for her, namely, preserving her from original sin and filling her with a fullness of grace beyond that of all the angels and saints. Then he told her that "sorrowful" referred to everything that our Lady did for him, namely, share in his sufferings, especially at the time of his crucifixion and death. Therefore, Jesus told Bertha that he wanted his mother invoked as the Sorrowful and Immaculate Heart of Mary.

During the first apparition at Pontevedra, after the Christ Child spoke, our Lady asked Sister Lucia to comfort her by observing five first Saturdays and by spreading this devotion. One can almost hear the heartfelt plea in our Lady's words: "Look, my daughter, at my Heart, surrounded with thorns. . . . You at least try to console me." Our Lady's instructions for five first Saturdays include two parts: one is a promise, and the other is an explanation.

Promise of the Graces Needed for Salvation

Our Lady makes a wonderful promise to those who observe five first Saturdays: assistance at the hour of death, with the graces necessary for salvation. What an extraordinary gift it would be to have our Lady near at hand at the moment of our death. Every time we pray the Hail Mary, we make this request of her, for we end with the words: "Holy Mary, Mother of God, pray for us sinners, now and at the hour of our death." We have seen the holy deaths of Francisco and Jacinta, whom our Lady promised to take to heaven. Would we not want to have our Lady do the same for us? What are the graces we will need for our salvation at the hour of our death? These graces would likely include receiving confession and Holy Communion on our deathbed, the strength to resist any temptations that may assault us in our final hours, protection from the devil who always tries to seize a departing soul, family and friends praying with us and for us, reconciliation with any of them with whom we have been estranged and the ability to forgive all who have injured us so that we might be forgiven by God and receive from him a merciful judgment.

Since our eternal salvation is the main goal of our life here on earth, how could we turn down this great promise of our Lady? We can be confident that if a person made the Five First Saturdays devotion even only once in his lifetime, our Lady would not forget it. However, we will see that Jesus said in another apparition to Sister Lucia at Pontevedra that we should not make this devotion only once, but over and over again, because he and our Lady want and even need our prayers for the conversion of sinners, especially of Russia, and for peace in the world. Many people have unfortunately put such a stress on the consecration of Russia by the Holy Father as the condition for the triumph of the Immaculate Heart of Mary and peace in the world, that they have forgotten or neglected the fact that our Lady also asked for the Five First Saturdays devotion. As we shall see, Pope John Paul II has done his part in making the consecration of Russia to the Immaculate Heart, but are we, as Mary's children, doing our part by devotion to first Saturdays?

Our Lady Outlined the Devotion

Our Lady outlined what is involved in observing the Five First Saturdays devotion. There are four main elements to the devotion and two conditions. We shall simply enumerate these elements here, and later in this book explain them more fully[3]: (1) go to confession either on the first Saturday itself or at least a week before or after, (2) receive Holy Communion, (3) recite five decades of the Rosary, and (4) keep our Lady company for fifteen minutes while meditating on the mysteries of the Rosary. The two conditions necessary for the devotion are that the practices be done on the first Saturday of five consecutive months, and that they be done with the intention of making reparation to our Lady for the sins of blasphemy and ingratitude against her.

Second Apparition at Pontevedra, Spain—
February 15, 1926

In the second apparition to Sister Lucia at Pontevedra, the child Jesus appeared to her, but she did not recognize him at first. He asked her if she had already done anything to spread the devotion of the Five First Saturdays. She answered that her confessor raised difficulties about the devotion, and that her own mother superior, though prepared to propagate the devotion, was discouraged when the confessor told her that alone she could do nothing.

> On the 15th (of February 1926), I was very busy at my work, and was not thinking of [the devotion] at all. I went to throw out a pan full of rubbish beyond the vegetable garden, in the same place where, some months earlier, I had met a child. I had asked him if he knew the Hail Mary, and he said he did, whereupon I requested him to say it so that I could hear him. But, as he made no attempt to say it by himself, I said it with him three times over, at the end of which I asked him to say it alone. But as he remained

[3] See Appendix B for a fuller explanation of the Five First Saturdays devotion.

silent and was unable to say the Hail Mary alone, I asked him if he knew where the Church of Santa Maria was, to which he replied that he did. I told him to go there every day and to say this [prayer]: O, my heavenly Mother, give me your Child Jesus! I taught him this, and then left him. . . . Going there as usual, I found a child who seemed to me to be the same one whom I had previously met, so I questioned him: "Did you ask our heavenly Mother for the Child Jesus?" The child turned to me and said: "And have you spread through the world what our heavenly Mother requested of you?" With that, he was transformed into a resplendent Child. Knowing then that it was Jesus, I said: "My Jesus, you know very well what my confessor said to me in the letter I read to You. He told me that it was necessary for this vision to be repeated, for further happenings to prove its credibility, and he added that Mother Superior, on her own, could do nothing to propagate this devotion." [4]

This was certainly a rather humorous situation. Young Sister Lucia did not recognize the Christ Child when she first saw him. Furthermore, when she tried to get him to say the Hail Mary on his own, he would not do it because the Son of God does not pray to his mother; his mother prays to him. When she finally recognized that it was Jesus, he asked her what she had done about spreading devotion to the Immaculate Heart of Mary. It was then that Sister Lucia mentioned the difficulties.

Her Confessor's Objections

Lucia's confessor was not convinced that Jesus was asking for the Five First Saturdays devotion to be spread around the world. As a proof, the confessor wanted the vision

[4] *Lucia's Memoirs*, pp. 196–97.

repeated, as were the apparitions of our Lady in the Cova. At the same time, he required further happenings to prove that Sister Lucia's devotion to first Saturdays was meant to be made universal. He questioned whether more ardent devotion to first Saturdays was needed, since many people were already receiving Holy Communion and praying the fifteen mysteries of the Rosary on the first Saturdays of the month. In other words, there was no need for this new devotion because something similar already existed. Jesus' answer to this question was that although some of his people may already be receiving Holy Communion and reciting the Rosary on first Saturdays, they might do so with more fervor and commitment if they knew about his request for five consecutive first Saturdays. Here are our Lord's words to Sister Lucia:

> It is true, my daughter, that many souls begin the First Saturdays, but few finish them, and those who do complete them do so in order to receive the graces that are promised thereby. It would please me more if they did Five with fervor and with the intention of making reparation to the Heart of your heavenly Mother, than if they did Fifteen in a tepid and indifferent manner.[5]

Mother Superior's Hesitation

Sister Lucia's superior hesitated in spreading the Five First Saturdays devotion because of the confessor's doubts. Mother Superior was actually prepared to propagate the devotion, but the confessor's remark that alone she could do nothing discouraged her so much that she ended up doing nothing. Our Lord responded to Sister Lucia:

[5] Ibid., p. 197.

It is true your Superior alone can do nothing, but with my grace she can do all. It is enough that your confessor gives you permission and that your Superior speak of it, for it to be believed, even without people knowing to whom it has been revealed.[6]

These words of our Lord remind us of what he said to his apostles at the Last Supper: "[A]part from me you can do nothing" (Jn 15:5). We must realize that of ourselves we can do nothing; but with God's grace anything is possible. Certainly, if the Lord wanted Mother Superior to promote devotion to first Saturdays, he would bless her efforts even if they seemed inadequate in the face of the task that had to be accomplished. After all, Jesus fed five thousand men (not counting the women and children) with five loaves of bread and two fish. The apostles didn't think it could be done. As Archbishop Fulton Sheen once said: "When men calculate according to their resources, there is never enough; but when God gives, there is always an abundance." Because of these doubts and hesitations, the message about the Five First Saturdays was slow in spreading, despite its importance. The devil always works on human weaknesses to foil or at least minimize the work of God, but in the end the Lord and his Blessed Mother will be victorious.

Third Apparition at Pontevedra, Spain— December 17, 1927

As a novice, Sister Lucia had another revelation from our Lord. While praying to Jesus in the tabernacle in the chapel at Pontevedra, she asked the Lord how she could answer questions from her superiors regarding the origins of the

[6] Ibid.

devotion to the Immaculate Heart of Mary without divulging the secret our Lady had told her to keep absolutely confidential. Lucia was unsure about how much of the three secrets, if any, she could make known to her superiors without going contrary to our Lady's directive not to reveal them. She wrote the following account of what happened:

> Jesus made her hear very distinctly these words: "My daughter, write what they ask of you. Write also all that the most holy Virgin revealed to you in the Apparition [July 13], in which she spoke of this devotion. As for the remainder of the Secret, continue to keep silence." [7]

Our Lord gave permission to Sister Lucia to reveal what we have called the First and Second secrets, but she was to continue to keep the Third Secret confidential. That is why she had to write separately about the Third Secret later on.

Revelation in Tuy, Spain—May 29–30, 1930

During her time as a novice with the Dorothean Sisters, Sister Lucia was transferred to a convent in Tuy, Spain. Here she was to receive a further understanding of the Five First Saturdays. She had been asked various questions by her confessor there, Father Jose Bernardo Goncalves, S.J., regarding the devotion, including "Why should it be five Saturdays and not nine or seven in honor of the sorrows of our Lady?" In a letter written to her confessor on June 12, 1930, Sister Lucia described a mystical experience she had when speaking with the Lord in the Most Blessed Sacrament:

> Remaining in the chapel with our Lord, part of the night of the 29th–30th of that month of May, 1930, talking to our Lord about [some of those] questions, I suddenly felt

[7] Ibid., p. 195.

possessed more intimately by the Divine Presence; and if I am not mistaken, the following was revealed to me: "Daughter, the motive is simple. There are five kinds of offenses and blasphemies spoken against the Immaculate Heart of Mary: blasphemies (1) against her Immaculate Conception; (2) against her perpetual virginity; (3) against her divine maternity, refusing at the same time to accept her as the Mother of mankind; (4) by those who try publicly to implant in the hearts of children an indifference, contempt, and even hate for this Immaculate Mother; and (5) for those who insult her directly in her sacred images." [8]

Our Lord ended this communication by telling Sister Lucia that it was his own mother who asked for these acts of reparation in order to move him to "forgive those souls who have the misfortune of offending her". Those who commit such blasphemies against our Lady are in grave jeopardy of losing their souls, for these sins seriously offend God himself. In spite of these terrible indignities, it is our Lady, as the Blessed Mother even of those who offend her so grievously, who is concerned for their eternal salvation. It is much the same love and compassion that prompted Jesus to pray on the Cross for those who were putting him to death in such pain and degradation: "Father, forgive them; for they know not what they do" (Lk 23:34). Jesus then added to Sister Lucia: "As for you, try incessantly with all your prayers and sacrifices to move me into mercifulness toward those poor souls." Our Lord's final words dealt with the proper carrying out of the Five First Saturdays devotion. Jesus told Sister Lucia that those who could not accomplish all the requirements of this devotion on Saturdays could do so on the Sundays following, if their priests were willing to make allowances for just reasons. That allowance was

[8] *Spiritual Guide*, pp. 128–29.

certainly very helpful for many of the poor people of the day, who may have been overly burdened by traveling to church on Saturdays for confession and Communion and then on Sundays to hear Mass. The Lord wants this devotion in reparation to his Mother to be available to as many people as possible.

Sister Lucia took very seriously our Lady's warning that another world-wide conflict, famines, wars and persecutions of the Church would result if men did not make reparation for their sins. She believed the Blessed Mother's promise that souls could be saved and disasters averted if people dedicated themselves to the Immaculate Heart of Mary through the Five First Saturdays devotion. This excerpt from a letter written by Sister Lucia shows her concern that our Lady's request for this devotion was not being faithfully carried out:

> Our Lady promised to postpone the scourge of war, if this devotion is spread and practiced. We see her putting off this chastisement in the measure that efforts are being made to spread it. But I am afraid that we are not doing all that we are able to, and that God, in no way satisfied, may raise the arm of His mercy and let the world be ravaged by this punishment, which will be as never has been, horrible, horrible![9]

Also during this time, Sister Lucia wrote that "peace or war depends on the [Five First Saturdays devotion] along with the Consecration." This second part of our Lady's request will be taken up in the next chapter.

---

[9] Robert J. Fox and Antonio Maria Martins, S.J., *The Intimate Life of Sister Lucia* (Hanceville, AL: Fatima Family Apostolate, 2001), p. 256.

14

THE APPARITION AT TUY, SPAIN—
JUNE 13, 1929

Our Lady Asks for the Consecration of Russia to Her Immaculate Heart

WHEN OUR LADY promised the conversion of Russia to avoid future wars, persecutions of the Church and the spread of Communism, she mentioned that two conditions had to be fulfilled. We have seen one of these already, namely, the devotion of Five First Saturdays. This was the task that we clergy, religious and laity were given to fulfill, and we must do so faithfully and with great devotion because our Lady wants and needs our prayers and sacrifices. The second condition, however, could only be fulfilled by the pope, who is the Vicar of Christ on earth and the successor of Saint Peter, whom Jesus appointed to be the head of the Church when he said: "And I tell you, you are Peter and on this rock I will build my Church, and the gates of Hades shall not prevail against it" (Mt 16:18). The second condition was that the Holy Father, in union with all the bishops of the world, consecrate Russia to the Immaculate Heart of Mary. Our Lady expressed these two requests in her July 13 apparition:

I shall come to ask for the consecration of Russia to my Immaculate Heart, and the Communion of Reparation on the First Saturdays. If my requests are heeded, Russia will be converted, and there will be peace; if not, she will spread her errors throughout the world, causing wars and persecutions of the Church. The good will be martyred, the Holy Father will have much to suffer, various nations will be annihilated. In the end, my Immaculate Heart will triumph. The Holy Father will consecrate Russia to me, and she will be converted, and a period of peace will be granted to the world.[1]

The fulfillment of our Lady's request for the consecration of Russia has not been easy. From the time our Lady returned to make the request in 1929 until it was fulfilled by Pope John Paul II in 1984, fifty-five years passed. In this chapter we will look at the apparition during which our Lady told Sister Lucia that the time had come for the pope to consecrate Russia. Then we will look at what the popes did in response to this request and what Sister Lucia said about what they did. We will end in the next chapter with the consecration made by Pope John Paul II, which Sister Lucia said "heaven accepted".

The Vision of the Most Blessed Trinity

Lucia was a postulant in the convent of the Dorothean Sisters in Pontevedra, Spain, when she received the apparition of the Child Jesus and the Blessed Virgin Mary regarding the Five First Saturdays. On July 20, 1926, she was transferred to the novitiate house in Tuy, Spain, to complete her postulancy and then be invested with the habit of the Sisters of Saint Dorothy on October 2, 1926. After

[1] *Lucia's Memoirs*, p. 162.

her two-year novitiate, she made her first profession of vows on October 3, 1928. She remained in Tuy until she made her perpetual profession of vows on October 3, 1934. A few days later she returned to Pontevedra. It was while Sister Lucia was in Tuy that our Lady told her the time had come for the pope to consecrate Russia to her Immaculate Heart and renewed her promise to convert Russia by this means. This communication came during a vision of the Most Blessed Trinity in the convent chapel. Here is Sister Lucia's description of this marvelous vision:

I had sought and obtained permission from my superiors and confessor [Father Goncalves] to make a Holy Hour from the eleven o'clock until midnight, every Thursday to Friday night. Being alone one night, I knelt near the altar rails in the middle of the chapel and, prostrate, I prayed the prayers of the Angel. Feeling tired, I then stood up and continued to say the prayers with my arms in the form of a cross. The only light was that of the sanctuary lamp. Suddenly the whole chapel was illumined by a supernatural light, and above the altar appeared a cross of light, reaching to the ceiling. In a brighter light on the upper part of the cross, could be seen the face of a man and his body as far as the waist; upon his breast was a dove of light; nailed to the cross was the body of another man. A little below the waist, I could see a chalice and a large host suspended in the air, on to which drops of blood were falling from the face of Jesus Crucified and from the wound in His side. These drops ran down on to the host and fell into the chalice. Beneath the right arm of the cross was Our Lady and in her hand was her Immaculate Heart. (It was Our Lady of Fatima, with her Immaculate Heart in her left hand, without sword or roses, but with a crown of thorns and flames). Under the left arm of the cross, large letters, as if of crystal clear water which ran down upon the altar, formed these words: "Grace and Mercy." I understood that it was the Mystery of the Most Holy Trinity which was

shown to me, and I received lights about this mystery which
I am not permitted to reveal.[2]

This beautiful vision of the Most Holy Trinity gives us
much for reflection. It seems most appropriate to compare
the vision to what happens at the Consecration of the Holy
Sacrifice of the Mass. At the Consecration, God the Father
receives Jesus, who renews the offering of himself that he
made on the Cross as the Victim for our sins. Then in turn
the Father gives Christ in the Eucharist to us as the Bread
of Life. The Holy Spirit is present, invoked by the priest to
come and sanctify the gifts of bread and wine by transform-
ing them into the very Body, Blood, Soul and Divinity of
Jesus Christ. The bread and wine are consecrated separately
to signify Christ's death, for a person dies when his blood
is separated from his body; thus, the death of Jesus on the
Cross is sacramentally renewed in every Mass. Our Lady is
present in the vision because she was at the foot of the
Cross on Calvary. For this reason Saint Padre Pio used to
say: "When you go to the Holy Sacrifice of the Mass, picture yourself standing below the Cross of Jesus, next to his
Blessed Mother, next to Saint John the Beloved Disciple,
and next to Saint Mary Magdalene, for in spirit that is where
you are!"
  Sister Lucia mentioned three other things in this vision
that we should reflect on for a moment. She mentions the
Blood of Christ coming from his pierced side and from the
wounds made by the crown of thorns on his head. This
Precious Blood falls onto the consecrated Host and then
falls into the chalice. Saint Peter tells us that the Precious
Blood of Jesus is the price of our redemption (1 Pt 1:18–
19). In the Old Testament, without the shedding of blood

---

[2] Ibid., pp. 199–200.

there was no forgiveness of sins (Heb 9:22). In other words, blood sacrifice was necessary for the remission of sins. In her vision, Sister Lucia saw Jesus offering his Blood to the Father for our salvation.

Below Jesus' left hand, Sister Lucia saw the words "Grace and Mercy". These are the fruits of Jesus' suffering and death, which flow upon mankind abundantly, especially through the Holy Sacrifice of the Mass offered all over the world. In the Mass Jesus renews the offering of himself that he made upon the Cross. He is both the Eternal High Priest who offers the sacrifice and the Victim who is sacrificed. The merits of Jesus' Passion and death, namely, his grace and mercy, are poured forth upon us in the Mass more abundantly than at any other time or in any other way because the Sacrifice of the Mass is really the unbloody renewal of the Sacrifice of the Cross. The sacrifice is unbloody because in the Mass Jesus neither suffers (for he is in heavenly glory) nor dies (for he has destroyed the power of our death by his Resurrection).

Finally, Sister Lucia wrote that Our Lady of Fatima was standing below the right arm of the Cross. In her left hand was her Immaculate Heart, aflame and surrounded by a crown of thorns. (In pictures of the vision, our Lady is often seen with the Rosary in her right hand.) The image suggests that Mary's sufferings are joined to those of Jesus on the Cross and that she offers both to our heavenly Father in reparation for sins and for the salvation of souls.

Our Lady Makes Her Request for the Consecration

After the vision of the Trinity, our Lady told Sister Lucia:

> The moment has come in which God asks the Holy Father, in union with all the Bishops of the world, to make the

consecration of Russia to my Immaculate Heart, promising to save it by this means. There are so many souls whom the Justice of God condemns for sins committed against me, that I have come to ask reparation: sacrifice yourself for this intention and pray.[3]

It was nearly twelve years since the time our Lady had told the children she would return to ask for the consecration of Russia to her Immaculate Heart. She had warned that another more terrible war would break out during the pontificate of Pius XI if people did not cease offending God. Our Lady had even told the three little visionaries by what sign the world would know this terrible war was about to begin, and we have seen that on the night of January 25–26, 1938, a great aurora borealis was sighted over all of Europe and parts of the United States. The night was lit up by various colored lights. Some people saw intense red lights in the sky, thinking there were huge fires happening nearby. Sister Lucia insisted that this was the God-given sign by which the world would know another war was about to begin. But we are getting ahead of ourselves. Let's first examine the responses to our Lady's request made by the various popes leading up to Pope John Paul II.

The Popes and the Consecration of Russia from Pius XI to Paul VI

Pope Pius XI (1922–1939)

If another world war could have been avoided by the consecration of Russia to the Immaculate Heart of Mary, then

[3] Ibid., p. 200.

that consecration would have needed to take place during the pontificate of Pius XI, who was pope from February 6, 1922, to February 10, 1939. For whatever reasons, Pius XI did not consecrate Russia to the Immaculate Heart of Mary, and the hostilities that would lead to the Second World War began heating up toward the end of his papacy. Sister Lucia insisted that World War II actually began with the German annexation of Austria in 1938.[4]

Some people have speculated about various possible reasons Pope Piux XI did not consecrate Russia. Some have said that he did not sense enough popular demand for the consecration from the people. Pope Pius XI certainly knew of the great Marian apparitions at Fatima. He also knew that Bishop da Silva had set up a canonical commission to study them. When the commission members reported to Bishop da Silva that they believed the apparitions were authentic, he issued a pastoral letter on October 13, 1930, declaring that they were worthy of belief and approving the public practice of devotion to Our Lady of Fatima. There is evidence that Pius XI had personal belief in the events of Fatima. For example, on January 9, 1929, talking to a group of students from the Portuguese College in Rome, he gave each of them two holy cards of Our Lady of Fatima, one for the student and the other to be sent to his family. Later in October of that year, the Pope himself blessed a statue of Our Lady of Fatima that was to be kept in the college chapel.

Pope Pius XI was a very holy man. His motto for his pontificate was "The Peace of Christ in the Reign of Christ". He proclaimed holy years in 1925, 1929, and 1933. He introduced the Feast of Christ the King to oppose the rise of anti-Christian regimes, and he consecrated the human

---

[4] Ibid., p. 113, see note no. 8.

race to the Sacred Heart of Jesus (which Pope Leo XIII had done before him). He canonized many saints, among whom were Therese of Lisieux, Bernadette of Lourdes, Robert Bellarmine, John Bosco, Thomas More, and John Fisher.

Pius XI wrote some very important encyclicals, including *Casti connubii* (on Christian marriage) in 1930 and *Quadragesimo anno* (on Catholic social teaching) in 1931. In 1937 he wrote *Mit brennender Sorge* (in German, though almost all encyclicals are written in Latin) attacking Nazism for its paganism and its belief in a "super race". He also canonized the Capuchin-Franciscan brother, Conrad of Parzham, who had been the doorkeeper at the busy Marian Shrine of Our Lady of Altotting in Bavaria, Germany. This humble brother was certainly a sign of contradiction to the Nazi ideal of the "superman".

Pope Pius XI also condemned Communism in his 1937 encyclical *Divini Redemptoris*. Looking at Communist revolutions in Russia, Mexico, and Spain, the Pope pointed out that each one had unleashed a horrible attack upon the Church:

> Not only this or that church or isolated monastery has been sacked, but as far as possible every church and every monastery has been destroyed. Every vestige of the Christian religion has been eradicated, even though intimately linked with the rarest monuments of art and science! The fury of Communism has not confined itself to the indiscriminate slaughter of bishops or of thousands of priests, and religious of both sexes; it searches out above all those who have been devoting their lives to the working classes and the poor. But the majority of its victims have been laymen of all conditions and classes. Even up to the present moment masses of them are slain almost daily for no other offense than the fact that they are good Christians or at

least opposed to atheistic Communism. And this fearful destruction has been carried out with a hatred and a savage cruelty one could not believe possible in our age.[5]

Knowing about the persecution going on in Russia, we wonder even more why Pope Pius XI did not make the consecration that our Lady requested. Some Church writers have offered as a possible explanation that Pope Pius XI followed the customary procedure to ignore pressure put upon the Holy See to act on the basis of a private revelation. There is one other possibility, granted very remote, that we should take into consideration. Let us use an analogy. An executive of a corporation depends greatly on the competence and fidelity of the people who work with him, especially secretaries who handle the messages. In a similar way, the pope must depend on those who work with him in the Vatican. During the pontificate of Pius XI, Padre Pio was often accused of various forms of misconduct. The previous pope, Benedict XV, never gave credence to these reports, but Pius XI, not knowing the saint, let the Holy Office investigate all the charges. The accusations came from Padre Pio's local ordinary and priests from his diocese encouraged by this archbishop to find fault with him. Gerardo Agostino Gemelli, a Franciscan priest and psychologist who believed all stigmatists were neurotic, also criticized Padre Pio, as did other clergy who doubted the possibility of supernatural phenomena. After the Holy Office investigated Padre Pio, harsh restrictions were imposed on him. Later, when Padre Pio's holiness became clear, Pope Pius XI greatly admired him. When he was asked why he had been so severe on the saintly man, he answered,

[5] www.vatican.va/holy_father/pius_xi/encyclicals/documents/hf_p-xi_enc_19031937_divini_redemptoris_en.html.

"I have not been badly disposed towards Padre Pio, but I have been badly informed." [6]

Could something similar have happened in regard to the request for the consecration of Russia? There are reliable reports that Communist sympathizers, especially Freemasons, had infiltrated the Vatican around this time. Bella Dodd, an ex-Communist who was received into the Church by Bishop Sheen, told him in 1950 that as a Communist in the 1930's she recruited men with no vocations to enter the ranks of the priesthood in order to destroy the Catholic Church from within. This plan, she said, had come directly from Joseph Stalin (a former seminarian, as we have seen), who was the head of the Communist Party throughout the world at the time. He had said that the Roman Catholic Church was the greatest enemy of Communism and that the way to destroy the Church was to infiltrate the priesthood. Dodd told Bishop Sheen that the Communists had "four contacts" high up in the Vatican. These were believed to be four cardinals who were Freemasons. Bishop Sheen forbade her to reveal their names.[7] Is it possible that Pope Pius XI had been "badly informed" about Our Lady of Fatima's request to consecrate Russia?

The Lord Complains of the Delay—Lucia wrote her spiritual director, Father Goncalves, that Jesus complained about the pope's failure to carry out his request. The Lord foretold that dire consequences would follow:

> They did not wish to heed my request. Like the King of France, they will repent and do it, but it will be late. Russia

[6] C. Bernard Ruffin, *Padre Pio: The True Story* (Huntington, IN: Our Sunday Visitor, 1991), p. 235.

[7] The information about Bella Dodd came to the author from the philosopher and religious thinker Alice von Hildebrand, who was a close friend of Dodd.

will have already spread her errors throughout the world, provoking wars, and persecutions of the Church; the Holy Father will have much to suffer.[8]

Jesus used an example from the history of the Church in France to show what can happen when his requests are neglected. In 1689 Saint Margaret Mary Alacoque, "the apostle of the Sacred Heart of Jesus", carried a message from Jesus to King Louis XIV. Jesus promised the king a blessed life and eternal salvation, as well as victory over his enemies, if he would carry out four requests: (1) to engrave the Sacred Heart of Jesus on the royal flags, (2) to build a chapel in his honor where he would receive the homage of the royal court, (3) to consecrate himself to the Sacred Heart, and (4) to use his authority and influence with the Holy See in order to obtain a Mass in honor of the Sacred Heart of Jesus. Nothing was ever done to respond to our Lord's requests. Approximately one hundred years later, in 1792, King Louis XVI was imprisoned by revolutionaries. He made a vow to consecrate himself, his family and his kingdom to the Sacred Heart of Jesus if he regained his freedom, his kingship and his royal power. But it was too late for the designs of Divine Providence. King Louis XVI, his wife and children were sent to the guillotine, and the anti-religious and anti-clerical French Revolution unleashed a violent persecution of the Church in France from which she has never totally recovered.

Other Requests for the Consecration—Sister Lucia's letters to Father Goncalves show that our Lord and our Lady made frequent requests for the consecration of Russia

[8] *Documents on Fatima and the Memoirs of Sister Lucia*, trans. Fr. Antonio Maria Martins, S.J. (Hanceville, AL: Fatima Family Apostolate, 2001), p. 324.

during the pontificate of Pius XI and were disappointed that it had not already been done.

"As regards Russia," she wrote January 21, 1935, "it seems to me that working so that the Holy Father may realize Our Lord's wishes, will give Him [Jesus] a lot of pleasure. Three years ago, Our Lord was quite upset at His wish not being fulfilled." [9] Then on May 18, 1936, she wrote:

> About the other question whether it would be good to insist in order to obtain the consecration of Russia, I answer in almost the same way as I answered at other times. I am sorry that it has not already been done. However, it is the same God who requested it, who has permitted this. [10]

In this same letter, Lucia explained that she had asked the Lord in prayer why he would not convert Russia without the consecration. He had answered:

> Because I want my whole Church to acknowledge that consecration as a triumph of the Immaculate Heart of Mary, in order to later extend its cult and to place devotion to this Immaculate Heart alongside devotion to my Sacred Heart.

In another conversation with our Lord in prayer, Sister Lucia expressed her conviction that the pope would not believe her unless God himself changed his heart. Our Lord responded:

> The Holy Father. Pray very much for the Holy Father. He will do it, but it will be too late. Nevertheless, the Immaculate Heart of Mary will save Russia. It has been entrusted to her. [11]

[9] Ibid., p. 299.
[10] Ibid., p. 324.
[11] Ibid., p. 325.

Pope Pius XII (1939–1958)

Pius XII was elected pope on March 2, 1939. He began his years as the Vicar of Christ on earth facing the great challenge of World War II. He combined a strong religious character with vast diplomatic experience and a winning openness of spirit. He was to need all of these qualities, as well as abundant grace from heaven, to carry out his enormous task. He was a man of great courage and even survived an assassination attempt on his life. In his years of service to the Church, he had been papal nuncio to Germany for about twelve years, beginning in 1917. During the pontificate of Pope Pius XI, he was made a cardinal in 1929 and became the Vatican secretary of state in 1930, a post he held until he was elected pope.

Pius XII was a deeply Marian pope. On November 1, 1950, he solemnly proclaimed the dogma of the Assumption of the Blessed Virgin Mary, the belief that Mary was assumed body and soul into heaven at the end of her days on earth. He also proclaimed a Marian Year (December 8, 1953, to December 8, 1954) to celebrate the centenary of the proclamation of the dogma of the Immaculate Conception of Mary, the belief that she was conceived without original sin and filled with a fullness of grace from her Divine Son. Also in 1954, he instituted the Feast of the Queenship of Mary and directed that there be a renewal of the consecration of the human race to the Immaculate Heart of Mary every year on this feast day, August 22, for she is the Queen of the World.

Pope Pius XII had a great interest in the events of Fatima. Providentially, he was consecrated a bishop on May 13, 1917, the very day our Lady was making her first appearance at Fatima. He felt that this linked him with the Fatima message in a special way. He was the first pope referred to as the Pope of Fatima. (Today this title belongs more properly to

Pope John Paul II because he fulfilled the requests of Our Lady of Fatima.)

We will now examine the two appeals for a consecration to the Immaculate Heart of Mary that moved this new Marian pope to act. One came from a Portuguese mystic, and the other from Sister Lucia.

The Request of Blessed Alexandrina de Costa (1904–1955)— The mystic Alexandrina de Costa lived in Balasar, a city in Portugal north of Fatima. She was injured in a fall while escaping from a man with evil intent and eventually became completely paralyzed. She offered her intense suffering, along with her prayers and penances, to Jesus in reparation for sins and for the conversion of souls. Eventually, the Lord allowed her to overcome her paralysis for three hours every Friday so that she might experience the sufferings of his Passion. God also permitted her to be attacked many times by the devil.

Alexandrina received a revelation from Jesus to ask Pope Pius XI to consecrate the world to the Immaculate Heart of Mary. Through her spiritual director, Father Mariano Pinho, S.J., she made this request in a 1936 letter to Vatican Secretary of State Cardinal Pacelli (later Pope Pius XII) and offered her sufferings for this intention. The following year, and again in 1939, the Holy See investigated the sanctity of Alexandrina. Meanwhile, in 1938, Father Pinho led the bishops of Portugal gathered in Fatima through the spiritual exercises of Saint Ignatius Loyola. At the end of the retreat, the bishops sent their own letter to Pope Pius XI requesting that he consecrate the world to the Immaculate Heart of Mary.[12]

[12] Umberto Pasquale, *Alexandrina* (Turin: Libreria Dottrina Cristiana, 1960). Excerpts in "Alexandrina", ed. Francis Johnston, trans. Anne Croshaw, Eternal Word Television Network website, accessed Sept. 3, 2010, http://www.ewtn.com/library/MARY/ALEXDRIN.HTM.

Alexandrina lived the last thirteen years of her life nourished only by Holy Communion each day. She died on October, 13, 1955. Her last words were "I am happy because I am going to heaven." Alexandrina had asked that she be buried in her parish church near the Blessed Sacrament and that the following be inscribed on her tombstone:

> Sinners, if my ashes can contribute to your salvation, come closer, pass over them, trample them into the earth, but never sin again, never offend our Jesus again.... Be converted! You do not want to lose Him for all eternity. He is so good! Enough of sin. Love Him! Love Him![13]

Both of these wishes were fulfilled, and her final resting place has become a pilgrimage site. Alexandrina was declared "blessed" by Pope John Paul II on April 25, 2004. As we will see, her request to consecrate the world to the Immaculate Heart of Mary was also fulfilled, not by Pope Pius XI, but by his successor, Pope Pius XII.

Sister Lucia's Request to Pope Pius XII—In 1940, Sister Lucia wrote again to Bishop da Silva of Leiria to express her regret that the consecration of Russia had not yet been made. "Would that the world knew the hour of grace that is being given it and would do penance!" she wrote. Then later that year, in obedience to her spiritual director, she wrote directly to Pope Pius XII:

> If your Holiness would deign to make the consecration of the world to the Immaculate Heart of Mary, making special mention of Russia, and would order at the same time that in union with Your Holiness all the bishops should also make it, the days would be shortened by which God has decided to punish the nations for their crimes through

[13] Leo Madigan, *Blessed Alexandrina da Costa: The Mystical Martyr of Fatima* (Fatima: Fatima-Orphel Books, 2005), 81.

war, famine and persecutions against the Church and Your
Holiness.[14]

Sister Lucia's spiritual director at the time was Don Manuel
Maria, then titular bishop of Gurza. He instructed her to
broaden the scope of the consecration to include the world
in order to increase the chances of its acceptance by Pope
Pius XII. The exclusive mention of Russia created a two-
fold problem, diplomatic and theological. Europe was
engulfed in World War II, and Russia was on the side of
the Allies. Pope Pius XII was maintaining strict neutrality
in regard to the warring nations, as his predecessor, Pope
Benedict XV, had done during World War I. To say that
one belligerent (Russia) needed conversion and not others
(e.g., Nazi Germany and Fascist Italy) could have caused
reprisals from both the Communists and the Allies. Theo-
logically, some people questioned how the pope could consecrate a nation that had officially declared itself atheistic.

As we saw, the request to consecrate the world came from
Blessed Alexandrina. At first, Sister Lucia was distressed by
this request for an expanded consecration, so she prayed over
this matter for two hours to our Lord in the Blessed Sacrament, who told her to do as the Bishop had directed. Jesus
even added that he would reward this consecration by shortening the war. Writing her letter to Pope Pius XII, requesting the collegial consecration of the world with special mention
of Russia, was something Jesus wanted her to do.

Pope Pius XII Consecrates the World—In October of
1942, the Portuguese people celebrated the Silver Jubilee of
Fatima (1917–1942). Urged by the requests of Sister Lucia,

[14] Fr. Rene Laurentin, *The Meaning of Consecration Today: A Marian Model
for a Secularized Age*, trans. Kenneth D. Whitehead (San Francisco: Ignatius Press,
1992), pp. 71–72.

Blessed Alexandrina and the bishops of Portugal, Pope Pius XII consecrated the world with special mention of Russia to the Immaculate Heart of Mary at the closing of the Silver Jubilee on October 31, 1942. Note in the following excerpt that Russia is unmistakably referred to but not mentioned by name:

[reference to the world] To you, to your Immaculate Heart, We, as universal Father of the great Christian family, as Vicar of Him to Whom has been given all power over Heaven and earth, and from Whom we have received the care of all souls redeemed by His Blood, who inhabit the world; to you, to your Immaculate Heart, in this tragic hour of human history, we entrust, we offer, we consecrate, not only Holy Church, the Mystical Body of your Son Jesus, which suffers and bleeds in so many places and in so many ways, but also the whole world torn by mortal strife, ablaze with hate and victim of its own sins.

[reference to Russia] Give peace to the peoples separated from us by error or by schism, and especially to those who profess such singular devotion to you and in whose homes an honored place was ever accorded your venerable icon (today perhaps often kept hidden to await better days); bring them back to the one true fold of Christ under the one shepherd.[15]

Who made this consecration with Pope Pius XII? Only the bishops of Portugal gathered in the Cathedral of Lisbon joined the Holy Father in making the consecration on October 31. Six weeks later, on the Feast of the Immaculate Conception (December 8), Pope Pius XII repeated the consecration at Saint Peter's Basilica in Rome in the presence of

[15] Timothy Tindal-Robertson, *Fatima, Russia and Pope John Paul II: How Mary Intervened to Deliver Russia from Marxist Atheism May 13, 1981–December 25, 1991*, rev. ed. (Still River, MA: Ravengate Press, 1998), pp. 232–33.

forty thousand people, but only a limited number of bishops were present.

Because neither of the two consecrations included all the bishops of the world, as Mary had asked for the conversion of Russia, that conversion did not happen. However, the course of the war was affected. Sister Lucia said that Jesus appeared to her the following spring (1943) and expressed to her his great joy over the consecration. He had promised that the consecration would shorten the war, and in early 1943 the Allies began winning decisive battles, when previously they had been losing. In February, Germany lost the Battle of Stalingrad, turning the tide in favor of the Allies. It was the first significant German defeat, and the beginning of the end of the Third Reich. Unfortunately, Russia, which suffered horrendous casualties in repelling the German invasion remained committed to Communism.

Pope Pius XII Consecrates the Russian People—On July 7, 1952, ten years after he had consecrated the Church and the world, with special mention of Russia, to the Immaculate Heart of Mary, Pope Pius XII in a special apostolic letter, *Sacro Vergente anno*, explicitly consecrated the people of Russia to the Immaculate Heart of Mary. Unfortunately, the world's bishops did not participate, and so it also failed to fulfill our Lady's request for Russia's conversion.

It is interesting to note that on October 13, 1951, the Pope sent Cardinal Tedeschini as his legate to Fatima for the closing ceremonies of the 1950 Holy Year. In his address to the people, the cardinal mentioned that, while walking in the Vatican gardens, Pope Pius had seen a "miracle of the sun" like the one that had taken place in Fatima on October 13, 1917. Pope Pius XII was truly a Marian pope. He died on October 9, 1958.

Pope John XXIII (1958–1963)

Pope John XXIII was elected on October 28, 1958. Many Vatican observers felt that his papacy would merely be an interim until Cardinal Montini (who later became Pope Paul VI) returned to Rome after being Archbishop of Milan. Instead, Pope John XXIII surprised the world by convoking the Second Vatican Council. His personal life, so simple and poor in spirit, attracted many people to him. Despite making pilgrimages to shrines in Italy, such as Loreto and Assisi, he never visited Fatima as Holy Father; but as Cardinal Roncalli, patriarch of Venice, he visited Fatima on May 13, 1956. We know that Pope John read the "third secret", as we shall see in a later chapter; however, he did not attempt a full collegial consecration (that is, one with all the bishops) of Russia. The Council bishops did discuss the need to consecrate the world to the Immaculate Heart of Mary, but never mentioned Russia by name. Even Cardinal Wyszynski, the primate of Poland and a strong opponent of Russian Communism, asked for a consecration without special mention of Russia:

> It is of the utmost importance to us that the Church should be placed under the patronage of the Mother of God and that the human race as a whole should be solemnly consecrated to her Immaculate Heart.[16]

One reason the bishops avoided language that might offend Russia is that Pope John XXIII had persuaded Russian Orthodox observers to attend the sessions of the Council, assuring them that there would be no contentious debates concerning the Church and the Marxist government in their country. The policy of avoiding the direct mention

[16] Ibid., p. 79.

of Russia confirmed the approach of Pope Pius XII and became another precedent for Pope John Paul II's successful consecration on March 25, 1984.

Paul VI (1963–1978)

Pope John XXIII died on June 3, 1963, and his successor, Pope Paul VI, was elected on June 21. Paul VI inherited the leadership of the Second Vatican Council, and despite the controversy brewing at the sessions, he saw the Council through to its completion during the early years of his pontificate. As the third session of the Council began on September 14, 1964, Pope Paul asked the Council Fathers to put their trust in the help of the most holy Virgin Mary. During that session a great debate took place about whether to have a separate Council document on our Lady, or to include her in a special chapter at the end of the "Dogmatic Constitution on the Church" (*Lumen Gentium*). The Council Fathers voted for the latter. On November 21, 1964, the Feast of the Presentation of Mary in the Temple, the third session ended with the approval of *Lumen Gentium* and its chapter about Mary. That afternoon, at ceremonies in the Basilica of Saint Mary Major in Rome, Pope Paul VI proclaimed Mary to be the Mother of the Church. At that time, the Holy Father recalled the consecration to Mary made by Pope Pius XII on October 31, 1942, and *personally* renewed this consecration to her. However, he did not use the opportunity of the Council, which gathered all the bishops together in one place, to make the collegial consecration requested by Our Lady of Fatima.

On May 13, 1967, the fiftieth anniversary of the first apparition of Our Lady of Fatima, Pope Paul VI delivered an apostolic exhortation to all the bishops of the world entitled *Signum magnum* ("The Great Sign"), in which he called for national, diocesan and individual consecration to the Immaculate Heart of Mary. Since the coming October would mark the twenty-fifth anniversary of Pius XII's 1942 consecration of the Church and of mankind to Mary, the Mother of God, he exhorted all "the sons of the Church" to

> renew personally their consecration to the Immaculate Heart of the Mother of the Church and to bring alive this most noble act of veneration through a life ever more consonant with the divine will and in a spirit of filial service and of devout imitation of their heavenly Queen.[17]

Pope Paul VI died on August 6, 1978. His successor was Pope John Paul I, elected to the papacy twenty days later. This pope did not live long: he died a month later, earning himself the name "the September pope". The stage was set for Pope John Paul II and his dramatic fulfillment of the requests made by Our Lady of Fatima.

[17] http://www.vatican.va/holy_father/paul_vi/apost_exhortations/documents/hf_p-vi_exh_19670513_signum-magnum_en.html.

15

POPE JOHN PAUL II AND THE CONSECRATION OF RUSSIA

March 25, 1984—Heaven Accepts the Consecration

WHAT A SURPRISE the Church and even the world experienced on October 16, 1978. That was the day that the conclave of cardinals of the Roman Catholic Church elected Karol Cardinal Wojtyla, Archbishop of Kraków, as the two hundred sixty-fifth Vicar of Christ on earth. He was the first non-Italian to be elected pope since Hadrian VI in 1523. He was also the first Slavic pope, having been born in Wadowice, Poland, on May 18, 1920. His "coming", however, seems to have been foretold by a Polish poet, Juliusz Slowacki, a century before: "There shall come the Slavic pope: he shall be a brother to his brothers and he shall sweep the Church clean!" When we look back at the pontificate of John Paul II, we see how he fulfilled those prophetic words. Thus many believe that he will go down in history as Pope John Paul the Great. He was a gifted person, with both extraordinary intelligence and physical strength. He had done some heavy manual labor as a young man in a limestone quarry during the German occupation of his country, and his robust health and relative youth, as far as popes go (he was elected pope at the age of 58), provided him with the strength to carry out an enormous amount of activity.

As a young man, Karol Wojtyla was a brilliant student, who at the same time excelled in sports, particularly soccer, swimming and skiing. He combined a love of writing, especially poetry, with a talent for acting. In the fall of 1942, during the Nazi occupation of Poland, he began to study for the priesthood in an underground seminary in Kraków. When he was ordained a priest on November 1, 1946, the Communist Russians controlled his country. He later studied in Rome at the Pontifical University (the Angelicum) and obtained a doctorate in 1948. When he returned to Poland, he had many assignments before becoming Archbishop of Kraków on December 30, 1963. He worked a great deal with the youth of Poland, for he knew that whoever—whether the Church or the State—won the hearts and minds of the young generation would control the country for years to come. He wrote a great deal, and one of his most important works was *Love and Responsibility* (1960), a pastoral treatise on sexuality which Pope Paul VI used in writing his encyclical *Humanae vitae* (1968). Later it contributed to the spread of his teaching known as "theology of the body." Archbishop Wojtyla was active at the Second Vatican Council, making important contributions to the Council's work on the Church's role in the modern world, especially regarding religious freedom.

His Many Works as Pope

If his accomplishments before being elected pope were significant, his achievements as Holy Father were simply staggering. Let us look briefly at some of them. (1) Perhaps not as appreciated as some of his more obvious accomplishments, Pope John Paul II restored confidence in and even loyalty to the vocation of the priesthood. In the last years of Pope Paul VI's pontificate, thousands of priests were leaving the priesthood by dispensation each year. The new pope called this tremendous loss of priests a "gaping wound" in the Church. He made a study of the problem and was able to stop the hemorrhage. He reminded priests: "The God who heard you say yes does not now want to hear you say no." Other problems in the priesthood would emerge later, especially the sexual misconduct scandals. But he did restore to many priests the courage and conviction to believe in their priestly vocations. (2) He made many pilgrimages, visiting one hundred twenty-nine countries throughout the world. It has been said that he was the most photographed person in human history. His presence brought a message of hope, love and trust in God's care for his people. People responded in enormous numbers; sometimes several million people turned out to see him, as they did in the Philippines and Mexico. (3) His special love for young people continued during his papacy. He conducted many World Youth Days, drawing young people all over the world closer to Jesus and his Holy Mother. (This author personally met a young man who traveled for thirty days on foot and by bus all the way from Mongolia to attend the year 2000 World Youth Day in Rome.) So many young people were affected by him, his example and the challenge of his teachings, that they are often called the "JPII generation". (4) His talent for writing helped him produce fourteen encyclicals, fourteen apostolic exhortations, eleven apostolic constitutions, forty-five apostolic letters and other writings, like sermons. It has been said that it will take the Catholic Church seventy-five years to absorb all that he taught us. He also oversaw a needed revision of canon law and of the universal catechism that were called for by the Second Vatican Council. (5) His love for the saints moved him to beatify and canonize more holy men and women than almost all of the popes before him combined. He said we need the saints because we see in their lives the concrete working of the Holy Spirit. (6) Finally, he led the Church into the third millennium. From the day he was elected Holy Father, his fellow cardinal from Poland, Cardinal Wyszynski, told him it would be his mission to prepare and lead the Church into the new millennium, and this goal was a guiding influence in all he did.

Great Love of the Blessed Mother

But crowning all of these accomplishments was his fulfillment of the request of our Blessed Lady to consecrate Russia to her Immaculate Heart, so that the promised era of peace might finally come to the world. He knew only too well the evils of Communism, not by reading about them in a book, but by living under its oppression for many years in Poland. One of the great influences in his life was his deep, personal love for our Lady. For the Polish people, devotion to our Lady centers around her image as Our Lady of Czestochowa at the shrine near Kraków, and the young Karol often visited this sacred place. In addition to the traditions of his homeland, the classic work of Saint Louis-Marie Grignion de Montfort, *True Devotion to Mary*, also had a great effect upon him:

> The reading of this book was a decisive turning-point in my life. I say "turning-point," but in fact it was a long inner journey. . . . This "perfect devotion" is indispensable to anyone who means to give himself without reserve to Christ and to the work of redemption. It is from Montfort that I have taken my motto "Totus tuus" ["I am all yours"].[1]

[1] Quoted in Louis-Marie de Monfort, *True Devotion to Mary* (Rockford, IL: Tan Books, 1985), p. vi.

This Marian pope would do all he could to promote devotion to our Lady, for he clearly understood how important her role is in the overall plan of salvation, as well as in the particular life of each man and woman called to the fullness of life in Christ.

No Stranger to Suffering

Another significant factor that helped to form the strong character of Pope John Paul II was the suffering he endured in his youth and early adulthood, especially the losses in his immediate family. His mother, Emilia, who wanted her little son to become a priest someday, was sickly from the time of his birth and died when he was only eight years old. He had a sister who died in infancy before he was born, and though he never knew her he shared in his family's grief over her. He also had an older brother who died three years after his mother. Finally, his father who had raised him and to whom he was very close, died suddenly in 1942, leaving him with no immediate family.

During the German occupation of Poland in World War II, Karol Wojtyla supported the resistance movement and eventually entered an underground seminary. On two occasions when the Gestapo were searching for him, he narrowly escaped capture. Some of his friends and associates, however, did not. On top of the hardships and losses of the war years, Wojtyla was injured in two accidents that nearly took his life. It was during one of his convalescences that he heard the calling to the priesthood. The end of the war brought some relief to the people of Poland, but when the Russians took over their country and imposed a Communist government, they found themselves again under the yolk of tyranny.

As he courageously resisted the Nazis, so Karol Wojtyla resisted the Communists. The conflict with the regime that most formed the mettle of his character was his effort to build a church in Nowa Huta, a model town for workers built by the Communists outside of Krakow. After he was made an auxiliary bishop of Krakow in 1958, Wojtyla applied for a permit to build a church in Nowa Huta, and this the civil authorities refused. The next year, Bishop Wojtyla celebrated Christmas Eve Mass in an open field in the town, demonstrating that a parish already existed in Nowa Huta and that it needed a building, but still the authorities refused the permit. Over the next eight years, first as auxiliary bishop and then as archbishop, Wojtyla continued to say Midnight Mass in the field and to apply for building permits, which were repeatedly denied. Eventually the people of Nowa Huta began clamoring for their religious rights, and violent clashes between them and the police broke out. Archbishop Wojtyla negotiated with the state, never conceding anything of the people's right to religious freedom, and a permit for the church was at last granted in 1967, three months after Wojtyla was made a cardinal by Pope Paul VI.

> The Nowa Huta experience permanently shaped Wojtyla's pastoral program as archbishop, just as it permanently shaped the personality of the future Pope as an unyielding defender of human rights, of the rights of freedom of conscience and religion. In fact, you could say that the battle Wojtyla would wage as Pope on behalf of man, of the dignity of the human person, began right there in Nowa Huta, his first test as a young, newly consecrated bishop.[2]

---

[2] Cardinal Stanislaw Dziwisz, *A Life with Karol: My Forty-Year Friendship with the Man Who Became Pope*, trans. Adrian J. Walker (New York: Doubleday, 2008), p. 33.

Pope John Paul II and Our Lady of Fatima

When Cardinal Wojtyla was elected pope on October 16, 1978, he gave great moral support to the movement for freedom in Poland. In 1979, he made his first papal trip to Poland, which Leonid Brezhnev, president of the Soviet Union, tried to prevent. Brezhnev's interference stirred national feeling in Poland. Strikes erupted throughout the country, and there were hostile confrontations between the Communist Polish government and the Solidarity labor union. Fearing they might lose control of Poland, the Soviet leaders threatened to send Russian troops to stop the freedom movement. Pope John Paul II, on December 16, 1980, wrote to Brezhnev and expressed his personal concern, and that of Europe and the world, over the possibility of Russian aggression against Poland. The government of the United States, and that of other nations, also communicated to the Soviet leadership that they were unwilling to tolerate an attack on Poland. Since an invasion of Poland would be countered by the Americans and NATO, Brezhnev needed to find other ways to stop Solidarity, otherwise the desire for freedom would spread to other countries under Russian domination.

Saint Peter's Square, Rome: May 13, 1981

Were the Russians desperate enough to plot the assassination of Pope John Paul II? After the attempt on the Holy Father's life on May 13, 1981, there were many rumors that Brezhnev had ordered the KGB to hire an assassin to kill the Pope.

No one questions that the Soviet leadership would have benefited from the death of the Pope, but no hard evidence exists to prove they were behind the man who shot him at exactly 5:19 P.M. on May 13, 1981. The Holy Father, making his rounds in his open jeep throughout Saint Peter's Square, had just taken a little two-year-old girl named Sarah into his arms. After lifting her high for all to see, then giving her a little kiss, he handed her back to her parents with a big smile. All of a sudden the first gun shot rang out; a second shot followed immediately, and the Holy Father collapsed in the arms of his secretary, Father Stanislaw Dziwisz. He was rushed to Gemelli Hospital in Rome, where he lost consciousness. As he was fading, he kept praying: "Jesus, Mother Mary." The surgeons operated for five and a half hours, and they were successful. The Pope recovered and returned to the Vatican. However, a few weeks later he came down with a fever and was in great pain, so he was rushed back to Gemelli Hospital. The Pope was suffering from an infection and underwent another operation.

The Pope's Connection with Fatima

During his second stay at Gemelli Hospital, Pope John Paul II began to think about the events of the assassination attempt. He was struck by the extraordinary coincidence that the attempt on his life was made on May 13, the day Our Lady of Fatima first appeared to the children. It was at this point that he requested to see the Third Secret. At the time it was being kept in the secret archives of the Congregation for the Doctrine of the Faith. The prefect of the congregation, Cardinal Seper, delivered two envelopes—a white one with Sister Lucia's original Portuguese text and an orange one with an Italian translation—to the deputy secretary of state, Martinez Somalo, who brought them to the Holy Father. When Pope John Paul II finished reading the Third Secret, he saw his part in the Fatima story. His former secretary, Cardinal Stanislaw Dziwisz, described the Pope's reaction:

> When he was finished, all his remaining doubts were gone. In Sr. Lucia's vision, he recognized his own destiny. He became convinced that his life had been saved—no, given back to him anew—thanks to our Lady's intervention and protection.... It's true, of course, that the "bishop dressed in white" is killed in Sr. Lucia's vision, whereas John Paul II escaped an almost certain death. So? Couldn't that have been the real point of the vision? Couldn't it have been trying to tell us that the paths of history, of human existence, are not necessarily fixed in advance? And that there is a Providence, a "motherly hand," which can intervene and cause a shooter, who is certain of hitting his target, to miss? ... "One hand shot, and another guided the bullet" was how the Holy Father put it.[3]

There is one more part to the story of the assassination attempt which we must look at before moving on to the Holy Father's consecrations to our Lady. Pope John Paul II visited his would-be assassin in the Rebibbia prison in Rome on December 27, 1983. The Pope had already forgiven Mehmet Ali Agca, but now he wanted to do so in person. When Ali Agca met the Holy Father, he did not ask for forgiveness. Instead, he said, "I know I was aiming right. I know that the bullet was a killer. So why aren't you dead?" Secretary Dziwisz, who was nearby, felt that two things terrified Ali Agca: first, forces he could not control had protected the Pope; and, second, these forces were related to the other Fatima besides Muhammad's daughter, whom he referred to as "the goddess of Fatima". As for Ali Agca's question, "So why aren't you dead?", Dziwisz recalled that the Pope "carried it around with him for years, pondering it over

[3] *Life with Karol*, p. 136.

and over again". His first and more important answer was that our Lady had saved him.

> But there was a second answer, the one that had to be given, or at least attempted. And as [Pope John Paul II] was approaching the end of his life, he felt something like a need to communicate the conclusion he had reached about it. In his last book *Memory and Identity*, we read these words: "Ali Agca, as everyone says, is a professional assassin. The shooting was not his initiative, someone else planned it, someone else commissioned him."[4]

Pope John Paul II and the Consecration of Russia

June 7, 1981

The Holy Father was filled with immense gratitude to Our Lady of Fatima for saving his life or, as we have seen him say, given it back to him anew, and he immediately thought of consecrating the world and Russia to the Immaculate Heart of Mary. In 1981 he composed a prayer which he called an "Act of Entrustment". Here is the part of that prayer that refers to both the world and Russia:

> *Mother of all individuals and peoples*, you know all their sufferings and hopes. In your motherly heart you feel all the struggles between good and evil, between light and darkness, that convulse the world: accept the plea which we make in the Holy Spirit directly to your heart, and *embrace with the love of the Mother and Handmaid of the Lord those who most await this embrace*, and [reference to Russia] also those whose act of entrustment you too await in a particular way.

[4] Ibid., p. 138.

Take under your motherly protection the whole human family, which with affectionate love we entrust to you, O
Mother. May there dawn for everyone the time of peace
and freedom, the time of truth, of justice and of hope.[5]

We see from this prayer that Pope John Paul II, in imita-
tion of Pius XII, consecrated the whole world. Russia is
included by a special reference but without being mentioned by name. Like his predecessor, Pope John Paul II
had serious diplomatic reasons for discretion. As we have
seen, the situation in Poland was grave. The clashes between
Solidarity and the government were becoming more intense,
and the leaders of the Soviet Union were threatening to
invade in order to restore order. There is a widely quoted
statement made by Bishop Paul Josef Cordes, then vice-
president of the Pontifical Council for the Laity. He recalled
that the Pope had considered explicitly naming Russia but
had abandoned the idea because he did not want to pro-
voke Brezhnev.

The Pope wanted this Act of Entrustment to be made in
Saint Mary Major in Rome on June 7, 1981, the Solemnity
of Pentecost. That day also commemorated the anniversary
of the First Council of Constantinople (381), which reaf-
firmed the divinity of the Holy Spirit, and the anniversary
of the Council of Ephesus (449), which declared Mary to
be the Mother of God. Since the Pope was recovering from
the wounds suffered in the attempted assassination, he
recorded the prayer and had it broadcast at the basilica.
Because this consecration was not done in union with all
the bishops of the world, it did not completely fulfill our
Lady's request for the conversion of Russia. However, Pope
John Paul II would repeat his prayer of consecration twice
more.

[5] *Message of Fatima.*

May 13, 1982

As an act of special gratitude, Pope John Paul II went to Fatima on May 13, 1982, to thank our Lady personally at her shrine for saving his life and to repeat the Act of Entrustment. It was exactly one year after the attempted assassination.

The Pope had intended to make this second consecration in union with all the bishops of the Church. However, the letters that had been sent to the world's bishops, inviting them to join him in the consecration, arrived too late for them to be able to participate in the ceremony. Consequently, it also did not properly fulfill the request of our Lady for collegial union with all the bishops, as Sister Lucia afterward told the apostolic nuncio to Portugal.

Pope John Paul II's homily on that occasion stressed many important points. First, he said that the message of Fatima is "so deeply rooted in the Gospel [that it] imposes a commitment" on the part of the Church to respond.

> The message of Fatima is, in its basic nucleus, a call to conversion and repentance, as in the Gospel. This call was uttered at the beginning of the twentieth century, and it was thus addressed particularly to this present century. The Lady of the message seems to have read with special insight the "signs of the times," the signs of our time![6]

Second, the Pope said the Fatima message is accompanied by a struggle between, on the one hand, the heart of the Mother of God, interceding on behalf of all mankind for a new outpouring of God's love and mercy and, on the other hand, the hearts of so many who have rejected God's love

---

[6] *Fatima, Russia and Pope John Paul II*, p. 243.

and consequently wish to build an atheistic, amoral society based on human reason and power alone.

> In the light of the Mother's love we understand the whole message of the Lady of Fatima. The greatest obstacle to man's journey towards God is sin, perseverance in sin, and finally, denial of God. The deliberate blotting out of God from the world of human thought, . . . the detachment from [God] of the whole of man's earthly activity . . . the rejection of God by man.[7]

A final thought of Pope John Paul II was that he came to Fatima in the spirit of the popes who have gone before him to repeat the ever relevant call to penance that is at the center of our Lady's message.

> Today John Paul II, successor of Peter, continuer of the work of Pius [XII], John [XXIII] and Paul [VI], and particular heir of the Second Vatican Council, presents himself before the Mother of the Son of God in her shrine at Fatima. In what way does he come? He presents himself, reading again with trepidation the motherly call to penance, to conversion, the ardent appeal of the Heart of Mary that resounded at Fatima 65 years ago. Yes, he reads it again with trepidation in his heart, because he sees how many people and societies—how many Christians—have gone in the opposite direction to the one indicated in the message of Fatima. Sin has thus made itself firmly at home in the world, and denial of God has become widespread in the ideologies, ideas and plans of human beings. . . . But for this very reason the evangelical call to repentance and conversion, uttered in the Mother's message, remains ever relevant. It is still more relevant than it was 65 years ago! It is still more urgent![8]

[7] Ibid., p. 245.
[8] Ibid., p. 249.

March 25, 1984

Pope John Paul II realized that without the bishops join-
ing him for the 1982 consecration, he would need to make
the consecration again. He decided to do so on March 25,
1984, the great Solemnity of the Annunciation, at the closing ceremony of the Holy Year of the Redemption. This
time the Pope made very careful preparations. More than
three months in advance, the Pope sent out letters dated
December 8, 1983, inviting all the bishops throughout the
world to accompany him in the act of consecration. He
even invited Orthodox bishops to join in the prayer, and a
number of them did so. He carefully gathered all the facts
relating to the consecration and reviewed the texts that
were used in the previous ones. He even consulted with
Sister Lucia herself. (He had already spoken to her in person when he was in Fatima in 1982.) Never before in the
history of the Catholic Church had any pope gone so far
to fulfill the requests made by heaven through a private
revelation.

On March 25, 1984, Pope John Paul II made the collegial consecration at Saint Peter's Basilica in Rome with
numerous cardinals and bishops, who were personally present,
as well as in union with all the bishops throughout the
world. At the same time about two hundred thousand of
the faithful were gathered in Saint Peter's Square. The Holy
Father knelt before the statue of Our Lady of Fatima that,
at his request, had been specially sent from the Fatima
Chapel of the Apparitions in the Cova da Iria. The complete text of the consecration is quite long, but we will
quote some important parts: (1) the collegial aspect of the
consecration, (2) the reference to the consecration made
by Pope Pius XII, (3) the consecration of the world, and
(4) the consecration of Russia.

[collegial reference] We find ourselves united with all the pastors of the Church in a particular bond whereby we constitute a body and a college, just as by Christ's wish the Apostles constituted a body and college with Peter. In the bond of this union, we utter the words of the present Act, in which we wish to include, once more, the Church's hopes and anxieties for the modern world.[9]

The collegial union of the bishops mentioned by Pope John Paul II was the element missing from Pope Pius XII's two consecrations in 1942. For this reason Sister Lucia said that the 1942 consecrations were incomplete. The following quotes leave no doubt that the Holy Father was very conscious of how Pius XII had carried out the consecration he was requested to make by the bishops of Portugal, namely, of both the world and Russia, the people for whom our Lady has special love and care.

[reference to Pope Pius XII] Forty years ago and again ten years later, your servant Pope Pius XII, having before his eyes the painful experiences of the human family [World War II], entrusted and consecrated to your Immaculate Heart the whole world, especially the peoples for which by reason of their situation you have particular love and solicitude.[10]

[direct reference to the world] And therefore, *O Mother of individuals and peoples*, you who know all their sufferings and their hopes, you who have a mother's awareness of all the struggles between good and evil, between light and darkness, which afflict the modern world, accept the cry that we, moved by the Holy Spirit, address directly to your Heart. *Embrace*, with the *love* of the Mother and the Handmaid of the Lord, this human world of ours, which we entrust and consecrate to you, for we are full of concern

[9] *The Last Secret*, p. 153.
[10] Ibid., p. 154.

for the earthly and eternal destiny of individuals and peoples.[11]

As we have seen, the consecration of the world was requested by Jesus through the Portuguese mystic Blessed Alexandrina da Costa. The request was also made by the bishops of Portugal. Then Lucia's spiritual director told her to ask the pope to consecrate the world to the Immaculate Heart of Mary with a special mention of Russia. Jesus confirmed these requests in a revelation to Sister Lucia, in which he said he would reward a consecration of the world with a special mention of Russia by shortening the war. Pope Pius XII did consecrate the world and Russia. For reasons we have demonstrated, Pope John Paul II chose to follow Pius XII's formula for consecrating Russia not by name, but by a veiled reference.

> [special reference to Russia] In a special way we entrust and consecrate to you those individuals *and nations* that particularly need to be thus entrusted and consecrated. "We have recourse to your protection, holy Mother of God": *despise not our petitions in our necessities.*[12]

Bishop Amaral of Leiria told Father Robert Fox, an American expert on Fatima, that during the consecration there were moments when the Holy Father paused. When he thanked the Pope later for consecrating the world, John Paul II said "and Russia". Many Fatima observers have concluded that the Holy Father, with his special love for the peoples behind the Iron Curtain, consecrated Russia with the bishops in the spoken words of the prayer, as well as with the silent words in his heart.[13]

[11] Ibid.
[12] Ibid.
[13] *Fatima, Russia and Pope John Paul II*, pp. 25–27.

The Holy Father went on to offer many more beautiful petitions to our Lady, with special emphasis on protecting the world from every form of evil. Here is a striking petition:

> Immaculate Heart! Help us to conquer the menace of evil, which so easily takes root in the hearts of the people of today, and whose immeasurable effects already weigh down upon our modern world and seem to block the paths towards the future![14]

Sister Lucia and the 1984 Consecration

On March 26, the day after the act of consecration, in the presence of cardinals and bishops, including the Bishop of Leiria-Fatima, Pope John Paul II asked: "Have I done what our Lady asked in Fatima? What does Sister Lucia think?"[15] Father Luis Kondor, the vice-postulator for the causes of canonization for Francisco and Jacinta Marto, answered the Holy Father's questions:

> Holy Father, before leaving for Rome with the [Fatima chapel] statue, I informed Sr. Lucia about the act which Your Holiness was about to carry out on March 25, and I asked her if this now would fulfill our Lady's request. The reply she gave me was that now the Holy Father will do all that is in his power.[16]

The Pope was happy with this reply. After all, if the Pope did all he could and it was not enough, then the consecration could never be made by him or any other pope. He

[14] Ibid., p. 155.

[15] Fr. Luis Kondor, SVD, "Sister Lucia and the Collegial Consecration", *Soul*, vol. 47, no. 5, Sept.–Oct. 1996, p. 28.

[16] Ibid., p. 27.

added: "It was also a great joy for me to know that five patriarchs of the Orthodox Church decided to unite with us in this consecration." [17]

Sister Lucia did not speak often about the consecration, but there were rumors that she did not approve of it. Finally she put her approval in writing. One letter, addressed to Sister Mary of Bethlehem on August 29, 1989, stated that the consecration made by Pope John Paul II on March 25, 1984 was both sufficient and effective. Here are her important words:

> Afterward [Pope John Paul II] wrote to all the bishops of the world asking them to unite themselves to him. He had the statue of Our Lady of Fatima [from the Cova da Iria chapel] brought to Rome on March 25, 1984. Then publicly, in union with those bishops who wished to associate themselves with His Holiness, he made the consecration in the way in which the Blessed Virgin had wished that it should be made. Afterward people asked me if it was made in the way our Lady wanted, and I replied: "Yes." From that time, it is made! [18]

Even with Sister Lucia's approval on record, so to speak, two questions have continued to circulate: (1) Why was she, who had stressed that the consecration required all the bishops, satisfied that it was done only with those bishops "who wished to associate themselves with His Holiness"? (2) Why did Sister Lucia accept the broadening of the consecration to include the whole world, while Russia was not specifically named? As a result of these questions, some people have disputed the validity of the 1984 consecration. Sister Lucia, however, was convinced that heaven accepted it. On

[17] Ibid.
[18] *Meaning of Consecration*, p. 87.

November 21, 1999, Sister Lucia wrote another letter in which she stated:

> [The consecration] was later made by the present pontiff, John Paul II, on March 25, 1984, this after he wrote to all the bishops of the world, asking that each of them make the consecration in his own diocese with the people of God who had been entrusted to him. The pope asked that the statue of Our Lady of Fatima be brought to Rome, and he did it publicly in union with all the bishops who with His Holiness were uniting themselves with the people of God, the Mystical Body of Christ; and it was made to the Immaculate Heart of Mary, Mother of Christ and of his Mystical Body, so that, with her and through her with Christ, the consecration could be carried and offered to the Father for the salvation of humanity.[19]

Despite these very clear statements by Sister Lucia, doubts continued to surface about the validity of the consecration. Pope John Paul II requested a meeting of Sister Lucia with Archbishop Tarcisio Bertone, then secretary of the Congregation of the Doctrine of the Faith. This meeting took place on November 17, 2001, at the Carmelite convent where Sister Lucia lived. Present also at the meeting were Sister Mary Lucy, prioress of the convent, and Father Luis Kondor, the editor of Lucia's memoirs. Archbishop Bertone asked Sister Lucia about those who were gathering signatures to petition the pope to consecrate Russia to the Immaculate Heart of Mary. She answered:

> Given the petition's stated purpose, the Carmelite community simply threw it away. I've already said that the consecration Our lady wished for was performed in 1984, and that it was accepted by Heaven.[20]

[19] *Fatima, Russia and Pope John Paul II*, pp. 27–28.
[20] *The Last Secret*, p. 56.

Sister Lucia was the last remaining visionary of Fatima and as such the last person who could verify whether or not heaven had accepted the consecration. She said heaven had accepted it. Let us believe her word; there will be no other.[21]

---

[21] For a fuller explanation of the controversy over Pope John Paul II's consecration, see Appendix C.

16

SISTER LUCIA—HER LIFE AND WRITINGS

The Message of Fatima and the Third Secret

Her Life

IN THE APPARITION OF JUNE 13, 1917, Lucia had asked our Lady if she would take the children to heaven. As we have seen, our Lady said she would take Jacinta and Francisco soon but that Lucia must stay on earth some time longer. Our Lady then told her she would have a special mission: "Jesus wishes to make use of you to make me known and loved. He wants to establish in the world devotion to my Immaculate Heart." As we noted before, Lucia asked our Lady with profound sadness, "Am I to stay here alone?" Our Lady answered Lucia with words of great reassurance, "No, my daughter. Are you suffering a great deal? Don't lose heart. I will never forsake you. My Immaculate Heart will be your refuge and the way that will lead you to God." [1] Our Lady had given Lucia her special mission, and though this mission would involve suffering, she promised to be Lucia's source of comfort.

[1] *Lucia's Memoirs*, p. 161.

Lucia's First Sufferings

The Angel of Peace had told the children that the Lord would send them sufferings, and these began even before the first apparition of Our Lady of Fatima in May 1917. Changes in the Santos family had already brought sorrow and worry to Lucia's mother, Maria Rosa. Her two eldest daughters had married and moved away, while two other daughters needed to leave home to work as servants for their income was needed because of losses incurred by Lucia's father. "My father had fallen into bad company, and let his weakness get the better of him," wrote Lucia in her memoirs; "this meant the loss of some of our property." [2] With four daughters gone from home, and Lucia in the fields grazing the sheep, all the household work fell upon Lucia's mother. Her anxiety and hardship were partially responsible for her refusal to believe that Lucia and her cousins were receiving visits from our Lady. She assumed the children were making up the story, and her disbelief had an effect on the rest of the family, who turned hard and cold toward Lucia.

As the apparitions progressed, the people going to the Cova were trampling the crops that her father, Antonio, had planted for food; and what the people did not trample under foot, the animals they brought along with them ate up. The lost crops caused Maria Rosa to become even more upset with Lucia and say to her, "When you want something to eat, go and ask the Lady for it!" Her sisters joined in the ridicule: "Yes, you can have what grows in the Cova da Iria." [3]

After the apparitions ceased, Maria Rosa became sick to the point the family thought she was dying. When little Lucia

[2] Ibid., p. 64.
[3] Ibid., p. 73.

went to hug her mother for what she thought might be the last time, her mother flung her arms around Lucia's neck saying, "My poor daughter, what will become of you without your mother! I am dying with my heart pierced through because of you." Maria Rosa clasped her arms tightly around Lucia, but Lucia's oldest sister pulled her away, saying: "Mother is going to die of grief because of all the trouble you've given her!" Filled with intense sorrow, Lucia offered this sacrifice to the Lord. Later, two of her other sisters said, "Lucia, if it is true that you saw Our Lady, go right now to the Cova da Iria, and ask her to cure our mother. Promise her whatever you wish and we'll do it, and then we'll believe." [4] Lucia rushed to the Cova with her Rosary in hand and there she wept intensely as she asked her heavenly Mother to cure her earthly mother. She was confident our Lady would hear her, and she did. When Lucia returned from the Cova, her mother was already feeling somewhat better. Three days later, she was able to resume her work around the house. Lucia had promised a certain sacrificial devotion which many pilgrims to the Cova imitate to this day when requesting special favors or healings from our Lady, namely, to process to the chapel in the Cova on bended knees:

> I had promised the most Blessed Virgin that, if she granted me what I asked, I would go there for nine days in succession, together with my sisters, pray the Rosary and go on our knees from the roadway to the holmoak tree; and on the ninth day we would take nine poor children with us, and afterwards give them a meal. We went, then, to fulfill my promise, and my mother came with us. "How strange!" she said. "Our Lady cured me, and somehow I still don't believe! I don't know how this can be!" [5]

[4] Ibid., p. 90.
[5] Ibid.

A final family sorrow to be mentioned is the death of Lucia's father, Antonio. He always had good health, but he got an attack of double pneumonia and died within twenty-four hours. Lucia mourned her father deeply.

> My sorrow was so great that I thought I would die as well. He was the only one who never failed to show himself to be my friend, and the only one who defended me when disputes arose at home on account of me![6]

Sufferings seemed to be continuous for Lucia at this point in her life. Some of these came in the form of her own fears and doubts that the visions of our Lady were false, especially after her parish priest suggested that they "might be a trick of the devil". But most of her daily struggles came from others. She suffered ridicule and scorn from many of her neighbors, probably motivated by a combination of disbelief and jealousy. She was also treated with disdain by two members of the government's cavalry who were assigned to keep people away from the Cova da Iria. One day when she arrived, they forced her to walk all the way back to her parent's home and even threatened to cut off her head when they found out she was one of the visionaries. They said killing her would end all of their problems. As we have seen, she had already suffered mistreatment from government officials when she was imprisoned with thieves and threatened with torture and death. Then there was emotional strain from the constant questions asked by clergy and others, some of whom were well-meaning while others were simply curious. All of these things caused her a great emotional suffering, but perhaps the greatest sufferings for Lucia were the deaths of her two little cousins Francisco and Jacinta. They had become her closest companions as they grazed their flocks together.

[6] Ibid., p. 91.

By sharing both the consolations and the hardships of the apparitions, a tremendous bond had formed between them. Still a child herself, Lucia bore these sufferings with supernatural grace. She knew all of them were allowed by God, and she accepted them with patience and offered them in reparation for the sins of others.

Lucia Receives an Education

Our Lady had told Lucia to learn to read and write, and after the apparitions her mother sent her to school. Because of her talents and good memory, she learned to read and write very quickly. However, a problem emerged because she was the "visionary" of Fatima. People were constantly questioning her and seeking her attention. A new bishop came to the Diocese of Leiria (Dom Jose Alves Correia da Silva) who was very concerned about her education as well as protecting her from the curious and from those who were always seeking "extraordinary phenomena". He arranged for Lucia to leave Aljustrel and to receive her education from the Sisters of Saint Dorothy at Vilar near Porto in northern Portugal. He did this secretly so that no one would know where she was. On June 17, 1921, she entered the college of the Dorothean Sisters. Though she received an excellent moral and religious formation, her education there was barely beyond elementary school level; and, she did a lot of domestic work. Aided by her good memory, her perseverance and her seriousness, she succeeded in acquiring for herself a fairly complete education. She was prepared to carry her mission further.

Lucia Enters Religious Life

For some time before going to Vilar, Lucia had thought of entering religious life. The life of piety at the college made her consider religious life even more seriously. At first, she wanted to enter the Carmelites to live a life of prayer, penance and solitude. But the example of the Dorothean Sisters who taught her coupled with her gratitude to them, made her decide to enter their community. Because of tensions with the anti-clerical government still in power in Portugal, the Dorothean Sisters sent their young candidates in formation to some of their convents in Spain. We have seen how Lucia was a postulant at the convent in Pontevedra, Spain, where she had the vision of the Christ Child and the Blessed Mother revealing the Five First Saturdays of reparation.

She then went to Tuy, Spain, to the novitiate house where she did her novitiate years, professed her first vows, and finally made her perpetual vows on October 3, 1934. After a short stay back at the convent in Pontevedra, she returned to Tuy in May 1937, where she remained until May 1946. At that time she went for a few days to the Cova da Iria and her little hamlet of Aljustrel, where she was asked to certify the places of the apparitions. Then she went back to a Dorothean convent near Porto.

Sister Lucia's long desire to live a life of prayer and solitude reawakened in her at this time. By the kind permission of Pope Pius XII, she was allowed to transfer to the Discalced Carmelites in Coimbra, Portugal, on March 25, 1948, taking the new name of Sister Maria Lucia of the Immaculate Heart. She did have some opportunities to leave her cloister, especially when two of the popes visited the Fatima shrine. Pope Paul VI expressly desired Sister Maria Lucia to be with him on May 13, 1967, at the Cova da Iria, for the Golden Jubilee celebration of our Lady's apparitions. She also went to Fatima when Pope John Paul II visited the shrine on May 13, 1982, to thank our Lady for sparing his life, and again on May 13, 2000, when he beatified Sister Maria Lucia's little cousins, Francisco and Jacinta Marto. We can only imagine the joy she experienced, seeing her little cousins declared "Blessed". She was to remain in the Carmelite convent in Coimbra till her death on February 13, 2005.

The Writings of Sister Lucia

In the years following the apparitions of our Lady, Sister Lucia carried out her mission to spread the message of Fatima throughout the world. In this way she made the Immaculate Heart of Mary known and loved. Sister Lucia originally began to reveal the messages of our Lady through letters; in fact, there were many letters. There were also interrogations by Church authorities and reports that were made. But her most important and influential writings were to be her first four memoirs (as well as the manuscript called "The Third Secret"). She wrote the memoirs in response to different questions about the apparitions put to her by those in authority. She later wrote two other memoirs that added details not found in the first four; toward the end of her life she also wrote the book *Calls*, in which she expressed her final thoughts on the spiritual message of Fatima. Because of limitations of space, we will focus only on the first four memoirs, since these are the ones that have made the greatest contribution to understanding and spreading the Fatima message.

First Memoir (December 1935)

This document was Sister Lucia's first long description of the events of Fatima. It was requested by Bishop da Silva of Leiria when the remains of little Jacinta were moved from her first resting place in a cemetery near Ourem to the little parish cemetery of Saint Anthony's in Fatima on September 12, 1935. Her body was found to be incorrupt. The Bishop asked Sister Lucia to write down everything she could still remember about Jacinta. The manuscript was written over a two-week period from the second week of December to Christmas Day 1935. It paints a wonderful picture of Jacinta in her natural character and in her supernatural graces. In describing Jacinta, Lucia had to tell about the apparitions of our Lady. Interestingly, the Bishop had sent Sister Lucia some photographs, including one showing the face of Jacinta after her incorrupt body had been removed from its original burial place. Sister Lucia sent a note of thanks to the Bishop in which she said:

> Thank you very much for the photographs. I can never express how much I value them, especially those of Jacinta.... I was so enraptured! My joy at seeing the closest friend of my childhood again was so great... She was a child only in years. As to the rest, she already knew how to be virtuous, and to show God and the most holy Virgin her love through sacrifice.[7]

Second Memoir (November 1937)

Sister Lucia wrote her Second Memoir under obedience to Bishop da Silva and her Dorothean Provincial Superior, Mother Maria de Carmel Corte Real. The Bishop knew that the young Sister Lucia was guarding in her heart many cherished memories which would be important for the Fatima story, so he commanded her in obedience to write what she could remember. Sister Lucia responded to the Bishop on November 7, 1937, saying: "I have already begun today, for this is the Will of God." She completed this memoir on November 21. It highlighted the events of the apparitions rather than the personalities of the visionaries. The Second Memoir dealt with certain events that were totally unknown up to this point. These included among other

[7] Ibid., p. 15.

things: the extraordinary blessings Lucia received at her First Holy Communion; the apparitions by the Angel of Peace; and the apparition of June 1917, concerning devotion to the Immaculate Heart of Mary. Sister Lucia expressed her great joy in being able to share these secrets of the love of Jesus and Mary, and the greatness of God's mercy, with others.

Third Memoir (July–August 1941)

In order to prepare for the Silver Jubilee Year of the Fatima apparitions (1942), plans were made to write a new book on Jacinta. So in July 1941, Bishop da Silva requested Sister Lucia to reveal more facts about Jacinta. As a result, she felt it was necessary to disclose the first two parts of the secret given during the apparition of our Lady on July 13, 1917 in order to describe the inner life of Jacinta in more depth. Sister Lucia completed her writing on August 31, 1941, and sent it to the Bishop of Leiria. This Third Memoir contained the first two parts of the secret: namely, the vision of hell and the devotion to the Immaculate Heart of Mary with the warning of another possible world war. Sister Lucia said the request of the Bishop to recall everything she could remember in connection with Jacinta "penetrated to the depths of my soul like a ray of light, giving me to know that the time had come to reveal the first two parts of the secret ... one about hell, and the other about the Immaculate Heart of Mary." Despite having written the account of what happened, Lucia still hesitated, not knowing "whether I should send it off [to the Bishop] or throw it into the fire". In the end she carried out the Bishop's request in complete obedience, for she became certain that this writing was "for the glory of God and for the salvation of souls".[8] Sister Lucia

[8] Ibid., p. 101.

never wrote anything on her own initiative, but only when she was commanded to do so by her superiors.

Fourth Memoir (October–December 1941)

This was to be the longest of all the memoirs. Again it was written at the request of Bishop da Silva. He and others working with him were seeking information about Francisco, so they submitted a number of questions to Sister Lucia. The Bishop stressed the need for her to write as quickly as possible. As a result, the memoir was written in two different notebooks. The first was completed on November 5 and sent to the Bishop, while the second was completed on December 8. The Bishop was seeking information about Francisco, the apparitions of the Angel, further recollections of Jacinta, and popular songs that the children sang. He also requested a new account of the apparitions of our Lady. Some additional material from the first two secrets was also included in the December 8 notebook. At the end of her writing Sister Lucia said to the Bishop: "I believe I have written everything which your Excellency has asked me to write just now."

The Third Secret—History, Revelation and Controversy

We read in the description of our Lady's July 13 apparition that right after the three little visionaries had seen the vision of hell, heard our Lady speak about another possible world war and saw the angel with the fiery sword, our Lady said to them: "Do not tell this to anyone. Francisco, yes, you may tell him." It was our Lady herself, then, who told the children to keep these three messages secret. We do not know precisely why she did so. Perhaps it was because the last two of them dealt with things that would happen in the future. Maybe our Lady wanted people to avoid excessive fear and panic, and not to fall into despair about what might come upon the world. Lucia, Francisco and Jacinta very faithfully kept these secrets. Even when the administrator in Ourem threatened to torture the children and kill them in boiling oil if they did not reveal the secrets, the children showed heroic courage in refusing to do so. As we have seen in Sister Lucia's Third Memoir, she felt inspired that the time had come for her to reveal the first two secrets, namely, the vision of hell and the devotion to Mary's Immaculate Heart together with her warning about another world war.

The Third Secret Is Revealed Separately

Sister Lucia wrote about the Third Secret on January 3, 1944. She was ordered to do this by the Bishop of Leiria, and she received the permission of our Lady to do so. She did not write the Third Secret in one of her memoirs, as she did the first two secrets; rather she wrote it as a separate, single manuscript, which she then placed into an envelope. This sealed envelope was initially kept in the custody of Bishop da Silva of Leiria. To ensure better protection of the Third Secret, shortly before his death, the Bishop transferred the envelope to the secret archives of the Holy Office in Rome on April 4, 1957, and he informed Sister Lucia that this transfer had taken place.

The Popes and the Third Secret

Pope John XXIII

When Sister Lucia placed the manuscript containing the Third Secret into an envelope, she wrote on the outside of the envelope that it could be opened in 1960, either by the patriarch of Lisbon or the bishop of Leiria. She had asked Bishop da Silva to read the manuscript, but when he had refused to do so, she made him promise that it would "be opened and read to the world either at her death or in 1960, whichever came first". When Archbishop Bertone, then secretary of the Congregation for the Doctrine of the Faith, interviewed Sister Lucia in 2000, he asked whether Our Lady of Fatima had fixed the date of 1960. "It was not our Lady," Sister Lucia replied. "I fixed the date because I had the intuition that before 1960 it would not be understood, but that only later would it be understood. Now it can be better understood. I wrote down what I saw; however, it was not for me to interpret it, but for the pope."[9]

According to Vatican records, Father Pierre Paul Philippe, OP, the commissary of the Holy Office, brought the envelope containing the Third Secret of Fatima to Pope John XXIII on August 17, 1959. In his personal diary for that date, the Pope wrote that he "brought me the letter containing the third part of the secrets of Fatima. I intend to read it with my confessor." Later, after the Pope had read the Third Secret, he wrote: "We shall wait. I shall pray. I shall let you know what I decide."[10] Pope John XXIII finally decided not to reveal the Third Secret and to return the sealed envelope to the Holy Office. Apparently, he discerned it was not the right time, and his decision to keep the Third Secret hidden from the world had a major impact on the faithful.

Because Sister Lucia had chosen the year 1960 as the time to reveal the Third Secret, a great deal of expectation, curiosity and even dread about what the message might contain heightened significantly over the years, especially as 1960

[9] *Message of Fatima.*
[10] Ibid.

drew near. It was common at the time to hear the expression "Zero 1960!" Many people expected Pope John XXIII to open the sealed envelope at one minute after midnight on January 1, 1960, and reveal its contents. They assumed the Pope was as excited to know the message as they were. At the same time, because of the long wait and the secrecy, many people thought the message would announce a cataclysmic event, either a great sign from God or a terrible punishment of the world. Thus, there was further disappointment when the Vatican published an official press release stating that it was "most probable the 'secret' would remain, forever, under absolute seal".

Pope Paul VI

On March 27, 1965, Pope Paul VI read the Third Secret with Archbishop Angelo Dell'Acqua. He decided not to publish the text and returned the envelope to the archives of the Holy Office. Like his predecessor, he apparently felt the time had not yet come for the message to be revealed.

Pope John Paul II

As we have seen, Pope John Paul II asked for the Third Secret to be brought to him while he was in the hospital recovering from gunshot wounds sustained in the attempted assassination. He recognized himself as the pope who was slain in the vision that Lucia, Francisco and Jacinta had seen. Some people have objected that Pope John Paul II could not have been the pope of the Third Secret because he did not die. Pope John Paul II knew about this objection, which is the reason he said he came to the very threshold of death and should have died, but our Lady prevented him from doing so. He used to say that our Lady did not so much prevent him from dying, as she gave him back his life. In his "Theological Commentary", Cardinal Ratzinger wrote that the vision of the Third Secret was not like a film about an unchangeable future. These events were not carved in stone. Rather, the vision was meant to challenge us to use the forces of good to direct the future in the right way. "The vision speaks of dangers and how we might be saved from them."[11] By prayer and penance, the life of Pope John Paul II was spared.

As we have seen, Pope John Paul II had his secretary of state, Cardinal Angelo Sodano, read the Third Secret at the Mass of Beatification for Francisco and Jacinta Marto at the Cova da Iria on May 13, 2000. After so much expectation and speculation, many were disappointed with the actual message, because, as Cardinal Ratzinger noted, "[no] great mystery is revealed; nor is the future unveiled."[12] Unfortunately, many people have allowed their disappointment to stir up doubts about the truthfulness of the Vatican. They question whether the Third Secret has been "softened" or "purged" so as not to discourage the faithful. They persist in supposing that the Third Secret contains doomsday prophecies about a global nuclear war or of a great apostasy in the Church, which the Vatican is refusing to reveal.

When Cardinal Bertone met with Sister Lucia on November 11, 2001, she put to rest the rumors that the Third Secret published by the Vatican was incomplete. "'Everything'— and when she said this, she paused to give the word its full weight—'has been published; there are no more secrets'."[13]

Cardinal Bertone told Lucia that some media both in Italy and abroad were saying that she had warned the pope in advance of the September 11 attack on the World Trade

[11] Ibid.
[12] Ibid.
[13] *The Last Secret*, p. 55.

Center and that she was spreading new apocalyptic inter-
pretations of the Fatima message. "None of it is true," she
said. "If I had had any new revelations, I wouldn't have
divulged them to anyone. I would have relayed them directly
to the Holy Father."[14]

According to Sister Lucia's prioress, the visionary suffered a great deal over the constant and widespread speculation about the Third Secret before it was revealed. When
she would hear of it, she would say,

> If they would just devote their energy to living out the real
> essence of the message, which has already been revealed. . .
> All they care about is what hasn't yet been said, rather than
> the fulfillment of Our Lady's request for prayer and penance.[15]

After the Third Secret was revealed by the Vatican, and some
people were questioning if the text were genuine, she said,
"Well, if they know what it [the Third Secret] is, then let
them tell us."[16]

The suspicion that the Vatican is withholding parts of
the Third Secret has laid the groundwork for a conspiracy
mentality that is revealing itself in mistrust and accusation.
This attitude has only made the spread of the true message
of Fatima more difficult.[17]

Pope Benedict XVI

Joseph Ratzinger has helped interpret the Third Secret of
Fatima not only in his previous role as prefect of the Congregation for the Doctrine of the Faith, but even now in his

---

[14] Ibid.
[15] Ibid.
[16] Ibid., p. 56.
[17] For a fuller explanation of the controversy surrounding the Third Secret,
see Appendix D.

current role as pope. During his apostolic journey to Fatima for the tenth anniversary of the beatification of Francisco and Jacinta, Pope Benedict XVI further interpreted the Third Secret in light of the attacks upon him and the Church caused by the discovery of sexually abusive clergy in Europe. His May 2010 visit to Fatima occurred shortly after new charges of abuse surfaced in Ireland and Germany. Some of the European cases were being blamed on the Holy Father himself. He was being accused of covering up misconduct while he was a bishop in Germany and then as the prefect of the Congregation for the Doctrine of the Faith. During an interview on the way to Fatima, the Pope linked the suffering caused by these accusations and the terrible sins committed by some priests with that seen in the vision.

> I would say that, here too, beyond this great vision of the suffering of the Pope, which we can in the first place refer to Pope John Paul II, an indication is given of realities involving the future of the Church, which are gradually taking shape and becoming evident. So it is true that, in addition to the moment indicated in the vision, there is mention of, there is seen, the need for a passion of the Church, which naturally is reflected in the person of the Pope... The Lord told us that the Church would constantly be suffering, in different ways, until the end of time.[18]

Pope Benedict did not blame the persecution he and the Church were experiencing on the media or on outside enemies of the Church, but on the sins of the Church's own children.

> Attacks on the Pope and the Church come not only from without, but the sufferings of the Church come precisely

[18] www.vatican.va/holy_father/benedict_xvi/speeches/2010/may/documents/ hf_ben-xvi_spe_20100511_portogallo-interview_en.html.

from within the Church, from the sin existing within the Church. This too is something that we have always known, but today we are seeing it in a really terrifying way: that the greatest persecution of the Church comes not from her enemies without, but arises from sin within the Church, and that the Church thus has a deep need to relearn penance.[19]

Penance! Penance! Penance! The word is at the very heart of the message of Our Lady of Fatima, especially of the Third Secret.

[19] Ibid.

Lucia Santos and Francisco and Jacinta Marto

Jacinta	Lucia	Francisco
Age 7	*Age 10*	*Age 9*

The Marto Family

Francisco Marto

Jacinta Marto

The Santos Family

Lucia Santos

Jacinta   Lucia   Francisco

This photo was taken immediately after the July 13th apparition of Our Lady of Fatima in which the children saw a vision of hell and heard of war and the persecution of the Church.

Crowds assembled at the Cova da Iria for the Apparition of October 13, 1917

Witnesses to The Miracle of the Sun, October 13, 1917

Inset photo: *The front page of the October 15, 1917 issue of the newspaper* O Século *reporting on the "The Miracle of the Sun"*

Sister Lucia as a Dorthean Sister

Sister Lucia as a Carmelite nun

Pope John Paul II and Sister Lucia (May, 2000)

Statue of Our Lady of Fatima, May 1946

On March 25, 1984, in St. Peter's Square in Rome, before the statue of Our Lady of Fatima from the shrine chapel, Pope John Paul II, together with all the bishops of the Church, consecrates the world and Russia to the Immaculate Heart of Mary.

Statue depicting the Angel of Peace distributing Holy Eucharist to the three children of Fatima

The Statue and Sanctuary of Our Lady of Fatima

A present day pilgrimage to Fatima

Sanctuary of Our Lady of Fatima

17

THE IMPORTANCE OF THE
FATIMA MESSAGE TODAY

A Defense Against Secularism, a Bridge to Islam

W HEN POPE JOHN PAUL II was recovering from the bullet wounds he suffered during the attempted assassination on May 13, 1981, he made a careful study of the
documents related to the Fatima message. He saw himself in
the description of the pope who was shot praying before the
large cross on the mountain. Realizing the significance of
this message for our present time, he said, "Fatima is more
important now than in 1917!" The Holy Father was convinced that the contemporary world is engaged in an enormous struggle between the forces of good and evil, between
a living faith in the Supreme Being and the absolute rejection of God. He recognized the consequences of this struggle: there will either be a civilization of love and truth based
on the sanctity of human life and those rights and responsibilities given by the Creator to each human person, or a
tyranny of hate and oppression based on contempt of God,
hatred of his Church and relativistic values. Let us recall a
statement made by Cardinal Karol Wojtyla on a 1976 visit to
the United States, two years before he was elected pope.

We are today before the greatest combat that mankind has ever seen. I do not believe that the Christian community has completely understood it. We are today before the final struggle between the Church and the anti-Church, between the Gospel and the anti-Gospel.[1]

These words of the man who became Pope John Paul II remind us of the underlying theme of Saint Augustine's great spiritual classic *The City of God*. Augustine wrote that since the advent of Christ, the world has been divided into two opposite cities: the City of God and the City of Man. The City of God is made up of all those men and women who love God so much that they are willing to hold themselves in contempt by self-denial, mortification and resistance to the temptations of the world, the flesh and the devil. The City of Man is made up of those who love themselves so much they are willing to hold God in contempt by sinful lives, selfishness and the perversion of all that God created. The conflict between the two cities will persist until the end of time, when the City of God will triumph.

Our Lady came to Fatima to warn her children that great evils would come upon the world if they did not lead good lives and offer reparation for the sins of mankind by prayer and sacrifice. These evils would include war, famine and persecution of the Church, as well as of the Holy Father. She exhorted her children to become fervent in working for the salvation of souls, for whom Christ her son died so painfully and yet so lovingly upon the Cross. Our penances and prayers for others are central to our Lady's message because she identified the salvation of souls as the key to peace in the world.

[1] This is a widely quoted passage from Wojtyla. According to George Weigel's *Witness to Hope*, it was cited on the editorial page of the *Wall Street Journal*, November 9, 1978, quoting the *New York City News*.

The Importance of Fatima in Today's Spiritual Battles

In that very important apparition of July 13, our Lady warned the children about the evils of Communism, which would begin in Russia and spread its errors throughout the world. She also said that Communism would cause wars and persecutions of the Church, in which the good would be martyred, the Holy Father would have much to suffer and various nations would be annihilated. Tragically, all of these things came true, and for this reason Pope John Paul II fittingly said that at Fatima our Lady foretold the main events of the twentieth century, a century characterized by extreme violence and the greatest destruction of human life that the world has ever seen. The threat of Communism and its many offspring remains to this day. Though the Soviet Union has collapsed, Communist regimes elsewhere in the world, particularly in China, still oppress the Church, while other forms of materialism oppose her in many countries that were once Christian. How can the Church do battle against the foes lined up against her?

Conversion from Our Sins

If sin is the cause of war and persecution, then the first thing we need to do is turn away from our sins and live lives of Christian virtue. God made us to know him, to love him and to serve him in this world so that we may be happy with him forever in the next. Holiness is God's will for us! Remember what our Lady told the children at the end of the October 13 miracle of the sun: "Do not offend the Lord our God anymore, because he is already so much offended!"

Blasphemy and the Rejection of God—What are the sins we must turn away from? First, the sins of blasphemy, which are directed against God, our Lady, the angels and saints and those things that are sacred because they are associated with the honor and worship of God. Such offenses express an actual, even if indirect, hatred of God. These sins must be overcome by the lively faith of believers, along with their authentic love of God and neighbor. In Saint Paul's words, "Do not be overcome by evil but overcome evil with good" (Rom 12:21). Remember, God's love is stronger than the world's hatred. Our Lady's message at Fatima will invigorate our faith and love if we only open ourselves to it.

The Culture of Death—Then there are the sins against life: abortion, euthanasia, embryonic stem cell research, assisted suicide and the whole "culture of death". Add to that list murder, physical abuse, gang wars, ethnic and racial cleansing, and all the other violent crimes that come from hatred in our hearts.

In the book of Genesis, we read the story of the first murder. Cain became jealous when his brother Abel's sacrifice was more pleasing to God than his own. When they were walking out in the field together, Cain killed his brother and buried his body in the ground. Then the Lord said to Cain: "Where is Abel, your brother?" Cain answered: "I do not know! Am I my brother's keeper?" The Lord then said to Cain: "What have you done? The voice of your brother's blood is crying to me from the ground!" Abel's innocent blood was crying out to God for justice. What about the innocent blood of the thousands of unborn children who are aborted each day worldwide? What about the approximately 50 million innocent unborn children who have been aborted in the United States since 1973, when the U.S. Supreme Court made abortion a constitutional right? Isn't their blood crying out to God for vengeance?

Archbishop Sheen said that unless we reverse the destruction of innocent life by abortion we will come to midnight on the clock of death, which he said will be a nuclear war.

It is important to recognize the connection between Communism and the culture of death. Under atheistic Communism, Russia did not recognize any God-given dignity to human life. A person was important only to the degree that he was useful to the state. Therefore, Russia became the first Christian nation in the world to permit abortion. It became so commonplace that there are women in Russia who have had as many as thirty-five abortions. Because the population of Russia has dropped drastically, the Russian government is now paying couples to have a second child.

How did the Communism that first planted itself in the Soviet Union spread abortion to western Europe and the United States? Communism teaches the radical equality of the sexes. Women in Russia, and later in Communist China, were required to enter the workforce in service of the state. What was forced upon the peoples taken over by Communism, was willingly adopted in western Europe and the United States in the name of equality. The movement for so-called women's liberation in these countries insisted that women could not take their equal place among men in the workforce unless they had complete control over their ability to reproduce and that control included the power to kill their unborn children.

As abortion has lessened the dignity of life, euthanasia to eliminate the terminally ill, the handicapped and the elderly has gained acceptance. In an atheistic society, these people's lives are seen to have no value, but only constitute a drain on the state's resources. Now in even formerly Christian societies, for many it seems too much of a bother to care for those in great need, while at the same time the Christian meaning of suffering is being lost. We need our Lady's help to reverse all of this.

The Attack on the Family—Another cause of the culture of death, which was fostered by Communism, is the attack on the traditional family. The family is the only place where the weak, whether they be very young, very sick or very old, are cared for by those bound to them through love. The family is the building block of society. If families are strong, the society will be strong; if they are weak, then the society will be weak.

As was noted earlier, Karl Marx saw the traditional family as an enemy of freedom and equality. The authority of husbands over their wives and that of fathers and mothers over their children create inequalities and are rivals to the absolute power of the state over each individual. This notion that the traditional family was the enemy of equality spread to Europe and the United States, where war was declared on those laws that supported traditional marriage. Little by little, the legal supports beneath marriage have been stripped away. First divorce was legalized, next cohabitating couples were given legal benefits that once were only granted to married couples. Now we see the push to give same-sex unions the same legal status as matrimony. Of course, when marriage is no longer honored and no longer understood as the only proper place for sexual relations, then sexual immorality runs rampant and weakens family life even further. Here we must recall our Lady's words to little Jacinta that more souls are lost by sins of impurity than by any other.

If we are to build a culture of love and life, then we must put into practice the essential message of Fatima: we must pray, make sacrifices for the sake of our souls and those of others, and strive to grow in true Christian virtue.

Our Lady of Fatima and the Muslim People

This chapter on the importance of Our Lady of Fatima's message in the world today would be incomplete without saying something about her unique appeal to the Muslim people. One of the greatest threats to world peace at this time is the growing tension between militant Islamic radicals and secularizing Western culture. Muslims and Christians have fought many battles over the last fourteen hundred years. Islam spread all through north Africa, nearly annihilating the Church there. The Muslims spread into Western Europe and were finally stopped near Tours, France, in 754 by Charles Martel. Later they spread into Eastern Europe and came to the very gates of Vienna, where they were finally stopped again by a heroic defense led by the Polish king, John Sobieski. After the battles of Lepanto (1571) and of Vienna (1683), there seemed to come a significant time of relative peace. Unfortunately, things changed when radical elements within the Muslim countries began to stir up jihad, or holy war, to spread the faith of Muhammad. That is why Archbishop Sheen has said that unless millions of Muslims convert to Christianity there will never be world peace.

When the Archbishop wrote his beautiful book on our Lady, *The World's First Love*, he included a chapter entitled "Mary and the Moslems." In it he wrote about a special link between our Lady under the title of Fatima and the Muslim people. We have already seen that Fatima was the name of Muhammad's first and favorite daughter, as well as of a Muslim princess in Portugal who converted to the Catholic faith. The only village in Portugal that bears a Muslim name is the place Our Lady chose for her appearances, and Sheen saw in this choice a sign of hope that the Muslims will convert to Christ through her.

[We may ask] why the Blessed Mother, in this twentieth century, should have revealed herself in the insignificant little village of Fatima, so that to all future generations she would be known as Our Lady of Fatima. Since nothing ever happens out of heaven except with a finesse of all details, I believe that the Blessed Virgin chose to be known as "Our Lady of Fatima" as a pledge and a sign of hope to the Moslem people, and as an assurance that they, who show her so much respect, will one day accept her Divine Son, too.[2]

In reaching out to the Muslim world, Catholics need to build upon the special respect which the Muslims show to our Lady. For example, she is the only woman mentioned in the Qu'ran. Muhammad said of his daughter Fatima after her death: "You shall be the most blessed of all women in Paradise, after Mary." Fatima herself is quoted as saying: "I surpass all the women, except Mary." Archbishop Sheen said that the Muslim veneration of Mary is shown in their believing in her Immaculate Conception as well as in the virgin birth of her son. Here are some references used by the Archbishop from the Qu'ran that refer to our Lady's holiness.

[The Qu'ran describes] the old age and the definite sterility of the mother of Mary [Saint Anne]. When, however, she conceives, the mother of Mary is made to say in the Koran: "O Lord, I vow and I consecrate to you what is already within me. Accept it from me." When Mary is born, [Saint Anne] says: "And I consecrate her with all of her posterity under thy protection, O Lord, against Satan!"[3]

[2] Fulton J. Sheen, *The World's First Love: Mary the Mother of God* (San Francisco: Ignatius Press, 2010), p. 207.
[3] Ibid.

The Qu'ran passes over Joseph in the life of Mary, but the Muslim tradition knows of him:

> In this tradition, Joseph is made to speak to Mary, who is a virgin. As he inquired how she conceived Jesus without a father, Mary answered: "Do you not know that God, when He created the wheat had no need of seed, and that God by His power made the trees grow without the help of rain? All that God had to do was to say: 'So be it', and it was done." [4]

In the Qu'ran there are also verses about the Annunciation, the Visitation and the Nativity of Jesus. The Archbishop saw all of these references to our Lady as signs that Muslims could form a more favorable attitude toward Christianity, and even to possible conversion, if they could be drawn to a greater veneration of Mary. He also saw as a hopeful sign "the enthusiastic reception which the Muslims in Africa, India, and elsewhere give to the Pilgrim Virgin statue of Our Lady of Fatima. Muslims attended the church services in honor of our Lady, they allowed religious processions and even prayers before their mosques. . ." [5]

The missionary efforts of the Church for the Muslim people have not born very much fruit. The Muslims for various reasons seem so far almost unconvertible. Muhammad wrote that Isaiah and Saint John the Baptist were prophets announcing the coming of Jesus, but then he added that Jesus was a prophet announcing his (Muhammad's) coming. It is hoped that through the love of our Lady, especially under her title of Our Lady of Fatima, the Muslim people will see that she is not simply the mother of a

[4] Ibid., p. 206.
[5] Ibid.

prophet, but of the incarnate Son of God. Let us end with a beautiful prayer in honor of our Lady taken from the Qu'ran, which says it was prayed by angels who accompanied our Lady at the Annunciation, the Visitation and the birth of Jesus:

O Mary, God has chosen you and purified you, and elected you above all the women of the earth!

18

"IN THE END, MY IMMACULATE HEART WILL TRIUMPH!"

Pope Benedict and the Continuing Challenge of Fatima

TOWARD THE END OF WORLD WAR II, a group of people survived the atom bomb dropped on Hiroshima, Japan, in a Catholic Church less than one mile from the epicenter of the blast. Everything around them was completely destroyed, and everyone in the area was killed. Yet, amazingly no harm was done to the church building or to the people inside, not even from the radioactive fallout from the explosion. When asked how he could account for this incredible situation, one of the priests who survived said: "I can only tell you that we have always tried to fulfill the message of Our Lady of Fatima!" Our Lady provides special protection to those who respond fully to her requests. She has given us this encouraging sign to remind us that she is always watching over us when we are trying to do what pleases Almighty God and to fulfill the requests she has made at Fatima for peace in the world through the salvation of souls.

We, too, must survive warfare, but it is most often the spiritual warfare brought on by the evils of our times, with its attacks on life, the family and our faith. No doubt our Lady is protecting us from many spiritual assaults that are not as obvious as an atomic bomb, but are nevertheless real. She is likewise preparing her spiritual sons and daughters for the struggles that will lead ultimately to the triumph of her Immaculate Heart. In earthly warfare, the general of the army is in charge. In spiritual warfare, Jesus is in charge. But he has chosen to direct some of us through his mother. (Someone once told me that if we were to think of our Lady as a general, then according to the book of Revelation (12:1), our Lady would be a twelve-star general.) A military general has to provide and direct the plans for battle. The general decides what will work to accomplish a victory, and what will not. The general must also determine which weapons will be most effective. Hasn't our Lady done something like this for us at Fatima? She has told us the evils that would come upon the world, especially with the rise of Communism. She told us how it could be defeated, not as a political or economic system, but as a spiritual evil intent on destroying God's order in the lives of men. She told us that to achieve a spiritual victory, we need to live holy lives of Christian virtue. We also need to pray and offer our sacrifices for the conversion of sinners. Finally, she told us that the most effective weapon, after the Holy Sacrifice of the Mass, is the Rosary. Saint Louis-Marie Grignion de Montfort and many other great Marian saints have stressed the point that our Lady prepares her faithful sons and daughters for battle.

Form Your Convictions

When I was a young novice over fifty years ago, my novice master repeatedly said: "Form your convictions now, because you will have to live the rest of your lives based on them." That was good advice. One of the things we must be absolutely convinced of is that our Lady is calling each one of us to be involved in this struggle. Convictions produce doers. Someone once said: "One person with a belief is equal in force to ninety-nine people who merely have an interest." Do we really believe in what our Lady is asking of us? Are we convinced of its importance, or are we merely interested in it?

Pope Benedict XVI Urges Us to Respond to Our Lady's Message

Pope Benedict XVI, when he was prefect of the Congregation for the Doctrine of the Faith, was closely involved with the proclamation and explanation of the Third Secret of Fatima. As the successor of Pope John Paul II, he has continued to be very active in promoting the Fatima message. He raised the World Apostolate of Fatima (commonly referred to as the Blue Army) to the level of a pontifical association of the faithful, so that it might have closer ties to the Holy See and greater prominence in spreading the messages of our Lady. As we have seen, the Pope made an important visit to Fatima in May 2010, in which he said,

> We would be mistaken to think that Fatima's prophetic mis
> sion is complete. Here there takes on new life the plan of
> God which asks humanity from the beginning: "Where is
> your brother Abel (. . .) Your brother's blood is crying out
> to me from the ground!" (Gen 4:9). Mankind has suc-
> ceeded in unleashing a cycle of death and terror, but failed
> in bringing it to an end. In sacred Scripture we often find
> that God seeks righteous men and women in order to save
> the city of man and he does the same here, in Fatima, when
> Our Lady asks: "Do you want to offer yourselves to God,
> to endure all the sufferings which he will send you, in an

act of reparation for the sins by which he is offended and of supplication for the conversion of sinners?" [1]

Perhaps the statement of Pope Benedict that best sums up his pastoral advice regarding Fatima is "Learn the message of Fatima! Live the message of Fatima! Spread the message of Fatima!"

We have hopefully learned more about the message of Fatima by reading this book and perhaps other literature on the subject, but how do we live the message?

1. **Strive to live good Christian lives.** We do this by obeying God's commandments and fulfilling the duties of our station in life. We also do this by growing in virtue, avoiding sin and being quick to confess our faults.

2. **Pray daily, especially the Rosary.** We are nothing without God, so we must pray if we are to have the strength we need to live as good Christians. In all of her apparitions, the request made most frequently by our Lady was to pray the Rosary every day.

3. **Observe the Five First Saturdays.** Our Lady asked for this devotion in order to bring about the complete conversion of Russia, peace in the world and the triumph of her Immaculate Heart. Our Lord asked that we observe five first Saturdays more than once. Because this devotion requires great commitment, it combines prayer with sacrifice into a powerful means of grace.

4. **Make sacrifices for the conversion of sinners and accept suffering patiently in reparation for**

[1] http://www.vatican.va/holy_father/benedict_xvi/homilies/2010/documents/hf_ben-xvi_hom_20100513_fatima_en.html.

our sins and those of others. There is no better way to grow closer to Christ than to unite our sacrifices and sufferings with his. By his Passion and death he has brought man back to God. By uniting our sacrifices and sufferings with his, out of love for God and love for souls who are far from him, we can participate in God's salvation of the world. There is no greater power than the sacrificial love of God, and we are called to share in it.

When adopting new devotions, or even when renewing our commitment to the ones we have already embraced, it is good to keep in mind these words of Pope Benedict XVI. The substance of the Fatima message, he said, "is not directed to particular devotions, but precisely to the fundamental response, that is to ongoing conversion, penance, prayer, and the three theological virtues: faith, hope and charity." [2] As we respond to the messages of Our Lady of Fatima, we will grow in our love for God and in our zeal for souls, and we will want to spread the word that the mother of our Lord helped us to become better disciples. We will be like the Samaritan woman who, after she spoke with Jesus at the well, could not help but tell her friends and neighbors about him.

Spread the Message

By Baptism every Catholic is called to the mission of evangelization. The word is derived from the ancient Greek words meaning "to proclaim good news". For Christians, the "good

[2] www.vatican.va/holy_father/benedict_xvi/speeches/2010/may/documents/hf_ben xvi_spe_20100511_portogallo_interview_en.html.

news" is primarily the Gospels, which contain what Jesus did and taught for our salvation. It was so important to Jesus that people receive the gospel message that he sent out his apostles to the very ends of the earth to proclaim it. Our Lady's message at Fatima likewise contains a message urgently needed for our time, and she is depending on us to spread it far and wide.

There are many ways we can do this. One is by the good example of living the message in our own lives, especially by the daily recitation of the Rosary and by the devotion to Five First Saturdays. You may even want to invite people to share in these prayers with you. Another way is simply to tell people about the events and message of Fatima. If you do this enthusiastically because it means a great deal to you, it will begin to mean something to others. Finally, provide literature and other media to inform and inspire others about practicing the message of Fatima in their own daily lives. Our Lady is calling us to be her apostles and evangelists.

Pope Benedict and the Mission of Fatima

In May 2010, Pope Benedict XVI became the third pope to visit Fatima, after Paul VI and John Paul II. He went to the Cova da Iria to celebrate the tenth anniversary of the beatification of Francisco and Jacinta Marto on May 13. At the same time, he was deeply concerned that progressive secularism and growing religious indifference were challenging Portugal's Catholic identity. During a Mass in Lisbon on May 11, the Pope said:

> [t]his local church has rightly concluded that today's pastoral priority is to make each Christian man and woman a radiant presence of the Gospel perspective in the midst of the world, the family, in culture, in the economy, in politics.

He urged Portuguese Catholics (and all Catholics):

> Bear witness to all of the joy that [Jesus'] strong yet gentle presence evokes, starting with your contemporaries. Tell them that it is beautiful to be a friend of Jesus and that it is well worth following him.[3]

On May 12, the Holy Father entrusted the world's priests to the Immaculate Heart of Mary, praying for "holy priests, transfigured by grace". He implored our Lady to keep priests from the temptations of evil, to let them focus on Christ as their model of holiness and to "restore calm after the tempest", especially the storm of the recent clerical sex abuse scandals.

At the end of the Mass on May 13, before an estimated five hundred thousand people in the Cova da Iria, Pope Benedict said the prophetic mission of Fatima is incomplete because: first, our Lady's message at Fatima, which contains fundamental truths of our faith, is still guiding and encouraging the Church in her present struggles; and second, we have not yet seen the glorious triumph of the Immaculate Heart of Mary, which the Pope prayed would occur by the year 2017, the one-hundredth anniversary of our Lady's appearances at Fatima. She has promised us it will come, the victory of the woman over the dragon portrayed in the book of Revelation. If we heed our Lady's call to personal holiness, prayer and reparation for sin, we will see the blessings promised at Fatima poured out abundantly on us!

---

[3] http://www.vatican.va/holy_father/benedict_xvi/homilies/2010/documents/hf_ben-xvi_hom_20100511_terreiro-paco_en.html.

APPENDIX A

FATIMA PRAYERS

Pardon Prayer

My God, I believe, I adore, I hope and I love You! I beg pardon for those who do not believe, do not adore, do not hope and do not love You.

Angel of Peace, Spring 1916

Angel's Prayer

O Most holy Trinity, Father, Son and Holy Spirit, I adore You profoundly. I offer You the most precious Body, Blood, Soul and Divinity of Jesus Christ, present in all the tabernacles of the world, in reparation for the outrages, sacrileges and indifference by which He is offended. By the infinite merits of the Sacred Heart of Jesus and the Immaculate Heart of Mary, I beg the conversion of poor sinners.

Angel of Peace, Fall 1916

Eucharistic Prayer

Most Holy Trinity, I adore You! My God, my God, I love You in the Most Blessed Sacrament.

Our Lady of Fatima, May 13, 1917

Sacrifice Prayer

O Jesus, this is for love of You, for the conversion of poor sinners and in reparation for the offenses committed against the Immaculate Heart of Mary.

Our Lady of Fatima, July 13, 1917

Decade Prayer

(Say at the end of each decade of the Rosary.)

O my Jesus, forgive us our sins, save us from the fires of hell. Lead all souls to heaven, especially those most in need of Your mercy.

Our Lady of Fatima, July 13, 1917

APPENDIX B

THE FIVE FIRST
SATURDAYS EXPLAINED

Our Lady's Spiritual Formation Program

The Five First Saturday's Devotion

When young people enter religious life, they go through different stages of training for living their religious calling, for example, being a postulant, a novice, or a temporary professed member of the community. We call these stages of religious training a "formation program". In a similar way, we may say that our Lady has given her spiritual sons and daughters, through a private revelation to the Fatima visionary Sister Lucia, a formation program to help them to be faithful in loving and serving her Divine Son and doing the heavenly Father's will. This formation program is the Five First Saturday's devotion. We will look at the four actions our Lady asked us to do on five consecutive first Saturdays and see how they help us grow spiritually: go to confession, receive Communion, recite five decades of the Rosary, and keep our Blessed Mother company for fifteen minutes while meditating on the mysteries of the Rosary.

Go to Confession

Going to the Sacrament of Penance assures us that we will be prepared to receive Jesus worthily in Holy Communion, especially if we need to have any mortal sins removed from our souls. Today we are experiencing a kind of crisis in the Church regarding confession; so few Catholics seem to be receiving this sacrament. Even seemingly good Catholics, who live in the state of grace and attend Mass daily, may go for a year or more without confessing their sins. How many graces are they failing to gain by neglecting this sacrament?

Pope John Paul II commented that it was good to see so many people going to Holy Communion, but where were these same people when it came to confession? He said that we have lost a "sense of sin". Unfortunately, many people no longer recognize that they offend God by the wrongs they do. There are many reasons for this blindness: a widespread decline in faith; the rejection of Church teaching, especially regarding morality; the fact that many ways of acting that were clearly seen as sinful years ago, are now accepted as legal and therefore considered as moral, for example, abortion, homosexual acts and euthanasia. There is much confusion about morality in the post-Vatican II Church.

Jesus said that in the end times evil will increase so much that the love of most will grow cold (Mt 24:12). To prevent this coldness from entering our hearts, our Lady is asking us to receive the Sacrament of Penance at least once every month. This frequency is important for so many reasons. We have seen clearly in the words of our Lady that sin offends God. At the same time, sinning endangers our salvation and makes us run the risk of being separated from God for all eternity. Finally, sin is the primary obstacle to our spiritual growth. So by getting us to go to confession on a regular monthly basis, our Lady will help us remain in the state of grace. This means that God will always live in us.

Let us look at the benefits of a good confession. What are they? First, it helps us make a good examination of conscience. Many people neglect examining their behavior and therefore are unaware of the sins they commit each day. But since we have to tell our sins in confession to someone else, namely the priest, we have to know what to tell him. Examination of conscience before confession is one of the best ways to see how we are doing in our relationship with God. Second, by the absolution that the priest gives us in the confessional, our sins are taken away. So many people experience their sins as a great oppression which even a psychiatrist cannot relieve. Through the power Christ has given the priest to forgive sins, our sins are taken away and our soul receives a great peace. This is the peace of mind and heart that only Christ can give; the peace which Saint Paul said goes beyond all human understanding. Third, confession gives us sacramental grace. This is the special help that God gives us to avoid sins in the future. We all need this grace. Fourth, confession gives us the opportunity to make a good resolution to amend our lives. Perhaps we will resolve to avoid committing certain sins or to practice certain virtues. Fifth, by going to confession we may also receive the added benefit of good advice and encouragement from a kind priest.

During the February 15, 1926, revelation from Jesus at Pontevedra, Spain, Sister Lucia asked the Lord a question about confession: Since some people have difficulty going to confession on Saturday, would it be valid for the fulfillment of the Five First Saturdays devotion for them to confess within eight days of the first Saturday? Jesus answered: "Yes, and it could be longer still, provided that, when they

receive me [in Holy Communion], they are in the state of
grace and have the intention of making reparation to the
Immaculate Heart of Mary." She then asked: "My Jesus,
what about those who forget to make this intention?" Jesus
replied: "They can do so at their next confession, taking
advantage of the first opportunity to go to confession." [1]

Receive Holy Communion

The next requirement of the devotion is to receive Holy
Communion on five first Saturdays. No doubt, many practicing Catholics were already receiving Holy Communion
on Sundays, and for some who lived near the church, often
during the week. Unfortunately, however, there was a widespread negative influence from the heresy of Jansenism,
which caused many people to put off going to Holy Communion for long periods of time. Jansenism held we are so
corrupted that we are not worthy to receive Jesus in Holy
Communion. (It was because of such thinking that the
Church had to institute her precept that Catholics must
confess their mortal sins and receive Holy Communion at
least once a year.) As a result of such distorted thinking,
people were spiritually starving because they were not regularly receiving Jesus in the Eucharist, the Bread of Life.
We need the strength that Jesus gives us through our reception of him as our daily Bread to practice the virtues, to
perform the works of mercy, to endure suffering and persecution, to conquer sin and resist temptations. Our Lady's
concern was that we receive Jesus, her Divine Son, at least
one extra time a month, so that we may have the strength
we need.

[1] *Spiritual Guide*, p. 148.

Recite Five Decades of the Rosary

The third element of the devotion is reciting five decades of the Rosary. We have seen throughout our Lady's apparitions her constant requests that we pray the Rosary, which involves five decades, every day. We have seen how pleasing the Rosary is to God and to our Lady and how powerful are its effects in terms of converting sinners and spreading peace in the world. But I think we can see an even deeper underlying reason why our Lady wants us to pray the Rosary. In the home it is usually the mother who teaches her children how to pray. We may say that Mary gave us the Rosary to teach us, her children, how to pray! After all, for centuries Catholics have learned how to pray through the recitation of the Rosary. In the beginning of the spiritual life, there are three primary steps of prayer that we must all learn. In the Eastern Church, these three steps are called the prayer of the lips, the prayer of the mind, and the prayer of the heart. What do we mean by these?

Prayer of the lips—is what we call formal prayer. This is when we use the words and prayers of others and make them our own. In the Gospel of Luke (11:1–4), Jesus was praying one day and his disciples were watching him. When he finished, one of them requested: "Lord, teach us also to pray." He then taught them the Our Father, also known as the Lord's Prayer. By reciting the words Jesus taught us, we are praying a formal prayer. In the Rosary, we have many formal prayers: the Our Father, the Hail Mary, the Glory Be, the Apostles' Creed, and the Decade Prayer, taught to the Fatima visionaries by our Lady. All through our lives, we will be praying formal prayers such as these, using the words of others and making them our own because we do not always know how to speak to God in our own words.

Prayer of the mind—is what we call meditation. As we pray the Rosary, we are asked to meditate or reflect on various episodes in the lives of Jesus and Mary. These are the mysteries of the Rosary. When we reflect on them, we try to understand them more deeply and apply the virtues they signify to our own lives. Meditating on the mysteries of the Rosary is really simple. One day two Franciscan Friars of the Renewal were on an airplane. A stewardess came over to them and began speaking to them. She told them she was a Catholic. She said she once wanted to learn how to meditate and was going to take a course in transcendental meditation, which would cost her three hundred dollars. She said that she picked up her Rosary instead, and learned to meditate for nothing! (What a bargain!)

Prayer of the heart—is a conversation-like prayer that comes spontaneously from the heart in one's own words. Praying the Rosary naturally stirs up affections in our hearts that we want to express to God and to our Lady. These affections may be of love, faith, trust, contrition, thanksgiving, praise and petition. The prayer of the heart is generally, but not necessarily, a deeper level of prayer than that of the lips and of the mind. It tends to be more personal because it comes from the heart. It is like speaking heart-to-heart with a friend! It is a wonderful fruit of praying the Rosary.

Keep Our Lady Company While Meditating on the Mysteries of the Rosary

Our Lady expressed to Sister Lucia this fourth element of the devotion in these words: "Keep me company for fifteen minutes while meditating on the fifteen mysteries of the Rosary, with the intention of making reparation to me." This part of the devotion is connected with the above prayers of the mind and of the heart. Our Lady wants us to begin by meditating (reflecting) on the various mysteries of the Rosary, but then end in a kind of heart-to-heart talk with her about what we reflect on in order to make reparation to her for the blasphemy and indifference that she suffers. This kind of prayer truly deepens our personal relationship with the Lord and his Blessed Mother.

We can gain much from meditating on the mysteries. The joyful mysteries help us to learn the meaning, the virtues and the trials of family life. The luminous mysteries help us to see how we must carry out our Christian mission in the world. The sorrowful mysteries teach us how to deal with the trials and sufferings of life. The glorious mysteries help us to focus on the goal for which God made us, namely, eternal life in heaven. Knowing the reward God is preparing for us, will help us to have joy and perseverance through the difficulties of life. As we reflect on these sacred mysteries, the Holy Spirit will enlighten us to offer our thoughts and prayers to our Lady in the spirit of reparation for the sins by which she, and ultimately Jesus, are offended.

The Blasphemies against Our Lady's Immaculate Heart—What Are They?

In his revelation to Sister Lucia, our Lord mentioned that there are five blasphemies by which people offend the Immaculate Heart of his mother. Let us look briefly at each of them so that we understand more clearly why we need to make reparation for them.

Blasphemies against Mary's Immaculate Conception

We can only imagine how much Satan must hate Mary's privilege of her Immaculate Conception! Why? Because it made her the first and only human person over whom he did not have any control or influence, not even for a second. God told the serpent in the garden after the Fall of our first parents that he would put "enmity" between him (Satan, the serpent) and the Woman. This enmity was such a bitter hatred and revulsion that one could not get near the other. Mary was so filled with grace that Satan would neither desire nor dare to come close to her. (The only reason he came close to Jesus to tempt him was because Jesus permitted him to do so.) Mary's Immaculate Conception was the beginning, therefore, of the destruction of Satan's kingdom. For this reason, he inspires those who follow him to blaspheme Mary's Immaculate Conception, some by denying it, others by ridiculing it and still others by scorning it. Our Lady wants reparation made for these outrages as well as intercession to convert those who do these things against her, for they are at risk of losing their souls.

Blasphemies against Mary's Perpetual Virginity

It is Catholic belief that Mary was a perpetual virgin. The Old Testament prophet Isaiah had said that "a virgin shall conceive, and bear a son, and shall call his name Immanuel" (Is 7:14). Mary's perpetual virginity means three things. (1) Mary was a virgin before the birth of Jesus because she did not have sexual relations with Saint Joseph before their marriage, as can be seen when she tells the archangel Gabriel at the Annunciation, "How can this be since I have no husband?" (Lk 1:34). The angel answers that the Child Jesus would be conceived in her womb by the Holy Spirit; (2) Mary was a virgin during the birth of Jesus, because he miraculously passed from her womb into the world outside without destroying the physical integrity of her body; and, (3) In her reflection on the virginal motherhood of Mary, the Church has been inspired to profess that Mary remained a virgin throughout her life. According to the Catechism of the Catholic Church, Mary's perpetual virginity reveals that "with her whole being she is 'the handmaid of the Lord' (Lk 1:38)".

The devil hates the special purity of our Lady because it stands as a rebuke to the sexual excesses, distortions and sins of our age. Remember that our Lady told little Jacinta that more souls go to hell over sins of impurity than for any other sins! Mary's perpetual virginity reminds each one of us to be chaste according to our vocation in life: single life, consecrated celibacy and marriage. The devil has stirred great hatred in the hearts of many of his followers against the Virgin Mary. Let us make reparation for these hateful outrages against our Lady.

Blasphemies against Our Lady's Motherhood

When the Second Person of the Blessed Trinity took flesh and blood from the Virgin Mary at the Annunciation, God became man. This mystery we call the Incarnation. It is difficult to understand that Jesus has two natures (divine and human) but is only one Person (divine). He is the Divine Son, who, sharing in the divine nature of the Father and the Holy Spirit, assumed a human nature from Mary. Thus Jesus shared our humanity with us without losing his divinity. While on earth, the Divine Son acted as a divine person through a human nature—walking, talking, eating, sleeping, and even dying just as we do. Now since a mother is always the mother of a person (for example, John's mother; Teresa's mother), and the only person in Jesus is God, the Second Divine Person, then Mary is rightly called the Mother of God. Those who refuse to accept Mary as the Mother of God are actually denying, though they might not realize it, that the Second Divine Person really became man in Jesus Christ. To deny that Mary is the Mother of God is to deny the Incarnation. So we must make reparation for those who deny or show contempt for this great truth of our Catholic faith.

At the same time, since Mary is the mother of Jesus, the Head of his Mystical Body, then she is also the spiritual mother of all his members, the Mother of the Church. Since Christ died to save all, Mary is also the Mother of Mankind. We see this truth when Jesus gave his mother Mary to all of us as he hung upon the Cross. He said to her: "Woman, behold your son!" Then he said to "the disciple whom he loved", Saint John, who represented all of us at the foot of the Cross, "Behold, your mother!" (Jn 19:26–27). So let us make reparation for all those who reject and ridicule the wonderful truth of Mary's motherhood!

Reparation for Those Who Keep Children from Mary

Our Lord expressly asked for reparation "for those who try publicly to implant in the hearts of children an indifference, contempt and even hatred against this Immaculate Mother." We have just seen how Mary is Mother of us all. A mother has a right to the love and affection of all her children, while all her children have a right to their mother's love and care. Since Mary is the Blessed Mother of all, she has a right to the love and affection of all her children, while they in turn have a right to her love and care. Reparation is needed whenever this relationship is deliberately harmed. For example, atheistic and/or bitterly anti-Catholic governments (more recently, those controlled by Communists and Nazis) systematically indoctrinated the young with atheistic or anti-Catholic beliefs and forbade them from Catholic teaching and practice. They especially taught children to dishonor our Lady. Reparation is also needed for those parents who from their own personal prejudices do not allow their children to learn about God or our Lady or to practice any religious devotion. We must pray not only for such parents, but also for the children who have been deprived of the opportunity to grow close to God.

Blasphemies by Those Who Insult Our Lady in Her Sacred Images

One of the ways people show their hatred toward God is to destroy or disfigure sacred places or images, especially those of our Lady. During periods of fierce persecution of Catholics, and even now in our own country, Marian statues have been destroyed on church property. Immodest images have been made of Mary, and her likeness has been made out of reviling materials, which would not be tolerated for images of people in public office. Her images are used in neo-pagan religious practices and sold in shops that encourage idolatry, witchcraft and deviant behavior. These are signs of a bitter hatred against God by people who may be deeply disturbed psychologically or involved in satanic cults. Such people will surely be subject to the judgment of God if they do not repent; therefore, we must pray for their conversion and make reparation for their sins. Our Lady herself requested that we do so, showing her compassionate love for even the most wayward of her children.

Conclusion

As a mother, our Lady wants none of her children to be lost, but all to be saved. So, let us faithfully and generously carry out her wishes in this great devotion of the Five First

Saturdays. Sister Lucia has assured us that prayer and penance are absolutely necessary for the peace of the world through the conversion of sinners. The Five First Saturdays devotion, with its unique combination of confession, Communion and the Rosary, holds a special place in our Lady's plan.

THE CONTROVERSY OVER THE CONSECRATION

Objections and Responses

Over the years since Pope John Paul II made the consecration of Russia to the Immaculate Heart of Mary, I have heard many people claim that it was not made properly, and so our Lady's request still has to be fulfilled. Many Catholics are confused and disturbed by things they hear and read. How often I have been asked, "Father, was the consecration really made?" At the same time, so much attention is given to the controversy over the consecration that little attention by comparison is given to responding to our Lady's call for prayer and penance, especially the Five First Saturdays devotion. So here, because it is such an important topic, I would like to address some of the main arguments challenging Pope John Paul II's consecration.

Objection: Our Lady never asked for the consecration of the world, only Russia.

This is true. As we have seen, it was Jesus himself who told Blessed Alexandrina da Costa to ask the pope to consecrate the world to the Immaculate Heart of Mary. This private revelation was the reason the Portuguese bishops told Sister Lucia to request Pope Pius XII consecrate the world with "special mention" of Russia. Our Lord told Sister Lucia to go along with what the bishops had asked of her. So Pope Pius XII consecrated the world with a special reference to Russia; Pope John Paul II followed his precedent.

Our Lady never said that the pope had to consecrate "just Russia" or "only Russia". She simply wanted Russia to be consecrated to her, no matter how it was done. We must be careful not to lay down "conditions" to the consecration that our Lady never stated. We can safely assume that our Lady would have had no problem with the request of her Divine Son! After all, her words to us in Scripture are: "Do whatever [my son] tells you" (Jn 2:5). Since Our Lady of Fatima asked for the consecration of Russia, and Jesus asked for the consecration of the world, popes Pius XII and John Paul II combined both requests into one consecration. It defies common sense to think that our Lord and our Lady wanted the pope to make two separate consecrations in union with all the bishops of the world.

Some people claim that Sister Lucia was commanded "under obedience" to request the consecration of the world, even though she did not believe that would fulfill our Lady's desire. But remember, in prayer she heard Jesus tell her to do what the bishops asked. There would have been no conflict between her obedience to Jesus and her obedience to her superiors.

Others have claimed that Pope Pius XII consecrated the world because no one would object to that, whereas many would have objected to consecrating Russia alone. It is true that mention of the world made the consecration easier given the diplomatic situation posed by World War II, but that was not the reason Pope Pius XII consecrated the world.

He did so to fulfill the Sacred Heart's request, and Pope John Paul II followed his example.

Finally, other people have said that popes Pius XII and John Paul II consecrated Russia simply by consecrating the world since "the whole contains each part". But this assertion overlooks the fact that both popes made a special reference to Russia apart from their reference to the world.

Objection: Russia was not explicitly mentioned by name in the consecration prayer.

As we have seen, Pope Pius XII's consecration contained a descriptive reference to Russia but did not mention the country by name, yet Sister Lucia never raised an objection to this. Pope John Paul II used a formula similar to that of Pope Pius XII, and Sister Lucia did not object to his indirect mention of Russia either. The problem she had with the consecration made by Pope Pius XII in 1942 was that he did not make it with all the bishops of the world. This was why she said it was "incomplete".

Pope Pius XII had diplomatic reasons not to mention Russia by name. So did Pope John Paul II, who no doubt feared reprisals by the president of the Soviet Union, who was at the time threatening to send Russian tanks and troops into Poland to crush the Solidarity movement. There is a widely quoted statement from Bishop Paul Josef Cordes, who was then the vice-president of the Pontifical Council for the Laity: "I recall that [Pope John Paul II] thought, some time before [the consecration], of mentioning Russia in the prayer of benediction. But at the suggestion of his collaborators he had abandoned the idea. He could not risk such a direct provocation of the Soviet leader." [1] The Pope

[1] *30 Giorni*, March, 1990.

also decided not to mention Russia directly out of sensitivity to the Orthodox bishops whom he had invited to join in the consecration prayer. So for good reasons, he followed the discreet approach of Pope Pius XII and of the bishops at the Second Vatican Council, where he himself was very prominent.

Pope John Paul II's descriptive reference to Russia in the consecration prayer would have left no doubt which nation was most of all being included, and this consecration of Russia was made not only by the Holy Father, but also by all the bishops of the world. So our Lady's request for a collegial consecration of Russia was at last fulfilled. Some eyewitnesses of the consecration have said that the Pope made lengthy pauses during the prayer, leading them to believe that he may have also silently mentioned Russia by name. Regardless, the Pope certainly believed he had consecrated Russia. When the bishop of Leiria thanked him afterward for consecrating the world, Pope John Paul II added, "and Russia".[2] Furthermore, Sister Lucia herself said that the 1984 consecration of Russia was accepted by heaven.

Objection: Not all the bishops of the world joined with Pope John Paul II in making the consecration.

What was required for the Holy Father to make the consecration in union with the bishops of the world was not an absolute "numerical" unity with every single bishop, but a "moral" unity with the overwhelming majority of the bishops, who would represent them all. It is very important to keep a balance in our thinking here. At the time of the consecration, there were over three thousand bishops in the world. Even with the pope's authority, he could not

[2] *Fatima, Russia and Pope John Paul II*, pp. 25–27.

compel every single one of them to make the consecration. Let us use a comparison. The bishops are the successors of the twelve apostles. How well did the apostles do with Jesus at the very important moment of his Passion? One of them, Judas Iscariot, betrayed Jesus! Another of them, Saint Peter himself, denied our Lord three times! All the other apostles, except Saint John the beloved, fled from Jesus! If our Lord could not get the twelve apostles to remain faithful in the critical moment of his Passion, how could Pope John Paul II ever get three thousand bishops to carry out the consecration? That would have required a miracle.

Suppose that only ten bishops did not carry out the consecration, would that have made the consecration invalid since there was not an absolute numerical unity? It would be almost absurd to think that! Suppose some bishops did not make it because they never received the letters that the Pope had sent out well in advance. (We can only imagine what mail delivery must be like in many countries of the world.) Would that have invalidated the consecration? Suppose some bishops didn't care to do the consecration, or didn't believe it was necessary; would that invalidate a consecration made by the overwhelming majority of bishops?

We have already seen the words Sister Lucia spoke to Father Luis Kondor, vice-postulator for the causes of canonization of Francisco and Jacinta, about the consecration Pope John Paul II was about to make: "The Holy Father will do all that is in his power!" The Pope did all he could; would our Lady have expected him to do more? Since Pope John Paul II did everything in his power to fulfill our Lady's request for the consecration of Russia, how could she refuse to accept it on the basis of minor details, such as how many bishops actually participated or how Russia was mentioned? If she could, wrote Father Rene Laurentin, "then she bears little resemblance to the most merciful Virgin whom we know." [3] Furthermore, if John Paul II's efforts were not sufficient, could any pope ever make the consecration successfully? If not, then this would contradict our Lady's words to the visionaries during the July 13 apparition: "In the end, my Immaculate Heart will triumph. The Holy Father will consecrate Russia to me and she will be converted, and the world will be given an era of peace."

Objection: If the consecration was made correctly, Russia would have been converted.

This objection arises from a confusion regarding two important words: consecration and conversion. "Consecration" means a dedication or setting aside of someone or something to God or to the patronage and protection of someone holy, in this case the Blessed Virgin Mary. The consecration of Russia was fulfilled when Pope John Paul II offered his prayer of consecration in union with all the bishops of the world. Sister Lucia confirmed this when she said: "Heaven accepted it."

"Conversion" means a change of mind and heart, of what a person believes and how he acts. Sometimes conversions happen instantaneously, as in the case of Saint Paul. His experience on the road to Damascus was so intense that he immediately believed in Jesus and became his disciple. But most often, conversion involves a process of gradual changes. For example, Saint Ignatius of Loyola used to love reading worldly books of romance and chivalry; he was not attracted to religious literature. But after being wounded in a battle and convalescing in his family's castle, he found himself with only two books to read: one on the life of Christ and the other on the lives of the saints. In the beginning he read them merely to pass the time; but as he continued to read,

[3] *Meaning of Consecration*, p. 84.

he gradually became attracted to Christ and the saints until he reached the point where he said to himself: "If Francis, Dominic and Anthony could become saints, why can't I?" His conversion process was finally over, but it had taken some time for him to turn from his worldliness and embrace the holiness of Christ.

When it comes to conversion, perhaps Russia is more like Saint Ignatius than like Saint Paul. The Blessed Mother never said that the consecration of Russia would take place one day, and its conversion would happen the next day. This was a false expectation. We must be careful not to assume things our Lady never stated, and we must remember that for the conversion of Russia our Lady asked for not just one thing, but for two things: the consecration and the devotion of the Five First Saturdays. It is clear that she wants and even needs our participation in terms of prayer, sacrifices, acceptance of sufferings and living holy lives. She will use these to obtain from her Divine Son the graces needed for the conversion of the people of Russia and eventually of the world. After all, this is the very heart of the message she gave Lucia, Francisco and Jacinta in her six apparitions. Remember that Jesus himself asked us not to make the Five First Saturday's devotion only once, but to make it over and over again because he wanted and even needed the merits of these good works to bring about the conversions in Russia.

Objection: If Russia has been properly consecrated, there would be at least signs that conversions are taking place there.

Keeping in mind what we have just said about the conversion process involving a number of steps, we can point to a number of events that show us beyond any doubt that a change of mind and heart is happening gradually in Russia.

The leader of the Soviet Union at the time of the consecration was Konstantin Chernenko, who was a hard-line Communist. However, in March 1984 (the same month as Pope John Paul II's consecration), a party official named Mikhail Gorbachev became the head of the Foreign Affairs Committee of the Soviet Union. When Chernenko died on March 11, 1985, Gorbachev became general secretary of the Communist Party, almost exactly one year after the Pope's consecration. He was the youngest Soviet leader since Stalin. He soon set up his program of *perestroika* ("restructuring") and *glasnost* ("openness"), which radically changed the Marxist-Leninist tyranny that had dominated the Soviet Union for nearly seventy years.

In the late 1980s, Gorbachev greatly softened the government's attitude toward religion. He allowed prominent religious people to visit the Soviet Union, such as Mother Teresa of Calcutta and the Greek Orthodox Patriarch of Constantinople. He spoke of the right of believers in Russia to express their convictions with dignity and without any restrictions. He reached out to the leaders of the Russian Orthodox Church and recognized their religious rights and granted the country's fifty million Russian Orthodox and ten million Roman Catholics to begin reopening and restoring churches and monasteries in commemoration of the thousandth anniversary of the birth of Orthodox Christianity in Russia. Finally, on December 1, 1989, Pope John Paul II and President Gorbachev met at the Vatican for the first time. They talked for more than an hour. Interestingly, the Pope told Gorbachev he had prayed before their meeting. Gorbachev later said his interpreter told him: "Prayer is a sign of order, of spiritual values and we have such need of those." The Pope said that this historic meeting "was prepared by Providence". Since the time of Gorbachev, religious freedom has been growing. On

March 15, 1991, the Vatican announced the formation of formal diplomatic relations with the Soviet Union.

Other events hastened change within the Soviet Union. On April 26, 1986, the Chernobyl nuclear power plant in Ukraine exploded. Throughout the 1980s, the Russian military suffered from various disasters, for example the loss of two nuclear submarines due to mechanical malfunctions. Meanwhile it was losing the war in Afghanistan at a great loss to Russian lives. All of these failures unnerved the Russian people.

At the same time, throughout the Soviet Union, the spirit of nationalism and independence was spreading, largely due to the steps toward freedom and independence that had been taken in Poland by the Solidarity movement. Countries were declaring themselves independent of the Soviet Union. New political parties and movements were emerging in these countries. Perhaps the biggest sign of change came when the Berlin wall came down. It had been put up by the Russians and the East Germans on the night of August 13, 1961, to prevent the continuous exodus of East Germans to freedom in the West. It became the bitter symbol of the division between a democratic West and a totalitarian East. It was the symbol of the Iron Curtain. On October 18, 1989, East Germany began allowing its citizens to cross to the West through the Berlin Wall. It was finally taken down in November 1989. It did not collapse by itself or by any force of nature, such as an earthquake or a tornado. It was taken down by the same people who put it up because they had a change of mind and heart. This was a conversion!

Not long after, the Soviet Union itself ended without a battle or bloodshed, but there was one last struggle. Seeing how Communism was falling out of favor throughout the Soviet Union, some Communist hard-liners attempted a coup against Gorbachev on August 19, 1991, which was the seventy-fourth anniversary of our Lady's August apparition at Fatima. The coup attempt failed on August 22, the Feast of the Queenship of Mary. Finally, at midnight on December 25, 1991, the red flag with the hammer and sickle was lowered for the last time over the Kremlin. In its place, the national flag of Russia was raised. President Gorbachev announced his resignation and the end of the Soviet Union; the fifteen countries that had made up the Union of Soviet Socialist Republics were now free to become independent.

One of Gorbachev's last acts was to send a letter to Pope John Paul II, and the world soon began to recognize the influence of both the Holy Father and our Lady in the collapse of Communism. It is important not to dismiss the break-up of the Soviet Union as simply "political". It has deeply religious significance. Under Communism the state religion of Russia was atheism. The Communist governmental structure first had to fall so that its imposed atheism would fall with it, thus opening the way for religious renewal.

This renewal or conversion of Russia is taking time. Remember, after the Communist Revolution, most of the churches in Russia had been destroyed or changed into government buildings. In the nearly seventy-five years of atheistic indoctrination and persecution, three generations of Russian people had received only the most minimal of Christian education, if anything at all. In the most intense periods of religious persecution, only a grandma here or there taught religion secretly to her grandchildren. If the parents had done so, they could have lost their jobs, been fined or even imprisoned. With so many deprived of religious instruction, teaching and spreading the Christian faith in Russia will take a good deal of time. Meanwhile, we must aid the conversion process by our lives of Christian virtue, our prayers, our sacrifices and even our sufferings. This is why the devotion of the First Five Saturdays is so needed.

Much evidence can be offered to show that people in Russia are turning back to God. Let me mention a couple of little examples I have personally encountered. One was a comment made to me by a priest who is very active in the pro-life movement. He told me he was in Ukraine attending a pro-life conference of about five thousand people, half of whom were Russian Orthodox and the other half were Roman Catholics. He said that at the conference about a dozen Russian Orthodox priests came to him and said: "It was Our Lady of Fatima who saved our country!" Another indication of change occurred in Kazan, Russia. I went there with the first pilgrimage group since the fall of Communism to venerate the icon of Our Lady of Kazan, which Pope John Paul II had sent back to Russia around 2005. It is the only icon I know of that has been declared miraculous in all of Russia. When the Communists took over in 1917, the icon was smuggled out of the country to preserve it from being destroyed by the Communists. One of the people in our pilgrimage group asked a Russian Orthodox priest what it meant for the country to have this precious icon returned. He said: "It means that now once again the Christian faith can flourish in Russia!" Remember, Russia used to be called "holy Russia". By God's grace and under the mantle of Our Lady of Fatima, Russia will become holy again!

Question: For the sake of argument, let us ask, if Russia has not been properly consecrated, what does this imply about Pope John Paul II and about the possibility of there ever being a valid consecration?

Do the people who still insist that Russia has not been consecrated realize the implications? Pope John Paul II was absolutely convinced that he had made the consecration of

Russia properly. A priest who was a seminarian in Rome in the 1990s was standing in line with other seminarians as Pope John Paul II was passing by, greeting each one of them. When the Pope passed this seminarian, he said: "Holy Father, please consecrate Russia to the Immaculate Heart of Mary!" The Pope looked at him intensely and said: "I did!" The Holy Father took a few steps and then turned back to that seminarian and said, pointing his finger toward him: "I did consecrate Russia to the Immaculate Heart of Mary!" Obviously, the Pope was very upset! Now if the Pope believed in his heart that he had made the consecration properly, what are the people who still deny the consecration thinking? (1) Pope John Paul II didn't know what he was doing? But he prepared for two years for the consecration, from 1982 to 1984. (2) He was misled? But he himself studied all the texts of the consecrations made before him and even spoke to Sister Lucia herself in 1982. (3) He really didn't care about doing the consecration? I only mention this preposterous idea because I actually had someone write to me and say this. (4) He lied to us? This slander deserves no comment.

In a 2001 interview with Archbishop Tarcisio Bertone, then secretary for the Congregation for the Doctrine of the Faith, Sister Lucia said, "I have already said that the consecration that Our Lady wished for was accomplished in 1984, and that it was accepted by Heaven." [4] If people cannot accept her testimony that the consecration was accepted, and she was the last living visionary of Fatima, whom could they trust to confirm another consecration? Moreover, given the confidence of the Holy See that our Lady's request for a consecration has been fulfilled, it is extremely unlikely a future pope will attempt another

[4] *The Last Secret*, p. 56.

APPENDIX C 261

one, which risks contradicting our Lady's statement of July 13, 1917: "The Holy Father will consecrate Russia to me, and she will be converted, and a period of peace will be granted to the world."

Appendix D

The Controversy over the Third Secret

Objections and Responses

The Third Secret has been dealt with in two chapters in this book. Chapter 8 presented the content of the Third Secret as Lucia, Francisco and Jacinta saw it revealed to them. Chapter 16 presented how Sister Lucia wrote the Third Secret on a separate manuscript and then placed it in a sealed envelope. The chapter also traces what popes John XXIII, Paul VI and John Paul II did after reading it.

The Third Secret was first made public at the Beatification Mass of Francisco and Jacinta Marto on May 13, 2000, in the Cova da Iria where the secret was originally revealed to the three children on July 13, 1917. Unfortunately, controversy created by certain objections surrounded the Third Secret almost from the moment it became public. We will look at each main objection separately, and offer a response to each.

Objection: The original Third Secret was written on one sheet of paper.

Many clerics who were familiar with the original text, including bishops who worked with popes John XXIII and

Paul VI, said that the Third Secret was written on a single sheet of paper (e.g., Cardinal Alfredo Ottaviani, who read the Third Secret with Pope John XXIII).[1]

The controversy came about when on June 26, 2000, the Vatican released a copy of Sister Lucia's handwritten text in a four-page format.[2] Though there are several possible ways a single sheet of paper can be turned into more than one page (written on both sides, folded and written on multiple sides, etc.) or copied onto more than one page, some critics said that the Vatican copy could not have been made from the authentic text and that some other document exists that contains the real Third Secret.

The Vatican copy of Sister Lucia's handwritten manuscript appears in the document *The Message of Fatima* prepared by the Congregation for the Doctrine of the Faith. In the introduction, the secretary of the Congregation at the time, Archbishop Bertone, stated: "There is only one manuscript, which is here reproduced photostatically." Sister Lucia herself confirmed the validity of the Vatican text. Archbishop Bertone and Bishop Seraphim de Sousa of Leiria met with Sister Lucia at her Carmelite convent in Coimbra, Portugal, on April 27, 2000. The Archbishop presented two envelopes to Sister Lucia. The first or outer envelope contained the second envelope, which held the Third Secret. Touching it with her fingers, Sister Lucia said, "This is my letter." Then, while reading it, she said, "This is my writing."[3] When asked if this document was the one and only Third Secret, Sister Lucia answered, "Yes, this is the Third Secret, and I never wrote any other."[4]

---

[1] *The Last Secret*, p. 63.

[2] A copy of the 4-page format of the text of the Third Secret can be found in *From the Beginning*, pp. 251–54, as well as on the Vatican website.

[3] *Message of Fatima*.

[4] *The Last Secret*, p. 64.

We have additional proof from Sister Lucia that the photo-copy of the Third Secret was authentic. She met again with Archbishop Bertone on November 17, 2001. A communi-qué about that meeting carried this most important point:

> With reference to the third part of the secret of Fatima, [Sister Lucia] affirmed that she had attentively read and med-itated upon the booklet published by the Congregation for the Doctrine of the Faith [The Message of Fatima] and con-firmed everything that was written there. To whoever imag-ines that some part of the secret has been hidden, she replied: "everything has been published; no secret remains." To those who speak and write of new revelations, she said: "There is no truth in this. If I had received new revelations, I would have told no one, but I would have communicated them directly to the Holy Father." [5]

Objection: The text of the Third Secret released by the Vatican contains no words attributed to the Blessed Vir-gin Mary.

The message of the Third Secret was not conveyed in words by our Lady, but in the various visions the children saw. Our Lady spoke simply by her actions, as when she prevented the fire from the flaming sword of the angel from touching the earth and consuming it. Archbishop Bertone explained:

> The part of the text where the Virgin speaks in the first per-son wasn't censored, for the simple reason that it never existed. The text these people talk about just doesn't exist. I am not toeing some party line here. I'm basing my statement on Sis-ter Lucia's own direct confirmation that the Third Secret is none other than the text that was published in the year 2000.[6]

[5] "Sister Lucy: Secret of Fatima Contains No More Mysteries", Vatican Information Service, Dec. 20, 2001.

[6] *The Last Secret*, p. 66.

Objection: The Vatican's copy of the Third Secret contains no information about a nuclear holocaust, a great apostasy, or the satanic infiltration of the Catholic Church.

This objection is largely the result of the disappointment that some people felt when the Third Secret was finally revealed. Cardinal Ratzinger (now Pope Benedict XVI) predicted this disappointment. "A careful reading of the [Third Secret]", he wrote, "will probably prove disappointing or surprising after all the speculation it has stirred. No great mystery is revealed; nor is the future unveiled." [7]

The years of waiting for the revelation of the Third Secret combined with the discretion of the Vatican built up in many people's minds the idea that the Third Secret predicted some catastrophe, like a nuclear war, a world-wide natural disaster or a great tribulation within the Church. Some people even developed a "conspiracy mentality", in which they assumed the faithful were not being told the truth about what was going to happen in the Church and in the world. Some critics have accused Vatican officials of publishing a fraudulent Third Secret or of withholding important information. The problem here is that no one has ever seen any other Third Secret of Fatima than the one that has already been released to the public. The burden of proof lies with the critics. They must produce another document or at least reliable witnesses who have seen and read it. At this point none have come forward.

There is one final authority who should be quoted. He is Archbishop Loris Capovilla, who once served as private secretary to Pope John XXIII. He had read the Third Secret along with Pope John XXIII and actually held the manuscript in his hands. Certain people have claimed that he had

---

[7] "Theological Commentary".

said there were "two texts" of the Third Secret. However, Archbishop Capovilla made the following clear and definitive statement:

> There are not two truths from Fatima, nor is there any fourth secret. The text which I read in 1959 is the same that was distributed by the Vatican.... I have had enough of these conspiracy theories. It just isn't true. I read it, I presented it to the Pope and we resealed the envelope.[8]

As for the doomsday predictions, we know that a terrible world-wide natural catastrophe or a nuclear war could happen, but that would be the result of our sins. This is why we must heed our Lady's message for prayer and penance. We also know that with the spread of secularism and religious indifference, many Catholics are no longer practicing their faith. But again, the remedy for this is prayer, penance and a fervent Christian life, as our Lady requested at Fatima. As for any triumph of Satan over the Church, this is impossible. Jesus himself said so when he told Saint Peter: "You are Peter, and on this rock I will build my Church, and the gates of Hades shall not prevail against it" (Mt 16:18). It will not be Satan who will conquer, but Jesus with his Immaculate Mother who will crush the head of the serpent.

Objection: The text released by the Vatican is not written in the form of a letter.

Some of the clerics who lived at the time the Third Secret was written mentioned it in terms of a letter, but this was not an emphatic point they were making. The photocopy of the original manuscript released by the Holy See does

[8] "Last Surviving Witness Says Third Fatima Is Fully Revealed", Catholic New Agency, September 12, 2007.

not have a formal address to the Bishop, however it does have a certain likeness to a letter. The document begins with a title like those in Lucia's memoirs and has a kind of introduction that makes reference to the Bishop:

> [title] The third part of the secret revealed at the Cova da Iria-Fatima, on 13 July 1917.
> [introduction] I write in obedience to you, my God, who command me to do so through his Excellency the Bishop of Leiria and through your Most Holy Mother and mine.[9]

Archbishop Bertone said that the point about the document being written in the form of a signed letter is not very important. He said of some of his critics that "they look at everything through the magnifying glass of their own biases. As a result they latch on to the most unbelievable things."[10]

As a final plea, let us set aside our doubts and support our Holy Father in the present struggle with our prayers, our fidelity, our service and our love! This would be very pleasing to the Immaculate Heart of Mary! I am absolutely confident that the Holy Father has fully conveyed Our Lady of Fatima's message to us!

---

[9] *Message of Fatima.*
[10] The Last Secret, p. 66.

THEOLOGICAL COMMENTARY ON THE THIRD SECRET OF FATIMA

A careful reading of the text of the so-called third "secret" of Fatima, published here in its entirety long after the fact and by decision of the Holy Father, will probably prove disappointing or surprising after all the speculation it has stirred. No great mystery is revealed; nor is the future unveiled. We see the Church of the martyrs of the century which has just passed represented in a scene described in a language which is symbolic and not easy to decipher. Is this what the Mother of the Lord wished to communicate to Christianity and to humanity at a time of great difficulty and distress? Is it of any help to us at the beginning of the new millennium? Or are these only projections of the inner world of children, brought up in a climate of profound piety but shaken at the same time by the tempests which threatened their own time? How should we understand the vision? What are we to make of it?

Public Revelation and Private Revelations—Their Theological Status

Before attempting an interpretation, the main lines of which can be found in the statement read by Cardinal Sodano on 13 May of this year at the end of the Mass celebrated by the Holy Father in Fatima, there is a need for some basic clarification of the way in which, according to Church teaching, phenomena such as Fatima are to be understood within the life of faith. The teaching of the Church distinguishes between "public Revelation" and "private revelations". The two realities differ not only in degree but also in essence. The term "public Revelation" refers to the revealing action of God directed to humanity as a whole and which finds its literary expression in the two parts of the Bible: the Old and New Testaments. It is called "Revelation" because in it God gradually made himself known to men, to the point of becoming man himself, in order to draw to himself the whole world and unite it with himself through his Incarnate Son, Jesus Christ. It is not a matter therefore of intellectual communication, but of a life-giving process in which God comes to meet man. At the same time this process naturally produces data pertaining to the mind and to the understanding of the mystery of God. It is a process which involves man in his entirety and therefore reason as well, but not reason alone. Because God is one, history, which he shares with humanity, is also one. It is valid for all time, and it has reached its fulfillment in the life, death and resurrection of Jesus Christ. In Christ, God has said everything, that is, he has revealed himself completely, and therefore Revelation came to an end with the fulfillment of the mystery of Christ as enunciated in the New Testament. To explain the finality and completeness of Revelation, the *Catechism of the Catholic Church* quotes a text of Saint John of the Cross: "In giving us his Son, his only Word (for he possesses no other), he spoke everything to us at once in this sole Word—and he has no more to say ... because what he spoke before to the prophets in parts, he has now spoken all at once by giving us the All Who is His Son. Any person questioning God or desiring some vision or revelation would be guilty not only of foolish behavior but also of offending him, by

not fixing his eyes entirely upon Christ and by living with
the desire for some other novelty" (No. 65; Saint John of
the Cross, *The Ascent of Mount Carmel*, II, 22).

Because the single Revelation of God addressed to all
peoples comes to completion with Christ and the witness
borne to him in the books of the New Testament, the
Church is tied to this unique event of sacred history and to
the word of the Bible, which guarantees and interprets it.
But this does not mean that the Church can now look only
to the past and that she is condemned to sterile repetition.
The *Catechism of the Catholic Church* says in this regard: ". . .
even if Revelation is already complete, it has not been made
fully explicit; it remains for Christian faith gradually to grasp
its full significance over the course of the centuries" (No.
66). The way in which the Church is bound to both the
uniqueness of the event and progress in understanding it is
very well illustrated in the farewell discourse of the Lord
when, taking leave of his disciples, he says: "I have yet many
things to say to you, but you cannot bear them now. When
the Spirit of truth comes, he will guide you into all the
truth; for he will not speak on his own authority. . . He
will glorify me, for he will take what is mine and declare it
to you" (Jn 16:12–14). On the one hand, the Spirit acts as
a guide who discloses a knowledge previously unreachable
because the premise was missing—this is the boundless
breadth and depth of Christian faith. On the other hand,
to be guided by the Spirit is also "to draw from" the riches
of Jesus Christ himself, the inexhaustible depths of which
appear in the way the Spirit leads. In this regard, the *Catechism* cites profound words of Pope Gregory the Great:
"The sacred Scriptures grow with the one who reads them"
(No. 94; Gregory the Great, *Homilia in Ezechielem* I, 7, 8).
The Second Vatican Council notes three essential ways in
which the Spirit guides the Church, and therefore three

ways in which "the word grows": through the meditation
and study of the faithful, through the deep understanding
which comes from spiritual experience, and through the
preaching of "those who, in the succession of the episcopate,
have received the sure charism of truth" (*Dei Verbum*, 8).

In this context, it now becomes possible to understand
rightly the concept of "private revelation", which refers to
all the visions and revelations which have taken place since
the completion of the New Testament. This is the category
to which we must assign the message of Fatima. In this
respect, let us listen once again to the *Catechism of the Catholic Church*: "Throughout the ages, there have been so-called
'private' revelations, some of which have been recognized
by the authority of the Church... It is not their role to
complete Christ's definitive Revelation, but to help live more
fully by it in a certain period of history" (No. 67). This
clarifies two things:

1. The authority of private revelations is essentially different from that of the definitive public Revelation. The
latter demands faith; in it in fact God himself speaks to us
through human words and the mediation of the living community of the Church. Faith in God and in his word is
different from any other human faith, trust or opinion. The
certainty that it is God who is speaking gives me the assurance that I am in touch with truth itself. It gives me a
certitude which is beyond verification by any human way
of knowing. It is the certitude upon which I build my life
and to which I entrust myself in dying.

2. Private revelation is a help to this faith, and shows its
credibility precisely by leading me back to the definitive
public Revelation. In this regard, Cardinal Prospero Lam-
bertini, the future Pope Benedict XIV, says in his classic
treatise, which later became normative for beatifications and
canonizations: "An assent of Catholic faith is not due to

revelations approved in this way; it is not even possible. These revelations seek rather an assent of human faith in keeping with the requirements of prudence, which puts them before us as probable and credible to piety". The Flemish theologian E. Dhanis, an eminent scholar in this field, states succinctly that ecclesiastical approval of a private revelation has three elements: the message contains nothing contrary to faith or morals; it is lawful to make it public; and the faithful are authorized to accept it with prudence (E. Dhanis, *Sguardo su Fatima e bilancio di una discussione*, in *La Civiltà Cattolica* 104 [1953], II, 392–406, in particular 397). Such a message can be a genuine help in understanding the Gospel and living it better at a particular moment in time; therefore it should not be disregarded. It is a help which is offered, but which one is not obliged to use.

The criterion for the truth and value of a private revelation is therefore its orientation to Christ himself. When it leads us away from him, when it becomes independent of him or even presents itself as another and better plan of salvation, more important than the Gospel, then it certainly does not come from the Holy Spirit, who guides us more deeply into the Gospel and not away from it. This does not mean that a private revelation will not offer new emphases or give rise to new devotional forms, or deepen and spread older forms. But in all of this there must be a nurturing of faith, hope and love, which are the unchanging path to salvation for everyone. We might add that private revelations often spring from popular piety and leave their stamp on it, giving it a new impulse and opening the way for new forms of it. Nor does this exclude that they will have an effect even on the liturgy, as we see for instance in the feasts of *Corpus Christi* and of the Sacred Heart of Jesus. From one point of view, the relationship between Revelation and private revelations appears in the relationship between the liturgy and popular piety: the liturgy is the criterion, it is the living form of the Church as a whole, fed directly by the Gospel. Popular piety is a sign that the faith is spreading its roots into the heart of a people in such a way that it reaches into daily life. Popular religiosity is the first and fundamental mode of "inculturation" of the faith. While it must always take its lead and direction from the liturgy, it in turn enriches the faith by involving the heart.

We have thus moved from the somewhat negative clarifications, initially needed, to a positive definition of private revelations. How can they be classified correctly in relation to Scripture? To which theological category do they belong? The oldest letter of Saint Paul which has been preserved, perhaps the oldest of the New Testament texts, the First Letter to the Thessalonians, seems to me to point the way. The Apostle says: "Do not quench the Spirit, do not despise prophesying, but test everything, holding fast to what is good" (5:19–21). In every age the Church has received the charism of prophecy, which must be scrutinized but not scorned. On this point, it should be kept in mind that prophecy in the biblical sense does not mean to predict the future but to explain the will of God for the present, and therefore show the right path to take for the future. A person who foretells what is going to happen responds to the curiosity of the mind, which wants to draw back the veil on the future. The prophet speaks to the blindness of will and of reason, and declares the will of God as an indication and demand for the present time. In this case, prediction of the future is of secondary importance. What is essential is the actualization of the definitive Revelation, which concerns me at the deepest level. The prophetic word is a warning or a consolation, or both together. In this sense there is a link between the charism of prophecy and the category of "the signs of the times", which Vatican II brought to light anew: "You know how to interpret the appearance of earth and sky; why then do you not know how to interpret the present time?" (Lk 12:56). In this saying of Jesus, the "signs of the times" must be understood as the path he was taking, indeed it must be understood as Jesus himself. To interpret the signs of the times in the light of faith means to recognize the presence of Christ in every age. In the private revelations approved by the Church—and therefore also in Fatima— this is the point: they help us to understand the signs of the times and to respond to them rightly in faith.

The Anthropological Structure of Private Revelations

In these reflections we have sought so far to identify the theological status of private revelations. Before undertaking an interpretation of the message of Fatima, we must still attempt briefly to offer some clarification of their anthropological (psychological) character. In this field, theological anthropology distinguishes three forms of perception or "vision": vision with the senses, and hence exterior bodily perception, interior perception, and spiritual vision (*visio sensibilis—imaginativa—intellectualis*). It is clear that in the visions of Lourdes, Fatima and other places it is not a question of normal exterior perception of the senses: the images and forms which are seen are not located spatially, as is the case for example with a tree or a house. This is perfectly obvious, for instance, as regards the vision of hell (described in the first part of the Fatima "secret") or even the vision described in the third part of the "secret". But the same can be very easily shown with regard to other visions, especially since not everybody present saw them, but only the "visionaries". It is also clear that it is not a matter of a "vision" in the mind, without images, as occurs at the higher levels of mysticism. Therefore we are dealing with the middle category, interior perception. For the visionary, this perception certainly has the force of a presence, equivalent for that person to an external manifestation to the senses.

Interior vision does not mean fantasy, which would be no more than an expression of the subjective imagination. It means rather that the soul is touched by something real, even if beyond the senses. It is rendered capable of seeing that which is beyond the senses, that which cannot be seen—seeing by means of the "interior senses". It involves true "objects", which touch the soul, even if these "objects" do not belong to our habitual sensory world. This is why there is a need for an interior vigilance of the heart, which is usually precluded by the intense pressure of external reality and of the images and thoughts which fill the soul. The person is led beyond pure exteriority and is touched by deeper dimensions of reality, which become visible to him. Perhaps this explains why children tend to be the ones to receive these apparitions: their souls are as yet little disturbed, their interior powers of perception are still not impaired. "On the lips of children and of babes you have found praise", replies Jesus with a phrase of Psalm 8 (v. 3) to the criticism of the High Priests and elders, who had judged the children's cries of "hosanna" inappropriate (cf. Mt 21:16).

"Interior vision" is not fantasy but, as we have said, a true and valid means of verification. But it also has its limitations. Even in exterior vision the subjective element is always present. We do not see the pure object, but it comes to us through the filter of our senses, which carry out a work of translation. This is still more evident in the case of interior vision, especially when it involves realities which in themselves transcend our horizon. The subject, the visionary, is still more powerfully involved. He sees insofar as he is able, in the modes of representation and consciousness available to him. In the case of interior vision, the process of translation is even more extensive than in exterior vision, for the subject shares in an essential way in the formation of the image of what appears. He can arrive at the image only within the bounds of his capacities and possibilities. Such visions therefore are never simple "photographs" of the other world, but are influenced by the potentialities and limitations of the perceiving subject.

This can be demonstrated in all the great visions of the saints; and naturally it is also true of the visions of the children at Fatima. The images described by them are by no means a simple expression of their fantasy, but the result of a real perception of a higher and interior origin. But neither should they be thought of as if for a moment the veil of the other world were drawn back, with heaven appearing in its pure essence, as one day we hope to see it in our definitive union with God. Rather the images are, in a manner of speaking, a synthesis of the impulse coming from on high and the capacity to receive this impulse in the visionaries, that is, the children. For this reason, the figurative language of the visions is symbolic. In this regard, Cardinal Sodano stated: "[they] do not describe photographically the details of future events, but synthesize and compress against a single background facts which extend through time in an unspecified succession and duration". This compression of time and place in a single image is typical of such visions, which for the most part can be deciphered only in retrospect. Not every element of the vision has to have a specific historical sense. It is the vision as a whole that matters, and the details must be understood on the basis of the images taken in their entirety. The central element of the image is revealed where it coincides with what is the focal point of

Christian "prophecy" itself: the center is found where the vision becomes a summons and a guide to the will of God.

An Attempt to Interpret the "Secret" of Fatima

The first and second parts of the "secret" of Fatima have already been so amply discussed in the relative literature that there is no need to deal with them again here. I would just like to recall briefly the most significant point. For one terrible moment, the children were given a vision of hell. They saw the fall of "the souls of poor sinners". And now they are told why they have been exposed to this moment: "in order to save souls"—to show the way to salvation. The words of the First Letter of Peter come to mind: "As the outcome of your faith you obtain the salvation of your souls" (1:9). To reach this goal, the way indicated —surprisingly for people from the Anglo-Saxon and German cultural world—is devotion to the Immaculate Heart of Mary. A brief comment may suffice to explain this. In biblical language, the "heart" indicates the center of human life, the point where reason, will, temperament and sensitivity converge, where the person finds his unity and his interior orientation. According to Matthew 5:8, the "immaculate heart" is a heart which, with God's grace, has come to perfect interior unity and therefore "sees God". To be "devoted" to the Immaculate Heart of Mary means therefore to embrace this attitude of heart, which makes the *fiat*—"your will be done"—the defining center of one's whole life. It might be objected that we should not place a human being between ourselves and Christ. But then we remember that Paul did not hesitate to say to his communities: "imitate me" (1 Cor 4:16; Phil 3:17; 1 Th 1:6; 2 Th 3:7, 9). In the Apostle they could see concretely what it meant to follow Christ. But from whom might we better learn in every age than from the Mother of the Lord?

Thus we come finally to the third part of the "secret" of Fatima which for the first time is being published in its entirety. As is clear from the documentation presented here, the interpretation offered by Cardinal Sodano in his statement of 13 May was first put personally to Sister Lucia. Sister Lucia responded by pointing out that she had received the vision but not its interpretation. The interpretation, she said, belonged not to the visionary but to the Church. After reading the text, however, she said that this interpretation corresponded to what she had experienced and that on her part she thought the interpretation correct. In what follows, therefore, we can only attempt to provide a deeper foundation for this interpretation, on the basis of the criteria already considered.

"To save souls" has emerged as the key word of the first and second parts of the "secret", and the key word of this third part is the threefold cry: "Penance, Penance, Penance!" The beginning of the Gospel comes to mind: "Repent and believe the Good News" (Mk 1:15). To understand the signs of the times means to accept the urgency of penance—of conversion—of faith. This is the correct response to this moment of history, characterized by the grave perils outlined in the images that follow. Allow me to add here a personal recollection: in a conversation with me Sister Lucia said that it appeared ever more clearly to her that the purpose of all the apparitions was to help people to grow more and more in faith, hope and love—everything else was intended to lead to this.

Let us now examine more closely the single images. The angel with the flaming sword on the left of the Mother of God recalls similar images in the Book of Revelation. This represents the threat of judgement which looms over the world. Today the prospect that the world might be reduced to ashes by a sea of fire no longer seems pure fantasy: man himself, with his inventions, has forged the flaming sword. The vision then shows the power which stands opposed to the force of destruction—the splendor of the Mother of God and, stemming from this in a certain way, the summons to penance. In this way, the importance of human freedom is underlined: the future is not in fact unchangeably set, and the image which the children saw is in no way a film preview of a future in which nothing can be changed. Indeed, the whole point of the vision is to bring freedom onto the scene and to steer freedom in a positive direction. The purpose of the vision is not to show a film of an irrevocably fixed future. Its meaning is exactly the opposite: it is meant to mobilize the forces of change in the right direction. Therefore we must totally discount fatalistic explanations of the "secret", such as, for example, the claim that the would-be assassin of 13 May 1981 was merely an instrument of the divine plan guided by Providence and could not therefore have acted freely, or other similar ideas in circulation. Rather, the vision speaks of dangers and how we might be saved from them.

The next phrases of the text show very clearly once again the symbolic character of the vision: God remains immeasurable, and is the light which surpasses every vision of ours. Human persons appear as in a mirror. We must always keep in mind the limits in the vision itself, which here are indicated visually. The future appears only "in a mirror dimly" (1 Cor 13:12). Let us now consider the individual images which follow in the text of the "secret". The place of the action is described in three symbols: a steep mountain, a great city reduced to ruins and finally a large rough-hewn cross. The mountain and city symbolize the arena of human history: history as an arduous ascent to the summit, history as the arena of human creativity and social harmony, but at the same time a place of destruction, where man actually destroys the fruits of his own work. The city can be the place of communion and progress, but also of danger and the most extreme menace. On the mountain stands the cross—the goal and guide of history. The cross transforms destruction into salvation; it stands as a sign of history's misery but also as a promise for history.

At this point human persons appear: the Bishop dressed in white ("we had the impression that it was the Holy Father"), other Bishops, priests, men and women Religious, and men and women of different ranks and social positions. The Pope seems to precede the others, trembling and suffering because of all the horrors around him. Not only do the houses of the city lie half in ruins, but he makes his way among the corpses of the dead. The Church's path is thus described as a *Via Crucis*, as a journey through a time of violence, destruction and persecution. The history of an entire century can be seen represented in this image. Just as the places of the earth are synthetically described in the two images of the mountain and the city, and are directed towards the cross, so too time is presented in a compressed way. In the vision we can recognize the last century as a century of martyrs, a century of suffering and persecution for the Church, a century of World Wars and the many local wars which filled the last fifty years and have inflicted unprecedented forms of cruelty. In the "mirror" of this vision we see passing before us the witnesses of the faith decade by decade. Here it would be appropriate to mention a phrase from the letter which Sister Lucia wrote to the Holy Father on 12 May 1982: "The third part of the 'secret' refers to Our Lady's words: 'If not, [Russia] will spread her errors throughout the world, causing wars and persecutions of the Church.

The good will be martyred; the Holy Father will have much to suffer; various nations will be annihilated'".

In the *Via Crucis* of an entire century, the figure of the Pope has a special role. In his arduous ascent of the mountain we can undoubtedly see a convergence of different Popes. Beginning from Pius X up to the present Pope, they all shared the sufferings of the century and strove to go forward through all the anguish along the path which leads to the Cross. In the vision, the Pope too is killed along with the martyrs. When, after the attempted assassination on 13 May 1981, the Holy Father had the text of the third part of the "secret" brought to him, was it not inevitable that he should see in it his own fate? He had been very close to death, and he himself explained his survival in the following words: ". . . it was a mother's hand that guided the bullet's path and in his throes the Pope halted at the threshold of death" (13 May 1994). That here "a mother's hand" had deflected the fateful bullet only shows once more that there is no immutable destiny, that faith and prayer are forces which can influence history and that in the end prayer is more powerful than bullets and faith more powerful than armies.

The concluding part of the "secret" uses images which Lucia may have seen in devotional books and which draw their inspiration from long-standing intuitions of faith. It is a consoling vision, which seeks to open a history of blood and tears to the healing power of God. Beneath the arms of the cross angels gather up the blood of the martyrs, and with it they give life to the souls making their way to God. Here, the blood of Christ and the blood of the martyrs are considered as one: the blood of the martyrs runs down from the arms of the cross. The martyrs die in communion with the Passion of Christ, and their death becomes one with his. For the sake of the body of

Christ, they complete what is still lacking in his afflictions (cf. Col 1:24). Their life has itself become a Eucharist, part of the mystery of the grain of wheat which in dying yields abundant fruit. The blood of the martyrs is the seed of Christians, said Tertullian. As from Christ's death, from his wounded side, the Church was born, so the death of the witnesses is fruitful for the future life of the Church. Therefore, the vision of the third part of the "secret", so distressing at first, concludes with an image of hope: no suffering is in vain, and it is a suffering Church, a Church of martyrs, which becomes a sign-post for man in his search for God. The loving arms of God welcome not only those who suffer like Lazarus, who found great solace there and mysteriously represents Christ, who wished to become for us the poor Lazarus. There is something more: from the suffering of the witnesses there comes a purifying and renewing power, because their suffering is the actualization of the suffering of Christ himself and a communication in the here and now of its saving effect.

And so we come to the final question: What is the meaning of the "secret" of Fatima as a whole (in its three parts)? What does it say to us? First of all we must affirm with Cardinal Sodano: "... the events to which the third part of the 'secret' of Fatima refers now seem part of the past". Insofar as individual events are described, they belong to the past. Those who expected exciting apocalyptic revelations about the end of the world or the future course of history are bound to be disappointed. Fatima does not satisfy our curiosity in this way, just as Christian faith in general cannot be reduced to an object of mere curiosity. What remains was already evident when we began our reflections on the text of the "secret": the exhortation to prayer as the path of "salvation for souls" and, likewise, the summons to penance and conversion.

I would like finally to mention another key expression of the "secret" which has become justly famous: "my Immaculate Heart will triumph". What does this mean? The Heart open to God, purified by contemplation of God, is stronger than guns and weapons of every kind. The *fiat* of Mary, the word of her heart, has changed the history of the world, because it brought the Savior into the world—because, thanks to her *Yes*, God could become man in our world and remains so for all time. The Evil One has power in this world, as we see and experience continually; he has power because our freedom continually lets itself be led away from God. But since God himself took a human heart and has thus steered human freedom toward what is good, the freedom to choose evil no longer has the last word. From that time forth, the word that prevails is this: "In the world you will have tribulation, but take heart; I have overcome the world" (Jn 16:33). The message of Fatima invites us to trust in this promise.

Joseph Cardinal Ratzinger, Prefect
Congregation for the Doctrine of the Faith
June 26, 2000

Bibliography

Benedict XVI. Homily on the Tenth Anniversary of the Beatification of Jacinta and Francisco. Accessed September 10, 2010. http://www.vatican.va/holy_father/benedict_xvi/homilies/2010/documents/hf_ben-xvi_hom_20100513_fatima_en.html.

————. Interview on the Way to 2010 Apostolic Visit to Fatima. Accessed September 10, 2010. http://www.vatican.va/holy_father/benedict_xvi/speeches/2010/may/documents/hf_ben-xvi_spe_20100511_portogallo-interview_en.html.

————. Homily at Terreiro do Paco, Lisbon. Accessed September 21, 2010. http://www.vatican.va/holy_father/benedict_xvi/homilies/2010/documents/hf_ben-xvi_hom_20100511_terreiro-paco_en.html.

Bertone, Tarcisio Cardinal. *The Last Secret of Fatima*. New York: Doubleday, 2008.

Chrysostom, John. "On the Cemetery and the Cross" (*De coemeterio et cruce*). In *The Liturgy of the Hours*, vol. 4. New York: Catholic Book Publishing, 1975.

Congregation for the Doctrine of the Faith. *The Message of Fatima*. Accessed May 24, 2010. http://www.vatican.va/roman_curia/congregations/cfaith/documents/rc_con_cfaith_doc_20000626_message-fatima_en.html

De la Sainte Trinite, Frere Michel. *The Whole Truth about Fatima: The Secret and the Church*, vol. 2. Translated by John Collorafi. Buffalo, New York: Immaculate Heart Publications, 1989.

De Marchi, John, I.M.C. *Fatima: From the Beginning*. Translated by I. M. Kingsbury. Fatima: Edições Missões Consolata, 2006.

De Montfort, Louis-Marie. *True Devotion to Mary*. Rockford, IL: Tan Books, 1985.

Documents on Fatima & Memoirs of Sister Lucia. 2nd ed. Translated by Fr. Antonio Maria Martins, S.J. Hanceville, AL: Fatima Family Apostolate, 2001.

Dziwisz, Cardinal Stanislaw. *A Life with Karol: My Forty-Year Friendship with the Man Who Became Pope*. Translated by Adrian J. Walker. New York: Doubleday, 2008.

Fox, Fr. Robert J. and Antonio Maria Martins, S.J. *The Intimate Life of Sister Lucia*. Hanceville, AL: Fatima Family Apostolate, 2001.

Haffert, John M. *Meet the Witnesses of the Miracle of the Sun*. Spring Grove, PA: The American Society for the Defense of Tradition, Family and Property, 1961.

Irenaeus, "Against Heresies" (*Adversus haereses*). In *The Liturgy of the Hours*, vol. 1. New York: Catholic Book Publishing, 1975.

Kondor, Fr. Luis, S.V.D. "Sister Lucia and the Collegial Consecration". *Soul*, vol. 47, no. 5 (Sept.–Oct. 1996).

Laurentin, Fr. Rene. *The Meaning of Consecration Today: A Marian Model for a Secularized Age*. Translated by Kenneth D. Whitehead. San Francisco: Ignatius Press, 1991.

Lindsey, David Michael. *The Woman and the Dragon: Apparitions of Mary*. Gretna, LA: Pelican Publishing Company, 2000.

Madigan, Leo. *Blessed Alexandrina da Costa: The Mystical Martyr of Fatima*. Fatima: Fatima-Orphel Books, 2005.

"The Message of Fatima Part III: The August, September and October Appearances." *Soul* (Winter 2009).

Pasquale, Fr. Umberto. *Alexandrina*. Turin, Italy: Libreria Dottrina Cristiana, 1960. Excerpts in "Alexandrina". Edited by Francis Johnston. Translated by Anne Croshaw. The Eternal Word

Television Network website. Accessed September 3, 2010. http://www.ewtn.com/library/mary/alexdrin.htm

Paul VI. *Signum magnum* ("The Great Sign"). http://www.vatican.va/holy_father/paul_vi/apost_exhortations/documents/hf_p-vi_exh_19670513_signum-magnum_en.html.

Pius XI. *Divini Redemptoris* ("Divine Redeemer"). http://www.vatican.va/holy_father/pius_xi/encyclicals/documents/hf_p-xi_enc_19031937-divini_redemptoris_en.html.

Pope, Henry. *Benedict XV: The Pope of Peace*. London: Trinity Press, 1940.

Ruffin, C. Bernard. *Padre Pio: The True Story*. Huntington, IN: Our Sunday Visitor, 1991.

Santos, Lucia. *Fatima in Lucia's Own Words: Sister Lucia's Memoirs*. Edited by Fr. Louis Kondor, SVD. Translated by Dominican Nuns of Perpetual Rosary. Fatima: Postulation Centre, 1976.

Santos, Lucia dos. *Fatima in Lucia's Own Words: Sister Lucia's Memoirs, Volume II*. 3rd ed. Edited by Fr. Louis Kondor, SVD. Translated by Dominican Nuns of Perpetual Rosary and Dominican Nuns of Mosteiro de Santa Maria. Fatima: Secretariado dos Pastorinhos, 2004.

Sheen, Fulton J. *The World's First Love: Mary the Mother of God*. 2nd ed. San Francisco: Ignatius Press, 2010.

Solimeo, Luiz Sergio. *Fatima: A Message More Urgent than Ever*. Spring Grove, PA: The American Society for the Defense of Tradition, Family and Property, 2008.

Szulc, Tad. *Pope John Paul II: The Biography*. New York: Simon and Schuster, 1996.

Tindal-Robertson, Timothy. *Fatima, Russia and Pope John Paul II: How Mary Intervened to Deliver Russia from Marxist Atheism May 13, 1981-December 25, 1991*. Rev. ed. Still River, MA: Ravengate Press, 1998.

Weigel, George. *Witness to Hope: The Biography of Pope John Paul II.* New York: Harper Collins Publishers, Inc., 2001.

World Apostolate of Fatima, U.S.A. *Spiritual Guide: For the Salvation of Souls and World Peace.* Washington, NJ: World Apostolate of Fatima, U.S.A., 2008.